C000130129

Crime on the Line

by Adrian Gray

TRANSPORT

PUBLISHERS

Crime on the Line

Atlantic Publishers,
Trevithick House, West End, Penryn, Cornwall TR10 8HE

First published 2000

© Adrian Gray, 2000

ISBN: 1 902827 00 7

Layout and design: Richard Joy, Paris

Reproduction and printing by The Amadeus Press Ltd, Bradford

British Cataloguing in Publication Data: A catalogue record for this book is available from the British Library.

Contents

Foreword

The purpose of this book is to give a picture of the intimate connection between the life of Britain's railway system and patterns of crime that evolved around it. The subject is so vast that it is impossible to give more than a glimpse of typical crimes which reflect wider tendencies, and to provide more detail of some of the most famous crimes that shocked the nation. It is a story that ranges from the most daring political crimes, to criminal assaults and petty thieving.

In order to avoid dragging over too many crimes that may still trouble the memories of living people, I have generally drawn a line at the year 1963 which, because of the Great Train Robbery, marks a key moment in the history of railway crime in any case; it is interesting that this famous robbery, both in character and method, belongs very much to the past rather than the present. The extent and nature of crime seems to have begun to change as the 1960s drew on and crime became more extensive both on the railways and in general - it should be remembered that from the middle of the nineteenth century crime in the nation as a whole had shown a pattern of general decline. The British Transport Police Report for 1961 (published later in 1962) draws attention to a significant increase in the crime rate. This increase in crime may partly relate to the changing nature of society, but on the railways it was also encouraged by the withdrawal of so many railway staff from locations like stations and signalboxes where they had always acted as "policemen" of the passengers and other members of the public. Vandalism increased as railway servants became less visible.

CHAPTER ONE:
MURDER!

It is perhaps surprising that passenger railways had been in use for over thirty years before the first murder on a train occurred in Britain and there were only seven in the first hundred years until 1929. Railway carriages at the time were almost always compartment stock, generally with no lighting, and in the early years it was common practice to lock the doors before the train started. With no communication cords to sound the alarm, passengers must often have felt nervous about unknown travelling companions with whom they were more or less imprisoned for long periods of time.

In fact railway murders were very rare until after the First World War with an increase from the 1960s, notably in the vicinity of stations as much as on the trains themselves. However no British cases approached the extremes of two famous German mass-murderers, Fritz Haarmann of Hanover and Peter Kurten of Dusseldorf, who both used stations as ideal places to select and pick up their many victims between the Wars. This rarity in Britain led to great interest being shown in the first few cases, which have become "classics" of crime literature, and leading to brief spasms of panic among the travelling population which were satirised in *Punch*.

Murders of Passengers: The Muller Case

The murder of Thomas Briggs by Franz Muller on 9 July 1864 is famous simply on the grounds that it was the first murder of a railway passenger in Britain; the case prompted the LSWR to put "portholes" between the compartments in its carriages, which were called "Muller Lights", and may have influenced the Regulation of Railways Act of 1868 which introduced regulations on communication cords.[1]

Thomas Briggs was the chief clerk at Robarts Bank in the City, and caught the 9.50pm Chalk Farm NLR train to his home in Hackney. At least three witnesses saw him in the train, but were reluctant to testify to this effect. Two young clerks who boarded the train in Hackney found a compartment covered in blood and Guard Ames then found a hat, bag and stick - the latter also marked with blood. The severely injured Briggs was found on the side of the track between Hackney Wick

Franz Muller, the first known "railway murderer", bludgeoned a bank clerk to death in a London & South Western Railway carriage in 1864. The case led to special inter-compartment windows, known as "Muller Lights", being installed in the company's carriages.

and Bow by the driver of an empty stock train and taken first to a nearby pub and then home, where he died of head injuries. The first clue was the hat - which did not belong to Briggs.

Two days later a gold watch chain was offered to a jeweller named Death in exchange for other goods, the man who brought it in having a German accent. The jeweller read about the murder the next day and reported this to the police. James Matthews recognised the description of the hat as belonging to a German who had had lodgings in Victoria Park near the NLR; this man - Muller - had also given a jewellry box to Matthews' daughter, with the unusual name of "Death" inside it. Muller's landlady had seen the jewellery that he had got from Death in exchange for what he had stolen from Briggs.

By this time Muller had left for the USA but the Police gained a lead on him by catching another sailing via Liverpool and he was arrested in New York. A lot of public hysteria focussed on Muller's foreign origins and his defence was organised by the German Legal Protection Society. Much of the defence concentrated on the unsatisfactory nature of Matthews' evidence: this man said he had bought the distinctive hat for Muller, but it was known that he had once had a similar hat himself, and the whereabouts of Matthews' hat was not known. Muller's alibi depended only on the word of his girlfriend, a part-time Camberwell prostitute who was supported by her own landlady who claimed to have seen Muller at 9pm on the night of the murder, but this was not enough to save him.

Muller was executed on 14 November, but it was not the end of the story. One result of the Muller case was that it sent a spasm of terror through the travelling public - was that person sitting opposite you another Muller? This fear was brought home to three men in a 1st class compartment of the 8.40pm Euston to Glasgow express in October 1864. They were very surprised when another young man crawled out from under the seat and said, "Believe me, gentlemen, I am not another Muller." He told them that he had "consumption" (TB) and was going to Stafford "to die". They got him back under the seat and told the guard at Rugby.

The "Lefroy" Murder

Popularly known under his alias, Lefroy, this notorious Victorian railway murderer's real surname was Mapleton. He occupies a unique place in British crime history as the picture of "Lefroy" was published in the *Daily Telegraph* and was the first of a wanted man to receive such publicity in the UK.

The case began on the 2.10pm London Bridge to Brighton train on 27 June 1881. Passing through Merstham Tunnel, a passenger named Gibson heard loud reports like fog-signals, but thought no more of it until the train stopped at Preston Park for ticket collection. There a blood-drenched young man tumbled out of a 1st class compartment saying that two men had been in the compartment with him, there had been shots and he had been hit in the head. He gave his name as Arthur Lefroy of Cathcart Road, Wallington; he said he was going to Brighton in connection with a play he was writing for the Brighton Theatre Royal. However, two aspects of him brought suspicion upon him - there appeared to be a watch and chain tucked into his boot, and he returned to London without contacting the Theatre.

Ganger Thomas Jenkins found the body of a murdered man in Balcombe Tunnel and the train taking "Lefroy" back to London with a police officer made a stop at Balcombe so that the news could be passed to the officer. "Lefroy" was allowed to return to his Wallington lodgings. The body of the murdered man was taken to the *Railway* Inn in Balcombe where it was identified as Frederick Gold, a retired corn merchant from Brighton. The face was marked by gunpowder and knife wounds, there was a bullet in his neck, whilst his watch was missing. A woman at Horley reported seeing a train pass with two men fighting, which was after the shots had been fired in Merstham Tunnel, and Gold's umbrella was found near the line south of Hassocks showing that the murderer must have still been on the train at that point.

"Lefroy" was questioned about his watch and made some unsatisfactory answers, and his lodgings were "watched" - rather ineffectively, as he escaped out the back! However he was identified as Percy Mapleton, a man with a record of odd behaviour some of which was criminal, and whose sister believed him to be bordering on lunacy. The competence of the officer in charge of the hunt, George Holmes, was so vilified that the Metropolitan Police virtually disowned him.

Mapleton took new lodgings in Stepney but foolishly sent a telegram to an old friend at his former lodgings; he was arrested at 32 Smith Street on 8 July where he was using the name "Park". He was put on the train and taken to Lewes Gaol, having to change trains at Haywards Heath where a large crowd gathered to see him. There was much evidence against him at the trial, including the fact that he had redeemed a revolver from a pawnshop the very day of the murder. After being found guilty Mapleton accused the jury of "murdering" him, but confessed to the crime before his execution.

He was hanged at Lewes on 29 November 1881.

The "Lefroy" case was very similar to the murder committed by George Parker on a Southampton to Waterloo train on 17 January 1901. Parker had been dismissed from the Marines for stealing from colleagues, was wanted for robbery from the Lyceum Theatre in London, and had decided to kill his married girlfriend and possibly himself too. To this end he bought a revolver in Southampton and began his journey to London, going as far as Eastleigh with his young lady where they both got off. However Parker decided to get back on to the fateful train, causing a sensation by the passionate farewell he enjoyed with his paramour.

Parker was in a compartment with Mrs Rhoda King and a farmer named William Pearson, who got in at Winchester. Near Surbiton Parker went to the lavatory and returned with his gun ready - opening fire at both passengers. Pearson was shot dead, but Mrs King merely wounded in the cheek and Parker offered her some of the farmer's money. A resourceful lady, she persuaded him to throw the gun out of the window and at Vauxhall he jumped from the train, thrusting the ticket he had stolen off Pearson into the collector's hand. Mrs King promptly shouted "Murder!" and he was chased through the streets and a gas works. When arrested by PC Fuller, Parker said, "I wish I had killed that woman." The defence tried to argue that he was insane, but the prosecution pointed out that he was rational enough to

The *Illustrated London News* coverage of the "Lefroy" murder. The illustrations show:-
Top: Train passing some cottages at Horley, on the London to Brighton line.
Inset: The window in one of the cottages, through which a woman saw two men fighting in a carriage. *Centre:* Entrance to Balcombe Tunnel. *Lower left:* The spot in the tunnel where the body of Frederick Gold was found. *Lower right:* Cathcart Road, Wallington, where "Lefroy" – alias Percy Mapleton – lodged; he was charged with murder eleven days after the crime.

Mr A L Smith.

Mr Poland.

The Jury

Sir Henry James

T. Watson, the guard

Mrs Gold

J. Gibson, ticket collector

Mr H. Hall, surgeon

Mr Hall, Station Master, Preston

Lord Chief Justice Coleridge

The Prisoner

W. H. Franks, ticket collector

Mr Terry, Chief Constable, Brighton

J. Martin, Policeman.
Mr Forrest Fulton
Mr Kisch

Mr Montagu Williams

TRIAL OF PERCY LEFROY MAPLETON FOR THE MURDER ON THE BRIGHTON RAILWAY.—SEE PAGE 466.
SKETCHES FROM THE PRESS GALLERY AT MAIDSTONE ASSIZES.

take Pearson's ticket so he could get through the barrier at Vauxhall. He was executed for the murder on 19 March.

Murders of Railway Officials

Possibly the earliest "railway murder" was at Ballybrophy in Ireland, where the station opened in September 1847. On 13 November labourer John d'Arcy was full of bitterness after losing his railway job, blaming the misfortune on Michael Smith. Bringing in John Coonan to help, he set out to kill Smith but nearly slaughtered a lamp-cleaner called James Carey instead. When he found Smith he beat him to death near the engine shed, then went off to get a job in Cork - where he was also sacked. D'Arcy joined the army instead, but could not resist boasting of what he had done with the result that he was tried and executed in 1848.

In November 1856 an official of the Midland Great Western in Dublin, Mr Little, was murdered while working on accounts in his office. The canal at the front of the building was drained and the hammer used to kill him was found there.

One of the few cases where one railway employee murdered another occurred at the LCDR's Dover Priory station on 1 May 1868. The two principal characters were Thomas Wells, an eighteen-year old carriage cleaner, and a superintendent named Edward Walsh[2]. A dispute between the two had begun in April 1868 when Walsh ordered Wells to carry manure to the superintendent's garden. Wells was very angry about this rather doubtful task, so straight after work he went into Dover to buy a pistol and some "caps". This may not have been with murderous intent, for on 30 April Walsh complained that Wells had played some "pistol-firing" trick on him. The superintendent planned to make the most of this, though, telling Wells that "I have not done with you yet, you will have to go to the stationmaster."

Very early the next morning Wells was observed taking a gun towards the station. Meanwhile, Walsh kept his threat and reported Wells to higher authority, the stationmaster telling him that if he did not apologise the matter would become a disciplinary issue. Wells was then sent away for a few minutes so that the stationmaster could write a short report, which was then read back to him.

Wells must have known his job was at risk, but he was not remorseful. Instead, he walked straight from the stationmaster's office to a nearby office, paused in the doorway, and shot Walsh in the head before running off. The stationmaster of Dover Pier, Cox, was a witness of the murder. Walsh died almost immediately, but

Sketches made from the press gallery during the trial of "Lefroy" – Percy Mapleton. They include a number of London, Brighton & South Coast Railway staff and the victim's widow.

Dover Priory in 1867, the scene of a notorious station murder the following year when carriage cleaner Thomas Wells shot superintendent Edward Walsh over a petty dispute. Wells became the first person to be hung in private after the ending of public executions.

Wells' attempt to escape suggested no real plan of what to do. He was found sitting in one of the railway carriages with the murder weapon beside him.

  The only defence offered at Maidstone Assizes was that Wells' temperament had been affected by an accident at work which had unbalanced him. It was said that he had suffered a "squeeze in the stomach" between some buffers, but his own family gave evidence suggesting a malicious streak. His father said he had often given way to "gusts of passion." The Guilty verdict was almost a formality.

  The Judge was clearly struck by the petty reasons for the crime and told Wells it was "a terrible crime of murder committed under circumstances of such atrocity as to be dreadful and almost incredible, considering your youthful age." Then he donned the black cap and sentenced Wells to be hung. In death, though, Wells achieved a significance he never had in life - the first person to be hung in private after the ending of public executions. Walsh's widow applied to the LCDR Board for a pension, but this was refused; perhaps this reflected a view that Walsh brought his fate upon himself through his behaviour to others, or it could simply have been the case that the LCDR was permanently short of cash.

  In September 1895 two policeman working for the railways were checking on a pilfering problem at Kay's Siding, Wigan. Detective Sergeant Kidd and his assistant Osborne surprised a gang in the act of stealing, and a violent struggle took place. Kidd was stabbed nine times with a knife and died. Elijah Winstanley, William Halliwell and William Kearsley were arrested, with Halliwell electing to give evidence against the other two. At the first hearing Winstanley became hysterical, shouting "Kill me, kill me. Go on, it's murder. I did it."

The murder weapon, a penknife, was found only sixty yards away from the scene of crime two months afterwards; Winstanley was executed at Walton gaol.

Another policeman to die was Thomas Hibbs of Birmingham. On 10 August 1901 he saw three men pilfering coal from Curzon Street goods station and gave chase. The men turned on him and knocked him unconscious, throwing him into the canal where he drowned. Although three were arrested for the murder the case was discharged due to lack of evidence.

A mysterious case was the murder of stationmaster George Wilson of Lintz Green station on the NER in Durham at 11pm on 7 October 1911. Wilson saw the last train off at night then turned back to his house but as he approached the door sand was thrown in his eyes and he was shot in the chest. Four miners heard his screams and came running, but he died without saying a word. No money was taken, though robbery would have ben the obvious motive. A NER casual porter, Samuel Atkinson, was arrested on the basis that he had been seen hanging around the station although his shift finished at 3.45pm, but the case was not strong enough. A £100 reward was offered for the detection of a man aged 20-22, without known result, though there was much local suspicion that Atkinson was guilty.

A violent robbery at Pollokshields East station cost two lives on 10 December 1945. During the evening a man burst in to the stationmaster's room and fired three times, killing Miss Bradshaw the clerk and a fifteen year old porter named Robert Brown, but only grazing Kenneth Scott. The robber ran off with two empty boxes from the safe but Scott ran to tell the guard of a departing train - who thought he was joking, and carried on departing! On 9 October 1946 a young locomotive fireman surrendered himself and a gun to PC Byrne, saying that he had already attempted suicide due to the effects of committing the crime. As there were doubts over his sanity he was given life in prison rather than execution.

On 22 August 1952 the booking clerk at Ash Vale station, near Aldershot, Geoffrey Dean, was stabbed twenty times and £160 stolen; a murder hunt began immediately. Attention soon focussed on John Alcott, a railway fireman from Hither Green depot, who had been seen at the station on the two previous days and had befriended Dean. It was discovered that Alcott had left home unexpectedly on 18 July, had bought a sheath knife in Aldershot, and had been seen with a knife at Ash Vale station at 6.30am on 21 July. The evening of the murder he had been seen around the station and had made use of his BR connection to make some phone calls.

Dean usually locked up at 7.45pm but had stayed on in the office to finish his accounts; Alcott was inside with him, having used the phone, and a soldier who passed by the station recalled hearing noises from inside the closed office. At 9.20pm the door of the office was forced open and Dean's body discovered.

Alcott had taken lodgings at Aldershot, and these were searched. A bloodstained wallet and two bloody 10s notes were found whilst the murder weapon was found hidden in the chimney. He was arrested at 11.15pm that night with £109 on him. The trial was almost a formality and he was executed on 2 January 1953.

Something Nasty in the Left Luggage....

The left luggage office or automatic locker has a sinister history in the twentieth century, for a time being almost done away with completely due to the threat of terrorism. Before this, though, the locker was associated with a number of famous murder cases and especially when involving a "trunk".

In 1924 Mrs Patrick Mahon was very suspicious about his husband's frequent absences and so went through his pockets. She found a ticket for left luggage and got a friend to investigate. The locked bag that was collected turned out to contain a bloody knife, setting in motion a trail that led eventually to the dismembered body of Emily Kaye in a bungalow at the Crumbles between Eastbourne and Pevensey. Mahon had cut her up there and was trying to dispose of the body by getting rid of it out of the carriage window, having already disposed of some parts between Waterloo and Richmond. Mahon was hanged in September 1924.

On 6 May 1927 a trunk labelled "F Austin, St Leonard's", was opened at Charing Cross, and revealed the body of a woman cut into five pieces. Bizarrely, a constable refused to permit the removal of the trunk until a doctor had certified the woman as dead. Mr Austin was soon ruled out of enquiries. The woman was identified as a prostitute, Minnie Bonati, a former cook who had married an Italian waiter from whom she was separated. Police were suspicious of an estate agent named John Robinson, who was known to have had a bigamous marriage, and a bloodstained duster was found in his office. He had killed her in his office opposite Rochester Row police station in the course of an argument; they had had a fight and she had fallen, hitting her head on the fireplace. Robinson had then cut her up and taken her by taxi to Charing Cross, telling the driver that the trunk was full of books. He was hanged in August 1927.

On 6 June 1934 a plywood trunk was left at Brighton station, but after a few days its smell began to concern the two railway staff who had to work a long, sweltering shift in its company. Unable to stand it any more, on 17 June William Vinnicombe asked a policeman to open the trunk - who then summoned a more

Ash Vale station, near Aldershot. Geoffrey Dean, the booking clerk, was brutally stabbed to death by a railway fireman in 1952. *(D. Cullum)*

senior officer. The lid was forced to let out a ghastly smell, then to reveal the naked and dismembered body of a woman - with no head or limbs. A search of the luggage office for further clues revealed only another body - a young baby in a tattered basket.

A few days later a railway man at King's Cross became concerned about another offensive item of luggage - an old brown suitcase. Finding that it contained four objects wrapped in newspaper, he too called the police who uncovered two legs and two feet. It was soon established that the body pieces belonged to the same young woman, aged between 21 and 28, and pregnant. In the course of a lengthy and painstaking investigation, a second Brighton trunk victim turned up for the murder of whom a young pseudo-Italian waiter called "Tony Mancini" was arrested - and sensationally acquitted. The station victim's arms and head were never found, although there was a good report of a head being seen in a pool at Black Rock. Suspicion closed in on a wealthy and influential Hove doctor, Edward Massiah, who also practiced as an illegal abortionist to the rich and powerful classes; it was thought that the girl had died while being treated, but the case never came to court. In 1938, following another unusual death, he left England and went to live in Trinidad.

The luggage lockers at Bournemouth West featured in another scandalous crime, the murder of Margery Gardner by Neville Heath. A suitcase containing the whip that Heath used on Gardner was found at the station.

Other Murderous Cases

Several railway murders have been unsolved or, at least, never brought to a conclusion. The earliest of these was the murder of Elizabeth Camp, the manageress of the *Good Intent* in Walworth. She was returning to Waterloo in February 1897 on the 7.42pm from Hounslow, expecting to be met at the terminus by her fiancé Edward Berry, when she met a brutal death.

Berry was surprised when she did not appear off the train, but her battered body was found soon afterwards under a seat by a carriage cleaner. Her purse and ticket were missing yet a brooch and ring had not been stolen, but a pair of bone cuff-links were supposed to have been left by her assailant - they turned out to have been borrowed from her sister. There did not appear to have been a sexual motive.

A search of the trackside was begun and between Putney and Wandsworth a chemist's pestle was discovered, with human hair attached. Witnesses said they had seen a man get out at Wandsworth and attention centred on a former admirer of Miss Camp's, a barman named Brown. Also under suspicion was Thomas Stone, who owed her money. Brown was able to produce an alibi but Stone was unable to explain his movements at the crucial time, though there was no other evidence against him.

On 24 September 1905 the badly mutilated body of Sophia Money, aged 22, was found in Merstham Tunnel on the Brighton line. Marks on the tunnel wall showed where she had been thrown out of the train and almost bounced along the side before falling beneath the wheels. First thoughts was that this was a suicide, but a white silk scarf had been rammed into her mouth to silence her. She lived in Clapham and had told a friend she was "going out for a walk" to Victoria. Signalman Yarnley at Purley Oaks reported seeing a struggle in a 1st class carriage of the 9.33pm to Brighton, and the case had some eerie echoes of the "Lefroy" murder. Due to this evidence it was assumed the case was one of attempted rape and that she had been either pushed out of the train or had fallen while trying to escape. There was confusion as to whether a woman such as her would have got on a train with a stranger, or where she intended travelling to. Various known "admireres" were questioned, but the trail went cold.

In 1912 her brother Robert Money became notorious due to his very complicated love life. He was having an affair with one sister and married to another when he took them all to Eastbourne; there he shot the two sisters and his three children by them, only one of the sisters managing to crawl away, before setting fire to the bodies and shooting himself.

On 17 March 1910 John Nisbet, the wages clerk at Stobswood Colliery near Morpeth, went to Newcastle to collect the wages in the company of two other clerks. He collected a bag containing £370 and returned by train, but his two companions got out at Stannington leaving him alone with one other man. At Alnmouth Nisbet's body was found in the train, shot five times.

An early suspect was John Dickman, who had been seen getting off the train at Morpeth and was known to have money problems due to betting. At Morpeth, he had to pay excess as he only had a Stannington ticket. On 9 June the missing wages bag was found down the shaft of the Isabella Pit near Morpeth. Dickman was arrested and found to have a bloodstained suit and £17 in gold sovereigns; witnesses knew that he had had a gun. He was hung at Newcastle on 10 August 1910, though there was some debate about the strength of the evidence. He was also supposedly linked with the murder of Major-General Luard of Kent on 24 August 1908.

Another unsolved case was that of Nurse Florence Shore, aged 55, in January 1920. George Clatt and two friends boarded a Victoria-bound train at Polegate in Sussex on 12 January, climbing into a 3rd class compartments containing one other traveller. This was a woman who clearly seemed to be ill, so at Bexhill the friends summoned the guard. Although they spoke to her she said nothing, but she did at last open her eyes and moved her fingers. She was holding a paper in her lap, there was blood in several places, splashes of blood around her and a broken comb - yet although she was clearly unwell in some way, there was no other sign that a murderous struggle had taken place in the compartment.

She was taken off the train and found to have injuries to the skull caused by a heavy implement as well as torn clothing. When she died on 16 January, there was talk of a murder hunt, but although a man had been seen to get into her compartment and then leave at Lewes the trail went cold. The man had been far from inconspicuous - due to the short platforms at Lewes he had been forced to get out by climbing along the footboard.

Similarly unsolved was the case of Winifred East in 1929, at the time the ninth murder committed[3]. East's body was found on the line of the Southern Railway between Kidbrooke and Eltham, having been electrocuted and also decapitated. This may have been taken as a suicide except that an empty purse was found nearby and post-mortem analysis revealed damage to the kidneys as if struck by a fist. Miss East, aged 28, had been travelling in a first class compartment into which a young man had been seen to jump at Barnehurst[4] - and which he left at Kidbrooke. A passenger in another compartment reported hearing screaming and various items were found in Miss East's compartment including a National Savings book behind the heater. Speculation was that she had jumped from the train to escape an attacker, and whether this counted as murder - an 1894 case in Australia where a Chinese man had died when jumping out had been adjudged to be so. However the East case was never solved.

A number of other murder cases were committed close to railways or had strong railway links, such as the trunk murders. A murder case that did not take place on the railway, but involved a good deal of activity on and around the trains in 1885, was a plot to rob Netherby Hall near Carlisle - the home of Sir Frederick Graham[5]. The gang travelled by train to Gretna on 27 October 1885, and during the next day were seen "doing something with a key" at the *Graham Arms* in Gretna. They then burgled the Hall on the evening of 28 October by using a ladder to get in upstairs. As a hue and cry was set up to chase them, the gang was spotted near Kingstown just north of Carlisle, but shot at the police and escaped along the railway track towards Carlisle. There they probably hid out in a goods wagon[6], where a bloodstained jemmy was later found.

The next day they were still on the railway, for they were spotted by the signalman at Dalston Road Crossing, south-west of Carlisle, and the alarm raised again - but they escaped by beating a policeman. They then cut across country, seeking a way of returning to their London haunts, with one of the gang arriving at Southwaite station on the LNWR south of Carlisle at 7.10pm and three others reaching Plumpton - the next station south - at 8.20pm. Of the latter group, Martin was responsible for the shooting dead of PC Byrnes near Plumpton station[7].

Unable to get a passenger train, some of the criminals climbed onto a goods train at Keswick Junction - to the alarm of the guard. He refrained from tackling them himself, but wrote messages on paper and threw them out of the train. At Shap one of the messages was found by another driver, and so a telegraph warning was sent from Shap signalbox to Tebay. Police could not be sent to Tebay in time, so railway staff bravely ganged together and confronted the villains, capturing Rudge and Martin; Baker escaped, but was caught later at Lancaster. A valuable diamond star was found under a railway arch at Tebay.

The gang was put on trial in January 1886, with Martin also being wanted for the murder of Inspector Thomas Simmons at Romford in January 1885 - another occasion when the train had been used to make a visit to an area for robbery[8]. Three of the gang were hung for the murder on 8 February 1886.

In January 1914 the body of five-year old Willie Starchfield was found under the seat of a NLR train from Chalk Farm to Broad Street, after having left home on an errand. The boy had been strangled with cord which was later found on the track, and the signalman at St Pancras Junction thought he had seen the struggle as the train passed. However the inquest heard there was doubt whether the boy had been killed on the train or dumped there after the murder. Willie's parents were separated and his mother had left him with a Mrs Longstaff. His father John, a newspaper seller, lived in Long Acre and had been awarded a Carnegie Medal in 1912 for tackling a mad gunman.

John Starchfield was the only real suspect, but he maintained an alibi. The cord used to strangle Willie was similar to cord used to tie bundles of newspaper. A Mrs Clara Wood thought she had seen the boy and a man who looked like Starchfield, whereas another witness thought she had seen the boy with a woman. The case was dismissed by the Judge as it relied solely on identification.

On 4 April 1914 the body of seven year old Margaret Nally of Amberley Road was found in the ladies cloakroom at Aldersgate Street station. She was found by Inspector Groves when he was closing up the station at 11.50pm, wedged behind the door of the cubicle so that her murderer would have had to climb out over the partition wall. She had been sexually assaulted and suffocated with a cloth pushed down her throat.

Investigation found that she had gone to visit an aunt near Paddington and had last been seen at 8pm. She was probably dead by 9.50pm, but in the intervening period had eaten a meal and lost her hat - which was never found. Marks of blood on her teeth suggested that she bit her killer during the attack. Beyond this, the Police investigation stalled - there were contradictory reports that she had gone by omnibus to Kings Cross and by Metropolitan Railway to Aldersgate Street. A ticket from Royal Oak to Moorgate Street dated 3 April was found with the words "I intend to kill a girl tonight" written on the back - it was a forgery. An alcoholic soldier in Dover leant over to the man next to him in a cinema and "confessed" to the murder. A report that her hat had been seen in a cinema also was without foundation. This was one more railway murder that had no solution.

In the latter half of the twentieth century murders in the environs of railway stations have become more common, possibly linked to staff reductions. This has been the case in London in particular, though this does not explain the mysterious murder of a Polish countess, Teresa Lubienska, who got off a Piccadilly line train at Gloucester Road on 24 May 1957 but never reached the street above. Her corpse, with apparent stab wounds, was discovered some time afterwards and it was believed her assailant had escaped by the emergency staircase. There were suggestions that this was a "political" murder, but no-one conviction ever resulted.

Unwanted children could be disposed of from trains so that there was less chance of a body being connected with a woman of the immediate district. In November 1874 labourers on the Metropolitan District Railway actually saw a woman throw a little girl off a LNWR Willesden to Mansion House train; they picked up the child, who had only slight bruising, but could not stop the train and arrest the woman.

In 1913 a boy's body was found beside the SER between Wellington College and Reading, which was linked to a woman having been seen beating a child at Wellington College station and the discovery of a child's knickers labelled "AF" near

When an angry mother was seen beating her child on the platform at Wellington College in 1913, no-one realised it would culminate in murder. *(Lens of Sutton)*

Sindlesham Halt. Winifred Franks, aged 25, a servant, was charged with the murder of the child. She was a single woman living in "straitened circumstances" and had made a calculated decision to kill the child, stripping all his clothes off before throwing him out, then tearing up the clothes and disposing of them in the same way. She said she did not know what she was doing at the time and was found to be guilty but insane at the time; she was sentenced to be detained at His Majesty's pleasure.

It was not always clear whether a murder had taken place, or simply the disposal of an unfortunate birth. For example, in October 1915 a package was received at Derby labelled "Glass with care". When opened as unclaimed it turned out to contain the body of an infant - all that was known about it was that it had come from London.

In September 1938 the driver of the 4.45am parcels train from Waterloo saw a white bundle beside the track between Putney and Barnes, near the Dryburgh Road bridge. When investigated it turned out to be a small child dressed in a white vest. Patient detective work showed that the child could only have come from one of three trains the previous night and interest centred on a woman and child seen travelling from Barnes Bridge to Vauxhall.

Attempted assassination of Queen Victoria at Windsor station in March 1882.
The assailant, Roderick McLean, was "severely handled" by the crowd and
"belaboured over the head" by an Eton boy.

Media attention brought a response from the proprietor of a boarding house at Vauxhall Bridge Road, who reported that Marguerita Eastwood who had been staying there had "lost" her child - she had said that it had gone into foster care. When Mrs Eastwood was arrested at Caterham she told an elaborate story about the eight month child being the product of a union between her soldier husband and a prostitute. The prostitute had said that Mrs Eastwood must look after the baby or she would tell the Commanding Officer. Mrs Eastwood said she had held the child out of the window three times with the intention of dropping it, but had been unable to; then the train had lurched and it had fallen from her grasp. This story was unconvincing and she was given penal servitude for life.

A famous attempted murder occurred in March 1882. Queen Victoria left Paddington at 4.50pm and arrived at Windsor at 5.25pm after her usual sedate journey. She walked across the station yard to where her carriage was waiting. Then a man, "wretchedly clad who was standing at the gateway of the yard, deliberately raised a pistol and fired it at Her Majesty's carriage, which was about thirty yards distant.[9]" The attacker was immediately seized by the police and also John Frost, the locomtive foreman at Slough who always accompanied the GWR royal train; he was "severely handled" by the crowd "and belaboured over the head and shoulders with an umbrella by an Eton boy."

The assailant was Roderick McLean, aged 32, an unemployed clerk. He had walked from Portsmouth to Windsor with no food and had earlier been seen hanging about the station by Smythe, the stationmaster. There was much talk that he was a hardened anarchist but legal proceedings soon revealed that he was of unsound mind. Queen Victoria was unharmed.

[1] A & M Sellwood, *The Victorian Railway Murders*, Newton Abbott, 1979: p.69

[2] Walsh was erroneously described as a stationmaster in *The Times*, 2 May 1868.

[3] *British Transport Police Journal*, January 1951.

[4] Whitehead's version is that the young man was already in the compartment when East got in at Barnehurst.

[5] *British Transport Police Journal*, October 1952

[6] Whitehead's *Railway Police* suggests the wagon was at Blencow nearer to Penrith, which would have meant a curious route to their journey.

[7] The site of the murder was marked by a memorial, between the station and the *Pack Horse Inn*.

[8] *Essex Murder Casebook*, S Jarvis, Newbury 1994; Jarvis reports that the murderer was arrested after trying to pawn his gun at Euston.

[9] *The Times*, 3 March 1882

CHAPTER TWO:
ASSAULT

Assault is, of course, a criminal offence under most circumstances and prosecutions were usually under the normal criminal law except in cases where the assault had been fuelled by drink - covered by a number of other laws and bye-laws. Curiously, the railway company had no duty to protect travellers from the ill-will of others. The case of Cobb v GWR was based on an incident when 16 men entered a compartment and stole £90 from other travellers, but the stationmaster refused to delay a train so the men could be arrested; the House of Lords ruled that the GWR was under no obligation to do this. In Pounder v NER 1892 a passenger who had been evicting striking miners was assaulted by a crowd of them who invaded his railway compartment; the NER guard did nothing to stop them and it was ruled that the railway company had no contractual obligation to protect a traveller. So, when you started a train journey you were almost literally on your own....unless, of course, there was someone nasty lurking under the seat!

Assaults by Railway Staff

An interesting case in March 1839 was brought by a gentleman named Henniker against a "conductor" on the GWR, Ashby. The former had been travelling to London when he was ordered out of his carriage by Ashby in a dispute over a seat; Ashby was not in GWR uniform, so Henniker refused, whereupon he was "dragged out of the carriage with great violence." He sued for damages and won £25.

Even more extreme was a battle fought at Howdon station on the Newcastle & North Shields Railway on 11 November 1839. John Dobson, an architect of note in railway circles[1], and James Archibald, a councillor, were waiting to catch a train back to Newcastle when the latter was assaulted by an "over-zealous" railwayman named Newton, who dragged him to the station house on the excuse that he was drunk and had refused to "show his ticket" - which he had bought seconds before! This assault must have seemed almost piratical as John Allan joined on Newton's side - a fearsome figure with a wooden arm and iron crook. Dobson, who tried to intervene, was hit twice on the head and knocked down. The two were freed by Mr Cruddas, a railway director, who recognised them. The two railway servants were fined £10 and £8 - the fines being paid by their employer!

Almost more shocking was an assault carried out by a railway director, Heseltine, of the Sheffield & Rotherham Railway in 1839. John Carmley alleged that on 7 August he paid his fare and got into the train at Sheffield, but complained to Heseltine that it was late departing. Heseltine, presumably out of some bizarre form of wounded pride, called the passenger a "blackguard" and summoned several railway police to drag him off the train and throw him out of the station. He won £10 damages.

This is not the only known case of assault involving a senior official. Robert Gill, described as "managing director" of the Manchester & Leeds in 1841, was charged with assault on John Marsden a Wakefield solicitor. The two had shared a bad-tempered exchange in Gill's office, with Marsden using poor language, and Gill had then thrown him out - but was judged to have used excessive violence and so was fined £30.

In October 1843 a spectacular row between two railway directors hit the newspapers as it was planned to settle it with a duel. The subject of the row was the tolls charged by railways and the effect on company finances of increasing fares. The protagonists were W Wilkinson, chairman of the London & Croydon, and John Entwhisle a former director of the Greenwich and Brighton railways. On 4 October a dispute between the two had led Enwhisle to beat Wilkinson with his cane at Camberwell, and the latter had hit back. Enwhisle said that "a false charge upon his character" had been made which Wilkinson had refused to retract. When the plan for the duel was discovered, Mr Roberts - deputy chairman of the Croydon Company - reported the affair to Union Hall Police Court. Warrants for the arrest of both men were issued and Wilkinson admitted the situation, although he was a Surrey magistrate himself. £1000 had to be paid over to keep the peace.

Curiously the Brighton Company was involved in another case of board room scuffles in August 1850, when the Chairman Laing was accused by Mr Rastrick of assaulting him and unlawfully expelling him from the board room. Laing's defence was that Rastrick was not elected a director and

For many Victorian travellers, being locked in a compartment with a dangerous lunatic was one of the greatest dangers of going by train! An illustration from *Mr Punch's Railway Book.*

that no violence had occurred. It was found that confusion had been caused by the practice of electing directors by a show of hands - Rastrick had believed himself to be elected and thus had gone to the next board meeting. At the door "he was stopped by the porters with some rudeness, and pushed back and the door shut in his face." Thus the case went to Laing, but the sequel was a ruling in November 1850 that once a poll had been ordered a vote taken by show of hands became void.

The theme of excessive force was also used in an accusation by five men against railway staff at Walsall in February 1841. The Manchester express made an unscheduled stop to pick up a parcel of information about the local election, and the five men - who had tickets - boarded the train; railway staff then threw them off, using excessive force.

The same theme can be noted in the case of Mr Vyse of Ipswich, who "broke and entered" Ipswich station when drunk. Two EUR officials felt

AN EXCITING TIME

Poor Jones is convinced that his worst fears are at last realised, and he *is* left alone with a *dangerous lunatic*!! (It was only little Wobbles running anxiously over the points of his coming speech to the electors of Plumpwell-on-Tyme!!)

he was obstructing them in their duties and he was removed by force, being taken to the police station. Vyse then sued them for assault and won £5!

An early example of racial tension was behind a case in August 1956. A Jamaican porter, Francis, was working at Lime Street goods station where he felt continually picked on by a crane driver who was also a shop steward. Francis said that the crane driver threatened him with a file and spat at him until he eventually snapped and assaulted the man. The Jamaican porter was discharged conditionally by the court.

Assaults by Passengers and Others

Probably the earliest known assault with any railway connection was on the engineer William James when he was surveying for a Liverpool & Manchester line in 1822; he was attacked by colliers until he hired a prize-fighter as a defence.[2]

In November 1847 the 6pm down arrival at Ely was met by the police after a man, apparently mad, had launched a frenzied attack on fellow passengers. When the others had got into the compartment the man had been lying on the seat, but he suddenly rose up and attacked the others, "making the blood flow in all directions." The man also attacked stationmaster Newell and had to be put in the "cage" for the night. Magistrates found that he was "a respectable man" who suffered from "determination of the blood to the head" after drinking one glass of brandy, so fined him a mere £5.

A strange assault case involved a charge against linendraper John Reid, who assaulted Metropolitan Railway porter Henry Maunders at Gower Street station - by pulling a few hairs out of his beard. Reid and his friends had been waiting for a train in September 1867 when they had started to amuse themselves by "coughing" outrageously as a commentary on the smoky atmosphere; the porter had asked them to be quiet, after which the assault had occurred. Reid was fined £3.

In September 1882 two freemasons travelling back from London to Birmingham by a midnight train quarrelled over the whisky they were sharing and a "desperate fight" broke out. Charles Williams smashed the window with his hand so that the carriage was "saturated with blood."

Another case involving whisky was a "serious affray" in a 3rd class compartment between Liverpool and York in May 1884. The victim, Cannon, was found at Bury bleeding badly from the head and his compartment was spattered with blood. Attempts to discover who had attacked him were fruitless as Cannon, who had just arrived from Madras, had spent most of his time since docking in Liverpool in the company of the whisky bottle.

However the behaviour of W O'Brien MP could have been even more dangerous. O'Brien was a highly unpopular Irish MP in 1889 at a time when the country was in ferment, and his journey from Cork to Clonmel required police protection. At Charleville a hostile group met his train at the station and O'Brien so disliked "the demeanour of the crowd" that he took out a revolver and opened fire from the carriage window. Two railway porters received head injuries and O'Brien was arrested by his own police guard, though he was protected from prosecution by parliamentary privilege[3].

A railway servant was also injured when a drunkard decided to attack Thomas Humphries' signalbox at Custom House; Humphries succeeded in blocking both lines to avoid an accident when he saw the attack was imminent, an action which prevented him from escaping. His assailant got two months prison.

A most bizarre crime was inflicted on Miss Amy Smith, who got onto a GWR train at Oldbury in 1891. As the train was about to leave a young man jumped into the compartment. Miss Smith closed the window, but the man suddenly jumped up and opened the window again - and then he opened the door. At first she thought he was going to commit suicide, but instead he grabbed her round the waist and threw her out of the train! He then threw her possessions out afterwards. At Langley the guard saw someone get out the "wrong side" of the train and run off across the fields. Eventually canal clerk Sadler Silvester of West Bromwich was tried for aggravated assault, but he produced friends who swore he was in Evesham at the time. A booking clerk recognised him as having bought a ticket on the date, but he made the mysterious comment that "It is the other man you want." With only the girl's evidence against him he was discharged.

In August 1904 two ladies were travelling up to London on the LBSCR when a man got into their compartment at Redhill. Arthur Cole immediately filled them with concern as his first act was to lean out of the window, shouting wildly and waving his arms. Then he sat down near to them and pulled a clasp knife out of his pocket, opened two blades, and apparently "sprang" at Gertrude Ranson as the train passed South Croydon. The other lady, Sophia Wilks, managed to get in front of Cole and grabbed the knife, passing it to Ranson who threw it out of the window. Both women then pushed Cole into the corner until the train stopped at East Croydon. Cole's defence was that he had taken out the knife to trim his cigar, but he was given two months hard labour.

A number of assaults were due to the inadequate care of the mentally ill. In August 1910 William Frost was attacked with a revolver while travelling in a 1st class carriage between Baker Street and Aylesbury. A man who got into the carriage suddenly produced a revolver and fired at Frost, who was hit on the chin. He managed to struggle with his assailant, who leapt out and the open door was seen by a signalman at Marlborough Road, who rang Swiss Cottage to stop the train. William Simpson was found crouched in the tunnel near the station, apparently very dazed - probably due to an electric shock. It was revealed that he had only recently been let out of an asylum, to where he was returned. In his possession he had 43 bullets, two bottles of chloroform, one of laudanum and several pieces of cord.

A strange case occurred between Scarborough and Whitby in April 1914. When the train arrived at its destination a girl was found slumped in a first class compartment. When she revived she said she had been attacked by a man who had suddenly climbed out from underneath the seat. He was "short of stature and wild-looking" and had hit her across the head with a pistol; the pistol was found in the carriage. Unfortunately for the "victim", Gertrude Hopper, the police discovered that she had acquired the pistol herself the day before!

Fury at a level crossing sometimes led to acts of vandalism (see chapter five) but in March 1961 it resulted in an assault. John Simcock was stopped by the crossing gates at Broadheath Crossing and was so annoyed that he forced entry into the signalbox and attacked the signalman with a glass ashtray. The man was knocked unconscious so that he was unable to send the signal to the next box that the mail train had passed. For this very dangerous attack Simcock received a £25 fine. In July the same year the signalman at Kew Bridge reported eight youths gathered near his box, heard a shot fired and had two of them try to force their way into his box so that he sustained a gashed knee.

External Matters

Sometimes matters that had nothing to do with the railways caused a fracas on the platform or in the train. Wm McWhirter, a guard on the Manchester & Leeds, got himself into money problems in October 1843. His creditors sent round two men to see him as he was readying the 7pm departure from the Manchester station, and they dragged him off the train to force him to pay. They were both arrested under Seymour's Act for obstructing a railway official and fined, but as they refused to pay they had a month in prison.

One of the problems for the London & Blackwall Railway was that agents for the Thames steamers touted aggressively for custom at Brunswick Wharf, whilst the Railway tried to keep them off its premises. In December 1843 this led to Blackwall Railway policeman John Earl being assaulted by two men from the steamer *Fairy*. The magistrates dismissed the case under a technicality as it was being tried under Lord Seymour's Act, but the prosecution had been brought by the Metropolitan Police rather than the railway company.

Railways led indirectly to "a most disgraceful fight" taking place between two members of the Liverpool Stock Exchange during excitement over railway shares in April 1845.

Fights Between Railway Workers

Most of the railway workers who fought each other were navvies, of course, but occasional disputes between other workers ended in assault charges too. Two footplatemen on the London & Croydon got into a fight in January 1842, with the result that Robert Jobson fractured the skull of Thomas Archer with a hammer. Both were arrested, but also sacked.

More serious was the fight that broke out on the footplate of a Limerick to Cork goods train in April 1873. When the train stopped near Butterant the guard was mystified to find the footplate deserted and thought both driver and fireman must have fallen off. Looking more closely, he found blood on the tender footsteps and the dead body of driver Arthur Wall near the track. The crossing keeper at Shinanagh reported a bizarre vision of a man in a vest and no trousers - this turned out to be the fireman, Timothy Nagle, who had fallen off the footplate and lost his trousers in a bog. However, the two men were known to have hated each other and Nagle had been seen to hit Wall with his shovel, so when the trousers were recovered from the bog and turned out to be bloodstained it was clear that Nagle's story of falling off in the course of a fight was not the complete truth. He was given 15 years for manslaughter.

Sexual Assaults

The first railway passenger trains in England had very basic carriages, which were usually divided up into compartments with no corridor connections. Thus passengers were stuck in a compartment with whoever else happened to get into the train for however long it took to travel from one station to another. This led to many problems for young lady travellers who, in Victorian England, were not meant to be alone with male strangers. One of the earliest known examples was on the London & Greenwich in March

FOR LADIES ONLY

"RESERVED CARRIAGES." (*See " Day by Day " in
" Daily News ")*

" If you travel in one, you run greater risks than in
travelling in the ordinary carriages.   I have known railway
officials allow men to jump into them at the last moment
before the train starts, with a mutual wink at each other
and a very objectionable grin."

Punch commented on the dangers caused by "Ladies Only" carriages.

1841, when James Thompson was accused of assaulting Emily Stacey. As soon as he saw her in the train Thompson had begun his "insulting behaviour", and when she moved to a different place he followed her. He tried to "hold her in an improper manner" and "used vile language". Two officials of the L&GR assisted the prosecution and Thompson was fined £5.

At the Great Exhibition in 1851 a model of a device to allow passengers to raise an alarm was demonstrated - a handle was turned to blow a whistle and by pulling a handle the guard could see coloured glasses which told him the compartment where trouble had occurred. There was some demand for "Ladies Only" compartments and in October 1851 the Great Northern put up notices to say that staff would arrange for women on their own to travel with other women; the guard could place them "where they will be free from annoyance." There was also a call for a system of communicating with the guard which developed into the "communication cord". However it was the Muller murder case which caused the Regulation of Railways Act of 1868 to make the cord compulsory for trains travelling more than twenty miles without a stop.

James Woodhouse, a guard on the Blackwall Railway, got involved in a fight with another passenger in November 1840 when he left his "box" to go into a carriage where a young woman was travelling in order to "kiss her". James McIntosh struck him on the jaw, for which he was fined £5. Another errant guard was Beadle of the London & Brighton in October 1841; he persuaded a young lady travelling second class to go into first, where "he commenced taking indecent liberties." When she resisted he threw her out at the next station! He was fined 40s and sacked. This case attracted the attention of Home Secretary Sir James Graham, who told the Croydon magistrates that he thought Beadle's sentence was inadequate. Beadle himself produced a lengthy circular making insinuations about the girl's character.

Drink tended to encourage some characters to make improper advances. On a train from Hessle to Hull in June 1841 a young lady was subjected to the unwelcome attentions of a drunken butcher, Thomas Spears. He put his face right up under her bonnet and she had to keep moving away. Then his own hat blew off, so he broke her bonnet. Spears admitted he was "a bit fresh" and was fined £2.

In September 1847 John Latham, who worked at Somerset House, was arrested at Paddington and accused of grossly insulting a lady in a GWR carriage. He was also accused of not giving up his ticket at Paddington, but there was strong feeling that Latham had been unfairly and excessively dealt with: "It is not to be endured that ladies and gentlemen should be treated as common felons, and confined in a station house on the charge of every jack in office," *Herapath* blustered. However, "we have witnessed most improper conduct by passengers," although in this case the GWR was unable to produce the offended woman. No lady had actually made a charge.

One of the most important cases hit the headlines in an unusual way - one of the key witnesses in it wrote a letter to *The Times* describing what had happened. On 11th July 1864 a letter from "H.S." was printed, describing how he had caught the 1.10pm from Waterloo and shared a compartment with a youth - quite peacefully until after Surbiton. As they were travelling on the Southampton line through Surrey, H.S. was shocked to see a young woman hanging by one hand from the outside door handle of the next compartment whilst the train rattled through the Surrey countryside at a tearaway 40mph.

Reaching out from his own compartment, H.S. was able to grab the young lady round the waist and pull her up onto the running board of his own compartment. More he could not do, and he clung hold of her with a supreme effort for five miles until the guard's attention was attracted by the cries of farmers and labourers in the fields at the lineside. When the train was stopped the young lady was hauled to safety, and then at the next station - Farnborough, across the border into Hampshire - a man in the neighbouring compartment was arrested.

The identity of the heroic H.S., who nearly lost his own life in clinging to the young lady, was soon revealed as Mr Stokes, a military bootmaker. The young lady was Mary Moody, the daughter of the museum curator at Winchester, whilst her assailant proved to be Henry Nash, a yeoman farmer from Farnborough.

Nash was arrested and charged with indecent assault upon Miss Moody, who told her tale for the first time before Hampshire magistrates. She said that the train had started with Nash, another woman and herself in the compartment, and Nash had tried to "force a conversation" with the other woman until she got out at Surbiton. She tried to get out herself, but was too slow to move before the train started again.

As they left Surbiton, Nash lay down across the seat opposite to Miss Moody and stared at her. He asked personal questions about why she wore spectacles and her age. In a panic she stood up, so Nash grabbed at her round the waist and "I also felt my dress greatly raised in front," she said. Fearing for her virtue, Miss Moody opened the carriage door and tried to climb out - in her testimony showing a strange grasp of Victorian morality:

"I knew that if I got out of the carriage I was liable to be fined...(but)...if my character had been gone then my life would have had no value."

Perhaps the most sensational revelation from Miss Moody was that, after she had climbed out onto the running board to save her honour, Nash had closed the door behind her!

However the prosecution of Nash before the Hampshire magistrates was dismissed, for his offence had been committed while travelling through Surrey! When he first appeared before the Surrey magistrates there was a rumour that he had offered Miss Moody £200 to drop the case against him, but she maintained her determination. He was finally charged at the Surrey Assizes with attempted indecent assault and common assault. The first charge was dropped, but he was found guilty on the second and sentenced to nine months Hard Labour - but for an established farmer of his position the disgrace must have been almost as great a punishment.

In the atmosphere caused by this case it was easy for a man to get himself into legal difficulties, especially as there was considerable emotion among travelling women. On 13 December 1864 James Swaine got himself arrested for criminal assault on a young lady between Waterloo and Richmond. As the train arrived at Richmond a man was seen clinging to the side of one of the carriages shouting "Murder! Police!" and in another a young woman appeared to be fighting off a violent male. The latter was Swaine, who had spent the day getting drunk at Rotherhithe and claimed to have lost £20 on the way home. For some reason he had conceived the idea that the young lady had robbed him while he was asleep, and he had put his hands on her to see if he could get the money back. She had assumed his intentions to be of the grossest nature, but his story was supported by the discovery of his pocket book and the money in the carriage. He was lucky to escape with a 40s fine for being drunk.

Less lucky was Ian Sietring, who got 21 days hard labour after asking Elizabeth Howell for a kiss in Blackheath Tunnel - and then grabbing her round the waist. His defence that she had spoken to him first made little impression. William Hyde "persistently annoyed the daughter of a commander in the Royal Navy" by travelling with her making suggestions and threats; he was bound over for £100.

The second famous case began on 17th June 1875 when two gentlemen were travelling in a first class compartment of the non-corridor 3pm Portsmouth to Waterloo train of the London & South-Western Railway. The train stopped at Woking and was then due to run non-stop to London, but after a few miles the men were disturbed by the sound of frantic screaming coming from nearby. They were astonished to discover that the screaming came, not from the next compartment, but from a young woman standing on the carriage footboard and clinging to the door of her compartment as the train whisked along at 40mph.

The communication cord was not working, so there was no way the two men could stop the train. The young woman seemed to scream words to them, but they could not hear. Eventually some platelayers at the trackside saw the situation and managed to alert the train driver, who drew the express to a halt near Esher, and the woman was helped down after about three miles in this precarious position.

As help gathered around her, she was found to be "half dead with terror." As questions were asked, it was discovered that "she had been so grossly and persistently insulted by a "gentleman" in the carriage in which she travelled that, in self defence, she had bravely encountered what appeared to her to be the less danger to save herself from distress." The "gentleman" was led out of the compartment, the guard noticing that his "dress" (or trousers!) was "unfastened at the front." He was put in a separate compartment and taken to Waterloo where he was arrested.

This was the beginning of a sensational Victorian *cause celebre*, in which the accused was 44 year old Colonel Valentine Baker, the commander of the 10th Hussars and assistant quartermaster general at Aldershot. The young lady was Miss Kate Dickinson of Durnford, near Midhurst, who was twenty two. The high social standing of both those involved, and the sensational manner of the girl's escape, attracted huge press attention and great public interest.

Miss Dickinson had left Midhurst by the branch train to Petersfield, where she had got into an empty first class compartment of the London express. At Liphook Baker had got in, sat opposite to her, and began to talk about visits to the theatre. At first she had felt safe in his company as her brother was in the army and they talked a little about him.

After Woking he stood up and shut the compartment window, then began to "take liberties" - firstly, by asking her name. Then he seemed keen to arrange another meeting by asking, "Could you fix upon a time when you will be on the line again?" Having been rejected in this request, it was then alleged that Baker sat next to the defenceless young lady, took her hands and, even though she pushed him away, he put an arm around her and kissed her on the cheek. She tried to ring the communication bell to the guard but thought it was broken[4], but Baker "violently forced her back into the corner, sank down close in front of her, and violently kissed her again" according to a report in *The Times*. Almost pushing himself on top of her, he tried to put a hand into her skirts.

Fearing what would happen next, Miss Dickinson had managed to force her way to the door and get it open; she backed out onto the footboard, clinging to the carriage side as the train sped along for a distance that was at first claimed to have been five miles. Only when the train was halted and she had been put in the care of a clergyman could she feel safe again.

Baker was bailed for £500 on charges of "attempting to ravish" and assault, which was partly paid by his brother, a well-known polar explorer. The affair immediately provoked discussion of why Miss Dickinson had not used a "Ladies Only" compartment; one writer to *The Times* complained women's refusal to use such compartments was common on the Great Western Railway - "Does not their constant refusal to do so suggest some reflections in reference to the recent charge of assault?" However other female correspondents complained that the compartments were often made intolerable by the presence of screaming babies!

Miss Dickinson's family decided to press the case forwards. She had three brothers - a doctor, a barrister and an army officer - who were clearly determined that Baker should be punished. Baker appeared before Guildford magistrates and was committed for trial at Croydon. He attempted to delay the trial or to have it heard elsewhere, believing that "the feeling in the popular mind is, I believe, at the present time very unfairly excited against me, especially in Surrey." Vicious rumours circulated that Col. Baker had been involved with similar problems before.

Col. Baker was tried at Croydon Assizes on 2nd August 1875. From eight in the morning the streets were densely packed with onlookers and eventually the Judge ordered that the streets outside be cleared due to the noise. Baker seems to have decided not to contest the minor assault charges on the basis that "he could not use any defence"; it was not made clear whether this was because he did not wish to embarrass the young lady, or whether because his conduct could not be defended, for he never appeared in the witness box himself. The defence accepted he had "taken liberties" by sitting next to her after Woking. Instead the trial focused on whether he had intended to rape Miss Dickinson.

The Prosecution, led by Serjeant Parry, argued that "he raised her clothes; there could be no doubt what he was attempting." Much of the detailed discussion then concentrated on the extent to which Baker's trousers were unbuttoned. Both the guard and a Manchester merchant confirmed that they were still undone when the train had been stopped, and the merchant had actually told Baker to do them up on the way to Waterloo. This opened the possibility that there had been "an accidental omission to

LA BELLE DAME SANS "MERCI"

Close personal contact with an attractive young lady could be a stressful experience for Victorian passengers.

fasten them" and that, in the confusion, the young lady had assumed Baker's intentions to be worse than they actually were.

The defence relied solely on cross-examining the prosecution witnesses. Miss Dickinson handled it all very well, "she answered throughout with the utmost coolness, calmness and clearness." In the end it took the jury only fifteen minutes to convict Baker of indecent assault, but he escaped the attempted rape charge; his punishment was twelve months in prison, a fine of £500 and the end of a glittering career in the British Army.

After his release Baker left Britain, taking a post with the Sultan of Turkey and then moving to Egypt. He rose to become a General, though he never regained his reputation in his own country.

Passengers on a GWR train travelling south from Wellington near Shifnal were alarmed to hear screams from a nearby compartment in May 1891, and even more perturbed to see a lady's shawl and hat fly out from the next window. Former Birmingham detective William Bowen climbed along the footboard to see if he could rescue the young woman while other passengers pulled the cord. As Bowen inched along he found the girl trying to climb out of the window, and pushed her back inside. As the train stopped it was possible to arrest Alfred Jones, and discover the story. Jones had grabbed the lady's hand, thrown her to the floor and assaulted her.

The third famous Victorian case occurred on the MR between Tamworth and Burton on 11 January 1892, when passengers in a compartment were astonished by a woman knocking on the outside window. They saw a woman standing on the footboard, clinging to the carriage, but she then fell off. After stopping at Barton under Needwood a luggage train was sent to look for her and the badly injured woman was found at the bottom of an embankment. When the men from the next compartment went to her compartment the man there said, "Yes, this is the carriage; inform the guard".

Mrs Mary Siddals, "a prepossessing young woman 27 years of age"[5], was married with two children. She remained virtually unconscious for several days, delaying the legal investigation. Then it was discovered she had been left alone in the compartment with a man dressed in black, who immediately seized her hands, threw her on the seat "and tried to criminally assault her." She had said, "You want to take my character from me" and screamed. He had then tried to push her out of the carriage.

John Goodall, aged 33, was charged with assault and grievous bodily harm. His defence argued that Mrs Siddals suffered from hallucinations, but he was found guilty. Then two other young women came forward to say that he had assaulted them on trains as well, but "by sanctimonious hypocrisy he had acquired a character for piety and purity" in his home town of Stafford in working as a preacher and teacher to the young. A sentence of two years hard labour was perhaps rather lenient, and would have been more had attempted murder been included in the charges.

On 13 March 1911 Elizabeth Townson, a servant from Chorlton

cum Hardy who was travelling to Ulverston, was found beside the track 300 yards south of Carnforth station where her train had stopped. When the alarm was raised a man from the train who was talking to staff at the station suddenly ran off across the goods yard leaving his bag on the train. Miss Townson was able to give a good description of him as he had a prominent mole and a tattoo "In loving memory of my father." James Molloy was arrested at Dalton Cross.

Miss Townson was largely uninjured and told how Molloy had got on the train at Lancaster and appeared drunk. He had thrown her on the seat and tried to assault her, saying "If you don't I will throw you out of the train", then had placed his hands around her throat. He was given a ten year sentence, leaving a wife and four children to grieve.

Bernard Cook was given five years for assault on a woman between Crayford and Bexley in June 1917; the woman was rescued by Aircraftsman Hurst, who heard screaming from the next compartment and edged along the footboard to see what was happening, then pulled the cord.

In February 1920 James Carey was charged with assault on Annie Whittington on an Aldershot train. Carey was one of five soldiers in the compartment, but all the others got out and he took the chance to make improper suggestions to Whittington, and then he assaulted her. On this occasion the victim was able to pull the cord and the guard arrested Carey. Amy Beachcroft of Petworth also managed to pull the cord and stop the train when Edward Gillan tried to kiss her whilst travelling to Victoria on 26 April 1921. "Don't move or you're a dead 'un," he said, but he was arrested at South Coulsdon.

As the dark and gloomy carriages of the Victorian era came to be replaced by the bright electric lights of the twentieth century, assault on trains became less of a public concern although it was to return as an issue when the 1960s heralded unstaffed stations and driver-only trains. However it became a temporary problem again during the years of the Second World War, when considerable measures were taken to reduce the level of light in night-time trains. After a number of serious incidents, the gloomy blue bulbs were replaced by 15 watt clear bulbs.[6]

Because of cases such as this "Ladies Only" compartments remained a feature of Britain's trains until open-plan carriages became the norm in the 1970s, although they were never enforced by law and never seem to have been very popular. There were occasional problems of them being used by the wrong sex - thus on 2 November 1957 a guard was hurt when trying to eject three youths from a Ladies Only compartment between Shepperton and Waterloo.

However, not every assault of this nature was accurately reported by its "victim" and perhaps it was because of this that one young man was given the advice "Keep your finger nails clean and never get into a railway carriage where there is only one woman."[7] The following colourful account appeared in the *Braintree & Bocking Advertiser* in 1859:

"Some months ago I was seeking a second class carriage at the Shoreditch terminus. A pretty young lady attracted my notice by politely informing me that there was room in her compartment, politely pushing open the door at the same time. As soon as I was seated opposite to her she pulled the door, as much as to say there was enough. We started, I very ungallantly engrossed in my newspaper, she silent, having no-one in the carriage but myself to speak to. I felt the carriage very narrow, and feared I was crowding her, and I moved back as far as I could. In a few moments I still felt her dress against me, and soon was really crowded, being pressed by her. Now, I confess with shame that, being a young man, I felt a little vanity at her attentions, and I yielded to temptation so far as not to move from her. In half an hour a gentleman got in, which, from the lady's face, was not an agreeable thing; she looked vexed. However, our silly conduct proceeded, she throughout taking the lead. At length the gentleman observed us, and my companion, blushing crimson at being discovered, very wickedly drew herself away from me, and flying to the opposite side said I had insulted her. When she found, moreover, that she was known to the thirdcomer, she became very indignant and screamed for the train to stop; she had been grievously assaulted etc. I cannot tell you, sir, my confusion. I durst not charge her with being the first to commence - how cowardly it would have looked! - and upon reaching the terminus her brother was informed - not by the lady, but by the gentleman - how infamously I had insulted her. He flew at me like a tiger, thinking I had really ruined his sister; he smashed my new hat over my eyes, and being much bigger than myself, and assisted by the other passenger, gave me such an awful punishment that I shall never forget it. They were then going to give me into custody; but on my appealing to her, she said that she would gladly have given me into the charge of the Police, but was too bashful to appear in a court of justice to prosecute; and so I got off."

In November 1864 a young woman of "prepossessing appearance" reported to Rugby police station to say that she had been assaulted on a Rugby to Coventry train. The young woman said she had been followed into the compartment by a man who "tried to take liberties" with her, then drew a knife and demanded money. She had given him 5s and her ticket. As the train slowed down he had jumped out, but she now had no money or ticket to get home. The police decided, after a few questions, that she had lost her ticket and had made up the story in order to get home; more dangerously perhaps, her description of the attacker matched the appearance of one of the other passengers.

Ladies of "ill repute" took to the railways as an opportunity for hunting out opportunities, sometimes to the considerable peril of male passengers. In July 1866 Alexander Moseley, a surgeon and dentist of Westbourne Park, was tried for indecent assault on Ellen Allen. Mrs Allen said she had been to Watford for a walk in the fields and had got into a compartment on the return journey with Moseley. He had then locked the door, pulled up her skirts, and attempted to rape her. At Euston she had told the authorities and Moseley had been arrested, foolishly giving a false name and address.

In his defence Moseley, aged 26, said that Mrs Allen had approached him on the platform at Watford and followed him into the compartment. She had then started a "free conversation"; he accepted he had locked the door, but said this was because he wanted to smoke. When they arrived at Euston, Moseley said she had suddenly demanded his name and address on the grounds that he had "insulted" her. It seemed likely that professional ruin and a prison sentence lay ahead, but Inspector Cornelius Fowey from London Bridge station came to Moseley's rescue - he recognised her as a woman who often met men at the station and "went off with them", then a porter from Victoria identified her as one of a group of prostitutes who worked the station. Moseley was released, but Mrs Allen ended up with five years penal servitude for demanding money with menaces.

The following year it was the turn of Rev George Capel to be in the unfortunate position of answering a charge of indecent assault, this time on Mary Fraser at London Bridge on 13 April 1867. The case was "watched" by a moral watchdog, the Associate Institute for Enforcing the Laws on the Protection of Women. Capel must have felt the whole of his life was on trial, but the defence soon established that the prosecution's chief witness of the indecency was an Army deserter - and also Fraser's boyfriend! The only other witness to the "assault" said that, "He had a book in his right hand and appeared to be pushing her crinoline away with his other hand. I did not see him commit any act of indecency," but Fraser had suddenly said, "You nasty beast, how dare you put your hand on me like that!" The charge was dismissed and a perjury warrant issued against Fraser's boyfriend, with the suspicion that the couple were using indecency allegations as a means of extorting money.

In September 1875 Florence Wise was arrested for assaulting John

Dover at the Elephant & Castle station. This was a popular venue for prostitutes, some of whom pestered men and demanded money and it seems that Miss Wise grabbed at Dover and tore his coat. She was given a month in prison.[8]

Prostitutes were often a problem at major stations, especially in London. The "short" trains between Charing Cross and Cannon Street were often used by such women to conduct their business in the privacy of a compartment knowing that there would not be any intermediate stations, whilst the LBSCR's late-night trains between Victoria and East Croydon or Brighton were also popular.

Charles Coolishaw was charged with indecent assault on Harriet Hoole on 22 December 1866 whilst travelling between Croydon and Bromley by train. Hoole, aged about 14, had been a servant for Coolishaw and he was taking her to Bromley to meet her brother. She alleged that he kept "hugging and kissing her, and also behaved most indecently." At the hearing some doubts arose - the two had had to change trains and wait for 30 minutes at Beckenham, but Hoole had made no attempt to speak to the stationmaster who had been nearby. It then emerged that Harriet had made a similar false claim against her cousin a few months before, and Coolishaw was allowed to walk free.

Soon after the Siddals case a Woodhouse dressmaker named Amy Faulkner was found on the line near Holbeck. She said that she had been returning from Bradford when a man she had been trying to avoid followed her into the carriage. After Armley station he had tried to kiss her and as she had grabbed for the cord he had opened the door and pushed her out. Superintendent Parish of the GNR was unconvinced about her story and she withdrew her statement. In the revised version she said that a young man had tried to kiss her but he got out at Armley, after which she had leant on the door and fell out.

While dealing with sexual crimes, mention can perhaps be made of a case at Hull Botanic Gardens MPD in 1961. People living near the depot had been annoyed for some time by staff who climbed onto the wall and looked into their houses, so most had bought net curtains. One house without nets was especially interesting, as the young woman who lived there regularly "entertained" her boyfriend. In February 1961 a cleaner climbed onto the roof of a railway shed to get a better view, but was then spotted by the girl. He was easily caught as there was only one ladder down from the high roof. Charged under the 1361 Justices Act, he was bound over in the sum of £5.

Other Fights and Battles

An "omnibus war" broke out at Cheltenham station in April 1841, where railway police had been instructed to allow only two companies' cabs into the station approach. Another company's driver promptly assaulted policeman Groves of the Birmingham & Gloucester. Also during the 1840s railway staff at Colchester had to get used to being assaulted by belligerent cabbies arguing over exactly where they were allowed to "stand"; one cab driver was twice fined £5 for whipping porters.

There was another "war" at Chester in 1849. The case involved a dispute between rival railway companies and included the ejection by force of the Shrewsbury & Chester Railway's ticket clerk from the station on 16 November. Barricades had been put up to prevent the S&C's omnibuses gaining access to the station, and it was rumoured that the LNWR had a train "filled with navvies with clubs" ready to do battle. The driver of one omnibus was arrested for forcibly entering the premises of the rival railway, but the case was dismissed as magistrates considered the area a public thoroughfare. After a court ruling on 4 December the barricades were taken down by order of magistrates so that S & C omnibuses could serve the station.

Being assaulted by a dog could be worse than being assaulted by a person, and in 1889 a Mr Elsworth was bitten by a dog at Upper Sydenham station. Unfortunately the dog belonged to the stationmaster. A case was brought against the dog and its owner but a Judge ruled that a station was not a public place and therefore dog legislation did not apply; this ruling emphasised the situation that police had no right of access to a railway station.

1 He became the architect of Newcastle Central station.
2 G Body, *Great Railway Battles*, Peterborough, 1984.
3 *The Railway Press*, 5 July 1889
4 *The Times*, 28 March 1892
5 P Earnshaw & D Jenkinson, *The Last Years of the Big Four*, Truro 1997, p.129
6 *The Railway Press*, 4 October 1889
7 Another rare event was a case prosecuted in 1990 of a man charged with sexually assaulting a cat on a train in London; it is too disgusting even to describe in this book, but interested readers may care to consult *The Independent*, 27 June 1990.
8 It may have been that no working system was installed on this train. Regulations at the time only insisted on a communication system if the train travelled more than 20 miles non-stop.

CHAPTER THREE:
PASSENGERS' TALES

The behaviour of passengers was mostly regulated through the bye-laws of each company which could be approved by the Board of Trade and its successors. Railways were also affected by the successive Railways Regulation Acts, especially that of 1840. The 1840 Act made ticket offences like travelling without a ticket specifically criminal, though railways could also use the civil law to recover the cost of unpaid fares. Passengers might also be prosecuted under normal criminal laws and often were - the various assault cases are examples of this. The case of Saunders v SER in 1880 ruled that a railway company had the right to put a person off the train if they had no ticket. After a number of difficult cases where fare fraud had been detected, the railways powers to arrest such people were codified in the Regulation of Railways Act 1889, which specifically helped with the problem of people giving false names and addresses. However, Knights v LCDR of 1893 established that the railway could not keep a suspect prisoner while the name and address was checked.

Unwelcome Passengers: Ticket Problems
The most common type of problem was **people travelling without a ticket**. The opening of the Manchester & Leeds Railway was met with an unprecedented scale of fraud in July 1839 - there were 110 cases on the first day alone! This inspired Mr Edmondson, a chief clerk, to devise a ticket system based on different colour tickets for each station[1]. However, this did not solve all problems - in six months of 1882 the North London experienced 10,549 ticket offences![2]

Punishment could be severe - arrested for travelling from Derby to

Belper without a ticket in May 1841, Henry Weston was sent to the treadmill for a month.

The normal fine for travelling without a ticket was £2[3], but railway companies felt that this was too little and that Shame might be a more powerful weapon. £2 was the normal maximum fine, but new penal clauses in the Regulation of Railways Act meant that an extra £2 could be fined if the passenger gave false details from 1890.In 1905 the GER began putting a monthly placard up at its stations listing the names of all those convicted, a tactic which the SECR also tried. However, one mangistrate thought that "there should not be two sentences on a man for one offence" and reduced a fine to 5s in 1907. However a few days later an Alderman at the same court took a different view - a passenger who offered a ticket inspector £2 to "keep it quiet" was fined a total of £3.

In June 1875 William Rodgers was arrested at Kentish Town for travelling from Leicester with no ticket as he had not been able to produce one; Rodgers lost his temper when pushed and struck one of the porters on the head, but when he arrived at the police station the ticket was discovered. The magistrates reprimanded the MR for excessive force. There were many ways of getting a ticket if you did not have one, but a group of young men who went to Reading races by GWR in 1891 hit upon a clever way. At Reading they jumped out of their carriage and walked along pretending to be ticket collectors, which meant they soon had more than enough tickets for themselves.

In November 1946 a "stowaway" passenger was discovered on the up *Cornish Riviera* just after it had left Plymouth - but this passenger without a ticket was a seven year-old girl, who was also without shoes and socks. A message was thrown out as the train passed Hemerdon signalbox and the train stopped at Exeter, where it was discovered the girl was the daughter of a Plymouth labourer who had plainly thought of a way to lighten the family's burdens.

Another common trick was using a ticket that had expired. Charles Humble, a wealthy basket-maker, was charged with this on the Newcastle & South Shields Railway in September 1839 and prosecuted under the Vagrancy Act; the railway company then withdrew its prosecution, considering the shame of publicity enough. Shame proved too much for William Dunn of Shortwood House, Staines, who was caught at Mortlake in July 1854 with an out of date ticket; already shadowed by a £3000 debt this latest setback proved too much - he ordered a private bath at the Old Royal Baths in Newgate Street, placed his gold watch carefully on the table, and drowned himself.

A rare offence was the forgery of tickets. In December 1849 three men were travelling second class on the SER between Canterbury and Grove

Thomas Edmondson's ticket system was introduced in an attempt to stop widespread fraud on his own railway – the Manchester & Leeds line – but was quickly adopted by others.

WATERINGBURY TO
LONDON
FIRST CLASS
PAID A £0.8.6
356

8 JAN. 20
WATERINGBURY TO
BRICK. ARMS
FIRST CLASS
PAID B £0.8.6
352

Ferry, when two of them began to explain to their unknown companion how easy it was to forge tickets; after listening carefully he revealed himself to be an off-duty guard and they were fined 20s each.

Another type of forgery, in a way, was the practice of letting other people use privilege tickets. In March 1956 a regular fraud was discovered by BTC police among Irish workers on BR, who frequently sold their privilege tickets to others so that they could travel home to Ireland for only a quarter the normal fare. A number of people were found guilty of conspiracy to defraud the BTC, stealing privilege ticket order forms and forgery. A pub in the Strand had been used to sell vouchers for the tickets at £1 or 30s each - the BTC's loss amounting to over £300. Nine month sentences were handed out.

Of course this was a type of "transferring" of tickets, which was outlawed in itself. The case of Langdon v Howells in 1879 clarified this matter - a man who had bought a return ticket sold the other half to another, who was then convicted of "travelling without paying his fare and with intent to avoid paying it." The ruling supported the view that using an illegally transferred ticket was the same as no ticket at all! This was supported by a 1946 case where a married woman gave her return half to her husband to use.

An unusual method of dealing with people travelling without tickets was employed on the Durham & Sunderland Railway in July 1839, when three Chartists were returning from a demonstration in Sunderland. They refused to leave the train when asked, so near Hendon the railway authorities detached their carriage so they could be arrested; one hopes there was no-one else travelling at that end of the train.

Another offence was travelling in the wrong class of carriage. In March 1842 two men were fined 10s each for using 2nd class from Gosport to London with a third class ticket; their claim that they had never been on a train before and had been shown into the wrong carriage. The same fine was levied at Colchester in October 1847 on a man who had travelled first class from Ipswich with a second class ticket.

When Thomas Wright was arrested for "travelling in a superior class" on the Metropolitan District in 1875 it may have seemed like a simple case - until it got to court. The MDR's counsel said he intended to withdraw the prosecution as the wife of the Rev Hunt had written on Wright's behalf, and asked the court's permission to do so. At this point it turned out that Rev Hunt himself was there with his own solicitor, and declared that his wife had no right to abuse his name in this way. Furthermore, he was citing Wright as the co-respondent in the divorce case against his own wife, whilst Wright was suing Hunt for libel. The MDR withdrew its case.

AN UNDERGROUND SELL

First Passenger. " They say they've put on detectives 'ere, to catch coves as travels without tickets."

Second Passenger. " 'Ave they ? Well, all I can say is, *I* can travel as often as I like from Cannon Street to Victoria, and not pay a 'apenny ! "

Detective. " See here. mate ; I'll give you half-a-crown if you tell me how you do it."

Second Passenger (after pocketing the half-crown). " Well, —when I wants to git from Cannon Street to Victoria without payin'—*I walks !* "

Avoidance of paying for rail travel was a popular topic for discussion.

The London railways were especially skilled at spotting habitual law-breakers, and the Metropolitan District was not unusual in arresting a member of the middle-classes in 1880 - the music director of the London Aquarium. The station inspector at Earl's Court was already aware that Charles Dubois had a second class ticket, but had seen him getting into first class several times. After the simple procedure of checking whether he had paid an excess at St James's Park, it was an easy matter to bring him to court. The 5s fine was less than the shame of being criminalised.

The same offence was still being committed a hundred years later, when in the summer of 1949 a man was ejected by the guard from 1st class near Swindon as he only had a 3rd class ticket; unfortunately he lost his temper and pulled the communication cord to cause annoyance - a lapse which cost him £2.

Some passengers bought a ticket for part of the journey, hoping that they would be able to go the rest of the way for free. For example John Lester bought a Birmingham to Coventry ticket in July 1844, but was still on the train when it reached Camden at 5.30am! He owed 1 guinea extra but could not pay and was given eight days in prison. This assumption presumably lay behind the arrest of Mr Chilton QC by the London & Croydon in 1845; he was travelling from Sydenham to London Bridge but lost his ticket, offering to pay the 1s again. However the railway officials decided to charge him the fare from Croydon - 3d extra - which he refused. Chilton was arrested and "imprisoned" for 15 minutes, so decided to sue for wrongful imprisonment. He won £500 compensation after a legal battle lasting two years. The Railway Clauses Consolidation Act of 1845 made it a specific offence to stay in a carriage after the limit of the ticket had been reached.

In September 1867 the GWR brought a clergyman to court, who it accused of a series of frauds "perpetuated in a most ingenious and deliberate manner." Rev Edward Muckleston of Haseley, Warwickshire, had already been caught in 1865 but had been let off with a charity payment. This time he had bought a one-month "tourist ticket" between Leamington and Rhyl but he used it for several different journeys, on the trial charge going between Chester and Hatton Junction. He was fined £2.

Some people acquired forged passes for rail travel. A man arrested with a forged pass at Euston in December 1847 had his signed "Robt Stephenson", which may have looked impressive but was given away by the spelling of "Eauston."

Reserved carriages also caused some problems. In September 1913 a scoutmaster was charged with interfering with the comfort of passengers on the LBSCR in a dispute over reserved places. He was taking fifty scouts to camp at Crowborough from Poplar but the LBSCR had refused to reserve compartments in advance - but when they arrived at Victoria compartments were provided. At East Croydon two ordinary passengers got in as there were no "Reserved" stickers, and Sidney Marsh the scoutmaster tried to keep them out. He lost his temper and at Sanderstead one man was thrown out of the train and left behind. Marsh was fined 20s.

Unwelcome Passengers: Illicit Rides

The railway "hobo" is an enduring folklore figure in America, but has never been a tradition in Britain perhaps because freight train workings were markedly different. Nonetheless, there have been occasions when "hitching a lift" did occur.

The problem was noted by the *Railway Times* in January 1841, when it reported that two men had been fined 10s for climbing into a truck attached to a fast Southampton train. It reported two recent cases of people having been injured while trying to climb aboard goods wagons. The other danger of the practice was that the culprit might be assumed to be planning a robbery, for which the punishment would be far more severe! Henry Waddington was caught in a goods waggon at 11.30pm on the Manchester & Leeds in September 1843 after magistrates at Halifax had passed on information about a gang of twenty who were planning to rob trains. Waddington pleaded that he was only intending to avoid his fare and, since he was "of previous good character", he was discharged.

The practice was clearly high-risk, and there can have been few more bizarre cases than a man arrested in September 1842. Hoping to get to Bristol without paying, he jumped onto the rear buffers of the 10.15pm mail train as it left Paddington and got off at Slough. Unable to pay his fine, he received two months prison at Aylesbury. In November 1847 a goods train of the Edinburgh & Glasgow Railway arrived at North Bridge, where a man was found asleep on the locomotive's buffer beam. He was fined a derisory £1 by magistrates.

Another risky journey was made by a thirteen year old boy from Glossop in January 1914. Wanting to get back home from Manchester, he climbed underneath a carriage but made a serious error in his choice of train - he was found under the carriage at Nottingham some hours later by a wheel-tapper, having become so cold that he was incapable of getting out by himself.

Another foolhardy traveller was Angus McLeod in September 1938, who was fined £3 at Bletchley for travelling on the roof of the *Night Scot* express from Euston contrary to LMS bye-laws, and for travelling without a ticket. McLeod's escapade began with a nostalgic drinking session in the company of Glasgow cronies, and he made a sudden decision to return home. He decided to travel on the roof, but found it an alarming experience: "When it rolled I had difficulty in keeping on. Ten miles from where it stopped it rolled badly and I nearly fell off, so when it stopped in a station I lay flat on the top until I heard the guard shout, when I got down and ran off. It was a silly thing to do, but I was desperate to get home to Scotland." Unaware that the tide of future events would cast question over his choice of words, Sergeant Merry said that McLeod was "as black as a nigger" with red, inflamed eyes.

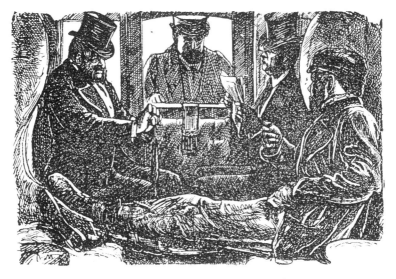

INJURED INNOCENCE

" Hulloa! *You've* no call to be in here! *You* haven't
got a fust-class ticket, *I* know."
" No!   I hain't!"
" Well, come out!   This ain't a third-class carriage!"
"*Hain't* it?   Lor!   Well I thought it *wos*, *by the look
of the passingers!*"

Many and varied were the excuses for travelling in the wrong class of carriage.

McLeod could very well have ended up like Christopher White,
whose body was found on the roof of the 10am Didcot to Paddington and
was removed at Southall West signalbox in July 1946.

In August 1956 passengers on the 11.30pm Manchester to Bury
train were horrified to see blooding streaming down across the windows of
their carriage, and ran to get staff at Woodlands station. Two youths had
drunk three pints of mild, two other beers and two whiskies each when they
got into the train for home. Under the effect of the drink, they decided to
climb out the window and onto the roof as a dare. Peter Hewitt sat on the
first carriage and his friend lay on the second, but Hewitt kept lifting his
head up and was killed when the train entered Collyhurst Road tunnel.

"Train surfing" became a popular phrase in the 1990s to describe
illicit pleasure rides on the outside of trains, but it is highly dangerous. In

September 1847 a youth was killed on the Midland Railway whilst riding a ballast wagon "for his own amusement."

Unwelcome passengers: Smoking, Drinking and Bad Language

One of the great terrors of Victorian railway travel was to be stuck in a compartment with a maniac, travelling for mile after mile with no means of seeking rescue. At least Lord Seymour's Act provided a framework for dealing dangerous passengers who had alcohol-related problems.

Firstly, it gave powers to refuse someone permission to travel if drunk and, in fact, to eject them from a station. For example, in October 1840 a frequent offender was ejected from London Bridge station and fined 20s. In January 1841 three drunken men were arrested for refusing to leave the platform of Blackwall station; they were kept in the cells overnight and fined between 10s and 20s. At Rochdale in 1844 William Cropper of Bury was ejected from the station for abusive language while drunk, but climbed back in over the wall and had to be arrested; he was fined 40s.

The main problem with drunks was the annoyance they caused to other passengers. Three men terrorised passengers on a Nottingham to Derby train of the Midland Counties Railway in May 1841; they were clearly inebriated, were rude to female passengers and struck the guard. They were fined £5-9-6d including costs, to which 40s was added for smoking. Joshua Bowden caused similar trouble on the Manchester & Leeds in December 1842, getting in drunk at Oldham and proceeding to swear, spit and push at other passengers; he was fined 20s. A year later the same company had problems with a man drunk and abusive at Rochdale; as he was unable to pay the 5s fine under the M&L Act, he had a month in prison to repent.

Worse behaviour was shown by three marine engineers on a Greenock to Port Glasgow train in October 1843, who were already drunk when they got in but took another bottle with them. When officials tried to eject them a fight ensued, and Mr Hood's "uniform coat was torn to pieces." They were fined 40s each. John Hay of Croydon was fined 20s for entering a L&CR carriage whilst drunk in November 1846.

In August 1864 a journey in a non-corridor compartment of a Kings Cross to Peterborough express could take nearly two hours: non-stop. This was a fair time to be trapped with a madman, but this unfortunate scenario occurred on 4 August on the 9.15pm. Just as the train was about to leave, a "strongly-built" sailor with a "wild and haggard look" got into the compartment to the terror of the other passengers. No sooner had the train left the station than he jumped up and said he had been robbed of £17 - "roaring and swearing" - then tried to jump out of the window. Kind but unwise, four passengers tried to drag him back in whereupon a fight started that only finished when the others managed to tie him up with straps. The passengers tried to get the people in the next compartment to alert the guard, but their cries of "Stop the train" only caused various women passengers to panic and start screaming. At Peterborough the sailor was taken off the train, but he assaulted four railway staff, while the stationmaster showed a marked reluctance to take him into custody! Alcoholism was suspected.

Of course passengers did not know whether an assailant like this was a drunk or a lunatic. You might suppose that 1st class was safer than 3rd, but this was not the case for James Quirey[4] who was travelling from Carlisle to Penrith in 1870. Thomas Bell of Manchester suddenly accused him of stealing his ticket, then seized him by the throat and beat him about the face. Passengers in the next carriage heard the commotion but could do nothing as "the passengers' signal was not workable." Only when the train stopped at Penrith was it possible to get help, and Bell was taken away to the lock-up where he tried to cut his throat with a penknife. He was charged with assault, damage to a railway carriage and attempted suicide, but was more likely a lunatic as the ticket that started the trouble was found in his possession.

Another unpleasant travelling companion was John Clark of Haywards Heath. In December 1870 he got into a 2nd class LBSCR carriage with a 3rd class ticket, then vomited over the legs of a Mr Toplis. When Toplis asked him for the use of his handkerchief to clear up the mess, Clark abused him. At Thornton Heath all the other passengers got out and the guard locked Clark in. When he arrived at his home town he was fined £2 with £2 costs.

John Simpson was fined 40s for terrorising passengers between Sidcup and London Bridge in July 1874. He began by using bad language, then started throwing his arms about and hit a man and his wife. He was removed by the guard, but when they left the train at London Bridge Simspon attacked the couple again and hit the man in the face. He was fined 40s for being drunk.

In September 1958 Countess Powlett was arrested for being drunk and disorderly at Waterloo. She was fined £2, but instead of accepting the punishment as her due she complained to the press that she had been imprisoned in a "Black Hole of Calcutta".

The sale of alcohol at stations was also regulated. In October 1841 the refreshment room keeper at Darlington was charged with selling brandy without a licence in a farcical case. The man had gone to help a traveller who had been taken ill and gave him some brandy; when the passenger insisted on paying, the refreshment room keeper contravened the law! The case was sensibly dismissed. In 1844 the landlord of an inn at Beeston near Nottingham was reprimanded by magistrates after refusing to open his doors for victims of a railway accident; he was told that his licence would not be renewed.

Smokers were a cause of continual debate. Railway companies deplored the effect that they had on upholstery, but also feared fire at stations. The Liverpool & Manchester banned smoking in 1st class as early as 1831 and many railway companies tried to prevent it altogether - in 1842 a "foreigner" was put off a Brighton line train for smoking a cigar. The Railway Clauses Act of 1845 made it much easier to regulate smoking through bye-laws, but in 1868 a pro-smoking clause in the Regulation of Railways Act forced most companies to include a smoking carriage for all classes in all trains which had more than one 1st class carriage. As early as 1839 there were suggestions for cigar-smoking carriages but many companies protected themselves with bye-laws. During 1840 the GWR brought a number of prosecutions with fines usually being 20s, which were donated to a hospital, in November 1840 the accused being "a respectably dressed foreigner." A man was fined 10s for smoking on the platform at Paddington in September 1841.

A letter to the *Railway Times* in December 1843 observed that smoking was always possible providing the guard received a tip; "Be kind enough to hold your cigar down as we pass the different stations", one smoker was advised. This apparent encouragement to smoke provoked a furious riposte in the next edition, which described smoking as "a very noisome personal gratification, most particularly offensive to female delicacy, and others unused to, and not liking to inhale, the slimy sticking smoke emitted from another's mouth."

On the GNR bye-laws provided for a 40s fine for smokers but from 1852 only the guard was allowed to eject a smoker, "not the common porter." The company maintained a non-smoking policy, yet allowed cigars to be sold at its stations, until it allowed smoking on most trains from 1867.[5] The ECR provided a smoking carriage on each train from 1854, but found that smokers still lit up wherever they happened to be; the *Cambridge Chronicle* described them as "thoughtless young men or callous brutes who care for nothing but their own gratification."

Smokers could be a belligerent lot, as was shown by the case of two Bedfordshire farmers - Roberts and Howell - who got onto a MR express at

Workman (politely, to old lady, who has accidentally got into a smoking compartment). "You don't object to my pipe, I 'ope, mum?"
Old Lady. "Yes, I *do* object, very strongly!"
Workman. "Oh! Then out you get!!"

Smokers and drinkers were hardly ideal travelling companions – especially if you got into the wrong compartment.

Irchester in November 1864. Henry Martin was already in the compartment, and they addressed him directly - "Hello Master, we mean to smoke here, whether you like it or not." They then opened both windows and began to talk in a jocular or sinister manner - depending on your viewpoint: "We'll serve him as Briggs was served, and then we'll throw him out," they said to each other, referring to the Muller murder case - it was the day before the execution of the first railway murderer. Howell then announced that he was really Tom King, the prize-fighter, and hit out at Martin but a man in the next compartment heard what was going on and told the guard at the next stop. Both men were fined 40s.

A smoker who risked several convictions was Henry King, who had a 2nd class season from Forest Hill on the LBSCR. He had acquired a carriage key, these having been openly sold at station bookstalls until just before this time, and he used this to lock himself into 1st class compartments for undisturbed smoking. Having smoked, he went to the 3rd class, presumably so he could say his journey was 2nd class "on average". He was fined 10s in September 1867.

Fines for smoking changed very little - in 1875 Charles King was fined 18s for smoking on the LCDR. Henry Johnson, a Windsor publican, was fined only 10s for smoking on the Metropolitan Railway in January 1867 as several others were smoking too. However in December 1892 Rugby magistrates fined a smoker £5 14s as he had continued to smoke even when other passengers and officials objected.

Another obvious assumption was that people should not travel by train with a gun, yet in November 1889 Charles Knight had to be fined £5 for travelling on the District Railway with a revolver.

Although Lord Seymour's Act was quite comprehensive in what it covered, a gap was found by magistrates in November 1840 when faced with the case of a group of men who engaged in a **conversation** "of a very disgusting nature" whilst in the presence of ladies travelling from Slough to Paddington in November 1840. The ladies were forced to move to another carriage, but magistrates had no power to punish the offence. However in July 1842 a tailor named Lewis was fined 40s for "insulting and disgusting language" at Paddington.

In July 1847 a correspondent to *Herapath's Railway Magazine* complained about male conversations, with men "who choose to make indecent conversation either directly [to a woman] or with another brute within their hearing." The correspondent wished to see more women-only carriages, as used on the GWR.

In August 1864 two Liverpool men were fined £5 each for insulting the wife of a GWR clerk on a train; they used "obscene and blasphemous language" and their conduct was "the most gross short of actual assault."

Homosexual acts remained criminal offences until the 1960s and occasionally took place on railway premises, though tending to receive little

Guard. " Some one been smoking, I think ? "
Passenger. "What! Smoking! That's very repre-
hensible. Perhaps it was the clerical gentleman who
has just got out of the next compartment."

Catching the offending smoker was not always easy!

press attention. Prosecutions were fairly rare and received little coverage in
the press, though one case that caused interest centred on the toilets at
Gloucester Road station in 1954. Two men, including W K Sam, were
arrested there for gross indecency and prosecuted; one man committed
suicide, but the court acquitted Sam who then launched his own case
accusing the police of wrongful arrest, malicious prosecution and conspiracy.

Sam's defence argued that he visited the toilets regularly as he drank
a lot of tea, the police view was that he was looking for other homosexuals.
Police officers had positioned themselves in the "stalls" to watch the
behaviour of men, and gave evidence that they had seen Sam come in and try
to kiss another man. The jury took the view that the police, if hiding in the
stalls, could not have seen what was happening outside and therefore must
have conspired together to produce the "evidence". Sam won £1600
damages, but could have gone to prison for two years.

Another unwelcome character was anyone begging. Charles Mills
was arrested for "soliciting custom" on the LSWR between Vauxhall and
Waterloo, over which he travelled several times a day singing and asking for

money. LSWR bye-laws covered this on a station, in a yard or at its premises, but not in a carriage so Mills was discharged.

We should also not forget spitting, which was outlawed in the bye-laws of many companies. Charles Emblin was fined 10s after spitting on the floor five times between Barking and Blackfriars. Another unwanted type of passenger was anyone with a communicable disease - sufferers were banned from travelling. In 1908 a Mrs Norton was fined £5 for allowing her son to travel on the SECR with scarlet fever.

Unwelcome Passengers: Hooligans

The sporting groups associated with problems on trains are normally football supporters. However horse races attracted some disreputable types too, such as Herbert Carter who also used the name Le Fevre. In July 1892 he got into a 1st class carriage at Sutton on his way to Goodwood via Victoria, and immediately began to annoy Lt Wilkie with foul language. At Clapham Junction he called Wilkie a liar, used foul names and threw paper at him as Wilkie got out - which constituted an assault. Wilkie told the guard who tried to lock Carter and his friends in, but they climbed out at the Grosvenor Road ticket platform - then jumped into another train going to Victoria. The case had to be dismissed as Wilkie had gone to India.

The 1950s was the era of the "Teddy boys", whose actvities occasionally affected the railways. At Blackpool in early 1957 two were seen fighting on a train and were removed by transport police - which then led to a fight between the police and five other "teddy boys". In August the same year up to thirty youths were involved in a fight on the 10.30pm Southport to Wigan in which windows, lights and tables were smashed - the tables disappearing into the darkness outside. Four were charged with disorderly behaviour and leaving the train in an improper manner, defending themselves buy arguing they had gone to help a friend who had been attacked by a drunk. They were each fined £1 plus costs.

Trouble was caused by Leicester "Teddy boys" during a day trip to Skegness in the summer of 1960. The gang caught the 7.52pm train back, but its progress became rather sporadic. Between Skegness and Sleaford the communication cord was pulled five times and the "Teddies" completely took over the eight middle carriages of the twelve carriage train. The guard locked the doors to keep them in that section and to protect other passengers. Police came onto the train at Sleaford and it eventually reached Leicester two hours late. By that stage the middle carriages had been devastated with seats and tables wrecked; carriage fittings were found scattered along the line between Firsby and Sleaford with damages costing £850. Arrests by the Sleaford police were complicated by the use of false names such as "Spuggy", "Smiggy" and "Mugs", and it took three weeks to collect 200 real names. 14 were charged and mostly fined.

The following Easter BTC expected further trouble and there were complaints about behaviour on the outward journey, so 40 young men were picked out at Skegness and put in one locked carriage with a number of officers, ensuring a more peaceful return trip to Leicester for everyone else. One youth who refused to use this special carriage was fined £5 for obstructing police. However South Wales officers were less successful and a Porthcawl to Llanelly return excursion was described as "a moving den of hooliganism." 700 young people were packed into ten carriages, of which nine were extensively damaged with slashed seats and broken windows. In the 22 miles between Porthcawl and Swansea the communication cord was pulled nine times and the train arrived at Swansea "only" three hours later as police disconnected the vacuum brake according to press reports. There had been problems on the way out to Porthcawl, so police had prepared for trouble on the way home by putting ONE officer on the train - although he was reinforced by another at Port Talbot!

Two Llanelly youths appeared in court for damaging lights (73 bulbs were broken), interfering with the comfort of passengers, using part of a train not provided for passengers and disorderly conduct on a train. Two young women had been grabbed, pulled down and kissed against their will, passengers had been splashed with beer and one of the youths sat on a window with only his legs in the train. They got two months prison and a £5 fine. Another youth of 16 was fined £15, but denied he was "showing off in front of the girls."

The same Easter weekend was also troublesome on the Blackpool trains which were disrupted four nights in a row. One Blackpool to Bradford working was 4hrs 42mins late due to the cord being pulled, another had no working lights left at all, while one passenger was taken off at Preston and needed stitches after being pushed through an internal window.

For the following Whitsun weekend there was a much stronger police presence at Blackpool and similar stations. Troublemakers were refused permission to board and when the trains reached Preston police came on board to look for signs of damage and eject suspects. The 11.30pm to Colne and 11.55pm to Rochdale were reputed to be the worst, made more problematic by the lack of corridor carriages; the guard on the Colne train complained that he had once had the cord pulled 16 times on a similar working.

The Glasgow suburban network suffered many incidents in the 1950s and 1960s, especially on Saturday nights. After a rash of assaults in 1967-8, Transport Police launched a campaign to get things under control by using a "commando squad." Within two weeks they had arrested 61 people in the Glasgow area, and then managed a further 35 on Glasgow to Stranraer trains.

Football traffic attracted a great deal of attention in the 1960s and 1970s, but was periodically a problem in earlier days as well.

Damage done on 5 March 1956 after Everton had played at Manchester City was described as the "worst in the history of railways" and was probably the first major incident of the modern era. Six excursion trains took spectators back to Liverpool, the last arriving at 11.20pm with 13 windows broken, 14 pictures ripped away, 2 mirrors broken, one door missing, several cushions heavily bloodstained, compartments slashed and luggage racks pulled off. Most of the other trains had received some damage as well. Superintendent Finney commented that "A number of young women were among the passengers on the damaged trains." One of the trains was stopped six times by people pulling the cord and drunken passengers had to be lifted off the lines.. It need not be said that Everton had lost the match, an FA Cup tie, 2-1 in front of 76,000.

The same set of supporters caused further trouble on 26 December 1957 when they were returning from a match at Bolton, even though police guards had been put on Everton trains since the "last train from Bedlam" incident of May 1956. On this occasion 600 Everton supporters were put in a non-corridor train, which rather reduced the effectiveness of the policing, but the cord was pulled and the train halted at Orrel station for 90 minutes. During the long wait in the dark many supporters got out and "swarmed across" the tracks, whilst other broke windows. There were further problems when Liverpool lost to Burnley in March 1958 and when Everton lost in the same town in August 1959.

Occasional problems continued to the early 1960s - in January 1962 four trains were damaged in Lancashire and two Watford supporters were taken to hospital after an incident in a train near Leyland; police asked trainspotters for help in identifying problems!

In 1969 a match between Portsmouth and Millwall resulted in trouble on the 10.50 from Waterloo to Portsmouth. A refreshment trolley standing on the platform was plundered of its cigarette stock just as the train was about to depart, and the fact that the buffet car was unstaffed and locked did not deter supporters from seeking other goods. At Woking the guard called for help and twenty police arrived, removing thirty supporters from

"I HOPE NOBODY'S GOT ANY BRIGHT IDEAS ABOUT 'DECENTRALISING' OR 'STREAMLINING' THIS LOT BEHIND OR WE'VE HAD IT."

"Youth" and railway vandalism – as depicted by a British Transport Police cartoon of the 1950s.

the train. 29 were charged for various offences including having no ticket and throwing things out of the windows; there were 28 convictions but Police commented that the public were not helpful in giving evidence.

This year was one of the worst for hooliganism, especially in March. On 19 March 200 "fans" were turned off a train at Norwood Junction by the Police following problems with the communication cord after a Crystal Palace versus Millwall game; windows were broken and other damage done. The same day three Underground trains were put out of service by criminal damage, though it was felt that better policing at grounds was causing the trouble to move to the railways.

One of the worst incidents on 30 March involved fans of Stockport County, 75 of whom had to be removed from a Crewe to Stockport special train to add to the six who had been arrested before even leaving Crewe!. A group in the first coach were singing, shouting and abusing officials, then the cord was pulled at Sandbach. The 75 in this carriage were made to get out so that the train could continue without them - there was no other train that night.

Railways also handled some other types of seasonal passenger traffic that produced a number of difficult incidents, most famous of which was the traffic to and from Kent in "hop-pickers" - people from the poorer areas of

"WHAT PRICE THAT BIT IN THE 'JOURNAL' NOW?. COMING IN ERE AND REPORTING THE LOSS OF HIS 'FLICK-KNIFE' TO OLD FRED WHO HAS SPENT THREE WEEK-ENDS ON 'ANTI-VANDALISM' DUTIES AINT GOING TO IMPROVE 'RELATIONS WITH THE PUBLIC' NONE."

Even the "Teddy Boys" of the 1950s had the right to report lost property to the Transport Police.

London who went out to the countryside on working holidays. Most of the trouble tended to occur on the return journey, as at East Farleigh in October 1874, when large numbers of police were employed to filter a few at a time through the ticket office. This tended to result in an impatient and bad-tempered crowd who pushed onto the platform, so it was unsurprising that as the train steamed up one drunken man fell onto the rails. The hop-pickers showed no interest in rescuing him, but the Police Superintendent dragged him out of the way in the nick of time, but immediately another drunk fell over and was injured. As the train stopped, a pitched battle took place to secure a seat.

At Maidstone East a special ticket office was set up in the goods yard; the railway staff locked themselves inside at the start of their shift and barricaded the door with iron bars. As tickets were issued, numerous attempts were made to defraud the railway with allegations of short-changing the most common. The local press gleefully reported all sorts of misdemeanours on the trains back to London - it was said that one woman had died and her corpse was robbed of 18s, that another woman had been assaulted by being bashed over the head with a salt cellar, and that there were numerous instances of people falling out. Here was a crowd who would have had nothing to learn from Teddy boys or football hooligans!

There were also occasional problems with military parties, such as the group of fifty soldiers returning to Bisley on a Guildford to Woking train in June 1958. At Woking they ran up and down the train "shouting and clambering about and alarming the passengers" - and were quite beyond the ability of local police to handle them, so military police were called in. The train had to be taken out of service but a spokesman for Army Southern Command was unmoved - "This sort of thing happens every year when Bisley Camp is open for shooting," he said[6].

Finally, a most unusual shooting incident caused terror in 1954. Four young men got into the 5.14pm Edinburgh to Leeds with an air rifle...and a snake. As the train proceeded southwards they let the snake loose and proceeded to shoot at it, with the result that the other passengers in the carriage fled in terror when they stopped at Dunbar. When the snake was dead they threw it out of the window and continued to shoot instead at the passing scenery. Each was fined £2.

In and Out of Trains

The relatively simple process of when to get on or off a train has caused many accidents, but is also well-defined by the law. With passengers accustomed to rooftop rides on stage-coaches, it was felt necessary at first to have bye-laws to stop them travelling on carriage roofs.[7] In the early days of railways, though, passengers persisted in acting spontaneously - often causing their own downfall. In December 1840 a passenger on the Taff Vale suffered the common problem of his hat blowing off - but he then leapt out to get it even though the train was speeding along at 35mph. In August 1843 Frederick Jenkins also jumped out of a train to get his hat - in this case the ECR train was travelling at 15mph and Jenkins was drunk. At his trial it was found that no clause in the ECR Act prohibited jumping out of a train, but he was fined 15s for being drunk.

This sort of case happened in the early days of railways due to ignorance. Two sailors making their first ever railway trip on the London & Greenwich in April 1841 jumped off the train at full speed - and were fined 10s. Sometimes people had made a simple mistake and then acted foolishly, like Albert Schuyler in 1867. He climbed hastily into a moving train at Crystal Place station, but then found he was in an empty stock working so the LBSCR was taking him to the sidings. His answer was to jump back out - through the window. He was fined 40s.

Drink also led to a few cases of self-defenestration, as exemplified by Thomas Langton in January 1884, who was travelling 3rd class on a Liverpool Street to Ipswich train. Passengers noticed that Langton, a demobbed soldier, had been drinking and after 13 miles he suddenly stood up and dived head first through the carriage window - which was closed at the time. Attempts to catch him by the feet were useless and no help was arranged until the train stopped at Colchester. He was found on soft ground near Romford, having cleared the up line and landed in someone's garden. He told Police that he had been in a compartment with two others who had started "foul play" and robbed him of £2, but he was taken off to the workhouse infirmary.

Often alcohol was involved. Thomas Sheppard was arrested for trespass and endangering his own life at London Bridge in May 1867 when he was found at 9.30pm lying between the tracks with cuts to his head. His explanation was that, after being a teetotaller for twenty years, he had been "induced to drink some spirits" at New Cross. He then became "so drunk he did not know anything about it." He seems to have got out at Spa Road by mistake and then decided to walk the rest of the journey. He was fined 10s.

Another reason was lunacy - in August 1889 W McNab jumped out of a St Pancras to Glasgow express near Knebworth when it was travelling at over 60mph. Amazingly he suffered virtually no injuries, but was adjudged to be mad rather than suicidal.

Edward Dawson, a Rochdale draper, just missed his train to Manchester in January 1841 so he ran after it and just managed to get hold of the step of the rear carriage. He was helped in by passengers, but then arrested and fined 15s. Dawson protested that he "often" caught the train in this way, and had been advised to do so by railway staff.

In July 1875 Thomas Crump was brought into court charged with leaving a NLR train when it was moving at Haggerston. Crump argued that the train was running late and had only stopped for 40 secs, thus not allowing him time to descend. He had fallen over as the train started again and another woman fell over as she could not get the door undone in the time. The case reflected badly on the NLR, which was shown to have used the threat of prosecution in an attempt to get Crump to drop his damages case. The charge was one that occurred many times until the introduction of sliding door stock managed to reduce the opportunities; for example, John Howard was fined 20s for leaving a LNWR train in motion at Willesden, compounding his offence by allowing the door to swing open. However a man who opened the door and jumped out at Cannon Street, when the train was going about 10mph, was only fined 2s6d in January 1867 although he had created a risk for "two or three" people on the platform.

Sometimes people had a good reason for jumping out. Henry Price was a passenger who combined two of the Victorians' fears - he was a thief and a lunatic! In December 1874 he robbed a sleeping passenger on a down mail train of the GNR, then tried to jump out of the window while passing Retford, sustaining nasty facial injuries which replaced the false beard he had worn earlier. He told a crowded hearing at Retford that he wanted to see York Minster, but it turned out he was an escaped lunatic from Wakefield. The case can be compared to the experience of a Dr Dunlop, who was unfortunate to be in the same compartment as two "seafaring witnesses" going to Durham Sessions with liberal liquid support. When the two "became excited" he decided to leap out of the window -and was knocked down by a train coming in the other direction, having to have a leg amputated.

In August 1961 a boy was fined £3 for opening a carriage door while the train was in motion at Denmark Hill. Six schoolgirls and seven schoolboys were in one compartment when two of their bags went out the window, so the cord was pulled and the door opened. The father of the arrested child complained that it was all the school's fault, while the boy said he had been threatened by another.

There has always been a tendency for passengers stuck in a train to all get out and walk, although this is illegal. On the ECR in September 1846 an up train was delayed at the Shoreditch ticket platform so a group of about forty got out and walked along the track to the terminus. Anthony Gibson resisted arrest, so was fined £5 for impeding ECR officials.

Passengers Fight Back

Passengers occasionally used the civil courts to fight back against railways that had let them down. One such case troubled the North British Railway, which found itself in the Small Debt Court after a train failed to stop at Portobello on 6 February 1848 - a passenger pursued it for two guineas costs and won the case.

A luggage dispute led to two LNWR porters being brought to court by F A Hardy for trespass and damages in May 1848. Hardy had gone to collect his trunk at Euston but refused to give the porter a clear description of it, so the porter refused to hand it over. Hardy grabbed the luggage, whereupon porter Evans hit him and Brown grabbed it back. The LNWR's Mark Huish supported the actions of his men, who could have been preventing a robbery, and the Judge dismissed Hardy's case.

Nineteenth-century railway journeys could be characterised by chaos and disorder.

A passenger named Goff sued the GNR in 1861 after it had treated him very shabbily. Goff gave in the wrong half of a return ticket and, although he had the correct half in his pocket, he was arrested; despite explaining his mistake, the GNR decided to prosecute him and he was taken to the magistrates, who sensibly dismissed the case. Goff demanded damages for wrongful arrest and the company lost this case.

An excursion trip from Leicester to Derby on 6 August 1866 resulted in the case of Shelton & Wife v MR. This seems to have been something of a problematic trip, with reports saying that at "Buxton" passengers were told to alight and transfer to the guard's van or they would get no further that night - there were eight passengers in this position. They reached Derby at about 11pm and were told to get out, but Mrs Shelton was unsure as they were not in a proper carriage with a footboard and they had not stopped in the platform. In trying to get out she broke her leg and had to spend seven weeks in a nearby hotel, during which time she was unable to help her husband run their pub. The MR's defence was that she was offered a place in a normal carriage but refused, and also refused to get into a normal carriage at Roseley. The MR won the case.

At Warwick Assizes in March 1868 a Birmingham surgeon named Jackson sued the Midland Railway for damages after an injury. He was travelling with his wife on a Birmingham to Leicester excursion for the "Foresters' Fete", when a "jerk" of the train near Narborough threw him forwards and then back so that he struck his head on the carriage partition. Jackson was faint and sick, having to be taken home in a cab and spending a month in bed. He claimed injuries for concussion, lassitude, deafness and being unable to work for two months. The MR's defence was that there had only been a slight jerk as the train crossed points and that Jackson's illness was actually rheumatic fever; the jury found no evidence that the MR had been negligent and Jackson lost.

A City merchant sued the GWR in 1889 after "receiving some slight injuries to his head" at the hands of the GWR at Westbourne Park. The merchant had been for a day out on the River Kennett and on his way back from Reading was found asleep with no ticket - so he was ejected. The GWR dealt with his suit by launching its own against him for being drunk!

Tricksters

Another danger of railway travel was that you could meet highly plausible characters who turned out to be rather dishonest. In 1954 one such character hung around Euston station looking for likely victims, eventually picking on a young soldier who was heading north. He took the soldier to the Rugby Hotel nearby to buy him a drink, offered him a lift to Lancaster, then asked for £6-10s to buy some whisky. With the money in his pocket, he disappeared. This character was found to have at least 28 similar offences in his record, as well as being married to one woman and "engaged" to another.

A game of cards was a popular way of wasting away time on a train, but playing with strangers was dangerous. A Swiss youth visiting Bletchley in 1867 was offered a game of cards while travelling back to London, by a gang who tricked him into getting onto a Manchester train. Once on the train the youth refused to play cards and the card-sharpers who had hoped to trick him lost their tempers at this, grabbbed him by the throat and proceeded to rob him anyway. To escape he had to smash a window and open the door. The same year Charles Williams, "a notorious sharper", was arrested for stealing £4-10s from a sailor; Williams' *modus operandi* was to pick up sailors at Waterloo and take them to a nearby pub, where he would "persuade" a few men to join a game of cards - all the men being secret members of the gang of sharpers.

A gang of card-sharps was acting on the Metropolitan Railway and one of them was caught at Uxbridge Road in 1890; he was sentenced to three months hard labour under the Vagrancy Act.

In 1957-8 a gang of card sharps worked the trains in an area around Barnsley, first tricking and robbing a Greek seaman near Retford. The cards they used were specially prepared with a linen square fixed at the centre and starched to make them easier to manipulate; they then travelled the trains but "set up" situations so it looked like they were strangers to each other. On 1 June 1957 they made the mistake of picking two victims who were travelling together between Cudworth and Leeds, and the two complained to police at Leeds that they had lost £20. The gang was arrested for conspiracy and given 18 month sentences.

Finally, two stories that don't seem to fit under any heading. In April 1867 Joseph Hopgood received a writ after libelling a Mr Watson - which he did by cutting offensive words about him onto a LBSCR carriage window with a diamond. In February 1939 a man and a woman were fined 40s each for an offence at Brixton station. Their crime - depositing a suitcase containing a live cat and a book on criminal psychology in the left luggage office at Brixton station, the cat being detected by staff after it had spent three days in its prison. More surprising still is that the couple returned to collect their suitcase after a week.

[1] *Railway Times*, 20 July 1839
[2] *The Graphic*, 24 Feb 1883
[3] In 1962 fines were raised at last from £2 to a maximum of £25, sentences from one month to two.
[4] It is a comment on reporting accuracy of the day that this man first appears in *The Times* as "Mr Tuasere."
[5] J Wrottesley, *The Great Northern Railway*, p.195
[6] *Daily Telegraph*, 21 June 1958
[7] L T C Rolt, *Red for Danger*, London , 1971: p.21

CHAPTER FOUR:
THEFT &
ROBBERY

Many different forms of robbery affected railways, ranging from the theft of railway materials to the stealing of goods and passengers' luggage in transit. This was nothing new, for robberies from stage coaches and horse-cabs had been a problem for years. The most difficult problem for the railway authorities to solve was the continual pilfering of goods by railway staff, which was an enormous problem in comparison to the occasional - but spectacular - "train robberies" such as the two "Great Train Robberies". For example, "losses in transit" rose from a value of £180,462 in 1938 to £2,778,367 in 1948, though fell to an average of about £1,000,000 per year in the mid-1950s. The years of the "black-out" were a boom time for the hundreds of petty criminals and corrupt railway staff who knew that wartime shortages meant that there were large profits to be made from crimes which could be committed under the protective blanket of wartime gloom; convictions rose by 300% between 1938 and 1944.

Robberies by Railway Staff

Thefts of goods came within the normal boundaries of the criminal law, but also gave rise to compensation claims within the civil law. For the owner of goods that had disappeared in transit to make a claim against the railway, there had to be proof of "wilful misconduct"; thus a theft from a stationary wagon might not be wilful misconduct as the goods could have been stolen by any member of the public, whereas goods pilfered by the guard from his van or compartment might give rise to a claim. This was underlined in H C Smith v GWR in 1922, when the GWR was able to say at what station the goods had last been seen.[1]

Honesty was expected of railway staff, but there were many temptations too. In March 1839 a porter at Lime Street station found a parcel of £305 in bank notes which he handed in to the authorities. This was several years' wages, but bank notes were highly identifiable in those days. In September 1841 a "gauger" on the Manchester & Sheffield at Holmfirth was given £50 to pay his gang but absconded with all the money; he was arrested at Huddersfield station booking office, by which time only £15 was left! Men employed to help with passengers' luggage were also involved in pilfering. Thomas Rollstone of the ECR was arrested in September 1842 for stealing an umbrella at Shoreditch - his house was then searched and many other items discovered. John Elmore, a police man at London Bridge in March 1844, took advantage of a mistake by a Mr Fisher who left a gold seal and ring in a taxi-cab, for which he was punished with 12 months hard labour.

One of the jobs of the passenger guard was to watch over the large quantities of luggage that passengers took with them in the early days, but this was a job that required total honesty. GWR guards seem to have been especially prone to temptation and one who was arrested for robbery was Frost, early in 1849. The Earl of Craven lost several items from his luggage which was delivered to Shrivenham station in November 1848, and then a few months later Frost was challenged by the head guard on a train between Bath and Chippenham when apparently stealing shirts and ties from passengers' luggage. Although the train was still moving - at 15mph - Frost jumped out of the window but was later caught and found to have a pistol.

In November 1852 the valet of H Foley took cases of his master's clothes from Birmingham to Hayford, but several items disappeared with a carpet bag. GWR police visited the house of passenger guard Henry Buckle and found two shirts, a silk scarf and a gold pin which were stolen. He was also found to have stolen a telescope between Birmingham and Warwick and gold bracelets between Cropredy and Leamington.

In July 1889 guard Owen Brannigan of the Great North of Ireland Railway was charged with stealing boots, knives and lace from luggage, all of which was found in his Dundalk house. Having found him guilty, the jury requested mercy - but the Judge rejected their plea and gave him five years penal servitude.

In the early days of the railways it was common for luggage to be handed over to porters, but the opportunity for this sort of theft has declined as passengers have become used to looking after their own luggage. However, until the early days of British Railways it was still the practice to have "travelling porters" on some trains, which occasionally gave rise to a pattern of thefts. In March 1948 it was noticed that there had been a number of losses from trains travelling south from Shrewsbury, and in June £50 of jewellry was stolen from a case going from Shrewsbury to Merthyr. On 24 August 1948 a policewoman in civilian dress boarded the train with a case, but by Pontypool Road a gold watch and some silk stockings had disappeared. A travelling porter was challenged and made to undress - the silk stockings were found under his shirt and the gold watch in his hand lamp. He was given three months at Hereford.

Goods staff were especially prone to pilfering. James Rigby, a watchman on the Manchester & Bolton Railway at the latter town, was caught stealing a basket of flour in October 1841 and his house was found to contain a stolen cart sheet. He was dispatched to Salford gaol. A "time guard" at Derby in 1842 was given twelve months hard labour for stealing cloth from a package, John James got the same for stealing a sack from Oldham Road station on the Manchester & Leeds in 1843 whilst a goods porter on the GWR was sentenced to seven years transportation for stealing a bale of goods in the same year.

A very mean arrest was that of Samuel Nell of the Leeds Railway in August 1842. His job was to sweep up spilt corn, which the railway then sold for 1s a sack to pig-farmers. Nell took a sack home. James Peak of the ECR was arrested at Colchester for putting a single mackerel into his pocket in 1843. The head porter at Shoreditch goods station was arrested for stealing game from packages in February 1844. A porter on the LCDR in 1875 stole some pears from a train stopped at signals near Grosvenor Road which must have been a sudden temptation - for which he received a week in prison and lost his job.

During 1848-9 the Lancashire & Yorkshire and the LNWR were the victims of a gang who organised a clever system of goods robberies. Goods guards changed the address labels on packages, which were thus diverted to a receiver named Wood, who was based in Manchester. Two others of the gang were arrested at Huddersfield in September 1849, but it was thought that up to fourteen were involved. One side result of all this was that the LYR at Huddersfield had paid out over £500 to customers whose goods had gone missing in the previous two years.

Petty pilfering was an established and frustrating problem from the first era of the railways. In 1853 the LNWR's goods manager complained that "Thieves are pilfering the goods from our waggons here to an impudent extent. We are at our wits' end to find out the blackguards. Not a night passes without wine hampers, silk parcels, drapers' boxes or provisions being robbed..."[2]

A man who should have known better was William Stones, a watchman on the MSLR at Sheffield Victoria in 1867, who had been a PC in the Lincolnshire force for four years. After only three months working for the MSLR he was arrested and his house searched - pilfered goods found there included blankets, rugs, boots, slippers, shawls, lard, cheese, cutlery, crockery, pipes, a hare, a duck and a revolver!

A fatal case of pilfering occurred in 1889. Eight employees of the LYR at Miles Platting stole a cask of brandy and spent the evening drinking it; two of them passed out, one dying of alcohol poisoning. Such cases where a group of goods porters worked together were quite common - seven LNWR men at Old Ford were stopped and searched as they were leaving work in April 1907 - the haul included ladies' boots, gramophone records, fancy shirts, children's shoes and whisky. When police visited the men's lodgings they found 77 other gramophone records. Punishments were three months hard labour.

Pilfering became an increased problem after 1918; claims for stolen goods against the NBR increased from £8610 in 1913 to £28,144 in 1918, and included £100 a day for whisky alone. The company blamed the many unsuitable men taken on during the war years for the almost constant pilfering.

Companies responded to this by sacking anyone found to be pilfering goods. This itself led to further problems, as when guard Fordham was sacked by the LNER in 1923 when a forequarter of beef was found beneath his jacket in the brake van. Although there was no satisfactory explanation of how the beef got there by itself, Fordham was acquitted at the Central Criminal Court and sued the company for wrongful dismissal - but he lost the case.

A driver and fireman who were regularly rostered to crew goods trains between Gloucester and Bristol realised that their load often contained cigarettes and used to take advantage of wayside halts to steal from the vans. This soon alerted transport police, who noted the connection between the disappearances of goods and who was on duty! In April 1948 the train came to a stop at Standish Junction and the driver walked back to steal from the cigarette van - only to find that it contained police officers. The fireman had not stolen anything but had accepted money to keep quiet, but the dishonest driver was given a three year sentence. In 1950 parcels of cigarettes were relabelled and sent to "Joe & Jim's Outfitters" in Eversholt Street, London. This establishment was set up as a secondhand shop, but nearly all the customers were men and they nearly all bought cigarettes! When the shop was raided it was found to contain 22,000 stolen cigarettes as well as some stolen clothing.

Railway goods sidings were often busy and labour intensive – and thus the opportunities for pilfering were immense.

The conspirators got between 15 months and three years hard labour.

The weakness for railway staff who stole regularly was that sooner or later a pattern of losses would become obvious to railway police. This was the case with a series of losses of parcels sent to Woking in 1948 and, rather than beginning a public investigation, police decided to watch the station in the belief that railway staff had an arrangement with taxi drivers to spirit away stolen parcels. On 28 September 1948, at 11pm, a porter was seen to move a barrow of parcels from the parcels office to a position very near the platform exit; almost immediately, a taxi driver came in and took a parcel of raincoats. When the taxi was stopped it was found to contain another parcel, of "New Forest" cigarettes. Three porters, three taxi-drivers and a lorry-driver were arrested and fined £20 each.

On 15 December 1949 the manager of Wellington Street goods depot in Leeds found 800 Christmas puddings were missing. These were found to be on sale via a Leeds grocer, who was arrested along with a railway van driver and the grocer's sister.

The use of an "outsider" to pass on or sell the stolen goods was essential to dishonest railway staff, but one gang at Trafford Park kept this role very much "in the family". In 1949-50 a gang of up to 17 railway employees pilfered regularly, delivering their thefts to the dustbin of a driver's

Woking station – the scene of a typical parcels "racket" in 1948 involving railway porters and taxi drivers. *(D. Cullum)*

wife who acted almost as a "general dealer" for the neighbourhood. When arrests were made, her stock included 20,000 cigarettes, shirts and coats. Another one who used a family connection was porter Broadfield at West Drayton in 1952, who handled the problem of how to get stolen parcels away from the station by getting his wife to leave the family pram in the parcels office; when she came in "to bring him his breakfast" in the morning, she collected the pram and put the child in it on top of the stolen goods. Perhaps it was the fact that the child was four years old that alerted police to this practice! Broadfield received three months in prison.

In 1950 British Railways estimated that pilfered goods cost it £3,000,000. A typical case occurred at King's Cross goods depot the following year, when a fish lorry was stopped leaving the depot with a sack of ladies shoes tied above the rear axle. The driver was acting for a group of goods porters, helping them to smuggle out stolen goods. He was fined £10. However a shunter at Euston who stole a parcel of seven silk blouses and passed them to an accomplice was given six months in prison.

The crime of "spiling" whisky received attention in 1951, when a good sporter was arrested for this highly-specialised offence at Longmorn station near Elgin. A police officer saw a goods porter kneeling on a sack on the floor of a wagon, and his curiosity was naturally aroused. The porter had two pint bottles, a rubber hot water bottle, a knife, a wooden "soile", six inches of copper pipe attached to the spile and an attache case. Using this equipment and a gimlet, he was extracting whisky from a barrel, but was easily caught. He was given a month in prison.

In 1959 police around Hardingham in Norfolk heard a rumour that "the village offered exceptional facilities for the easy purchase of household articles." Enquiries suggested that these came from parcels at the railway station, but no claims for losses had ever been filed - perhaps because the stationmaster responsible for handling the paperwork was also the person doing the stealing! With 37 offences to "take into consideration", he was sentenced to a year in prison.

A railway enthusiast's interest in Triang electric trains caused his downfall in March 1960. The man worked as a goods porter at London Road, Manchester, and was seen to hide away a package containing a Triang electric transformer. At the end of the shift he was challenged and found to have a total of 27 pieces of Triang equipment. At home he had 149 other pieces and ten model locomotives valued at £98. He also had a Triang price list with all the stolen items ticked off. The porter had been able to get away with this specialised robbery for such a long time by only robbing parcels sent to London Road in error, so they could not be traced.

Efforts were made to ensure that goods staff were honest men and checks were usually made. In March 1950 James Ross applied for a job at Kings Cross as a parcels porter, saying that he had previously worked for Charles Brown and had not been employed by the railways before. Brown confirmed the details, but officials were suspicious and investigated - they discovered that Ross had been a goods porter at Kings Cross until 1947 and had six previous convictions - including two for railway thefts and one for rape! Ross and Brown were both fined £5 under the Servants Character Act of 1792.

Had the same system been in use in all circumstances it might have prevented a number of robberies from Paddington goods station in 1956. The stationmaster there took on two men supplied by the Labour Exchange, but he was not given access to any other details about the men - the Labour Exchange could not pass on information about people without their permission. One of the men had 23 convictions for larceny and, with his colleague, now added another three offences with a series of goods thefts. A nine month sentence resulted.

Some of the efforts involved police closely observing staff working at goods stations, and this uncovered an unusual case in 1959. A goods porter at Leeds City was seen to be meeting two men, who appeared to be intimidating him. Suspecting dishonesty police interviewed the porter, who took the opportunity to unburden himself of a tragic story. Once owner of a prosperous coal business he had gone to a cinema in Leeds and met a boy with whom he committed an "indecent act". Two men had then turned up and demanded money, forcing the sale of the coal business so that he had to get a porter's job instead - but even this did not satisfy them. The police arranged for him to hand over marked notes to his oppressors and the two went for trial - receiving four years and 18 months respectively.

In 1951 two young Willesden firemen were sent to prison after committing over ninety offences, taking advantage of their right to travel up and down the Euston main-line. One of their robberies was from Polish Hostel coaches in sidings at Rugby, from which savings books were taken and then the money withdrawn in London. They then committed a number of burglaries in houses near the Euston to Rugby line, travelling back on night trains using the excuse that they had met some "girls" and often giving false names. On 27 November they were seen on the 12.05am from Euston and got out at Rugby, where they promptly broke into a house and were then arrested.

After this catalogue of dishonest railway servants, we must remember that the majority were of course very honest. However, the wages of honesty were not always excessive. In October 1957 a guard found a handbag containing the princely sum of £3829, which he gave in to the inspector at London Road, Manchester. A woman came to claim the bag and was so delighted with his honesty that she gave him a reward - 2s6d; this represented 0.003% of the sum lost!

Cab drivers were involved in many robberies of passengers and this was one of the reasons why railway companies regulated their access to station yards. Badges were introduced at London Bridge in 1841 and produced a sharp fall in the number of luggage robberies. The introduction of badges was unpopular with some cabbies and in August 1841 two cabsmen were arrested at London Bridge for refusing to show their badges. They were fined 10s each but refused to pay, so were sent to prison for five days.

Other Thieves and Robbers

Major stations were targeted by criminals who hoped to steal quickly away with a valuable consignment of goods. Some of this was opportunistic and some organised, but the severity of punishment declined quite sharply over the years. In January 1844 John Long was sentenced to seven years transportation for stealing a load of shoes from Nine Elms station - they were worth £150. Two men who stole blouses and shirts from the LNWR in 1921

Pilfering from sidings was a problem in the 1940s and 1950s – even on New Year's Eve, apparently!

received only three months hard labour in comparison!

Pilfering from the goods van on a passenger train was relatively uncommon - at least, when committed by passengers. In May 1841 two men were arrested on a Southampton to London train for climbing from a carriage into the luggage van and stealing oranges to eat. Both men claimed that they had bought the oranges before the journey and were in the luggage van as the train was overcrowded; without other evidence, the case was dismissed.

A speculative thief who stole a parcel out of the parcels van of a Euston to Liverpool train in November 1907 must have been pleasantly surprised when he opened the box to find it contained 2000 gold half-sovereigns, part of a consignment of four boxes being sent to Brazil. The consignee had unwisely sent these as normal parcels rather than registering them as bullion traffic and as the train had made several stops on its journey clues about the disappearance were hard to find.

The most common problem was with minor pilfering at sidings and stations. This could have serious consequences as trespassers had a high risk of being involved in an accident. In the 1850s the Taff Vale Railway had a

Even pilfering from colliery sidings could seem a joke in the late 1950s,
although the tears of the BTP officer may be for the demise of steam!

constant problem with pilfering of coal at Bute Docks in Cardiff, and railway
staff who tried to prevent theft had often been set upon - with Irish people
getting most of the blame. At the Docks coal was emptied into ships via a
shoot system and in December 1856 Caroline Murphy, aged 44, decided to
steal coal out of the shoots. Having removed a board, she put her head and
shoulders into the shoot to pull out coal and was struck by the falling
counterpoise weight with fatal results[3].

In April 1914 two labourers got into vans at Doncaster goods yard
but then lay low when they heard footsteps outside. The steps belonged to
the guard, who locked the van. They were stuck inside as the train ambled
off to Conisborough, where they were shunted into a siding. Death from
thirst or hunger could have resulted had their banging on the door not
attracted the attention of porters. It was commented that if they had been
put in the sidings at Immingham they might never have been released. Both
men got seven days in prison.

It was much harder for non-railway staff to pilfer goods at stations as their presence could lead to suspicions - unless they had other reasons for being there. Mary Eversden was a poulterer and egg dealer from Sandy, who often delivered her goods to the local station for forwarding to London; however in December 1890 she foolishly stole 20lbs of butter which another dealer had left there, relabelling it as her own produce. A tradesman might often need to be at his station to check for deliveries, and thus in 1948 a Faversham fishmonger began to steal fish from his local station which was consigned to others. Police became suspicious and a delivery of fish were specially marked - when they disappeared, it was a simple matter to trace them to his shop where they were on sale. He was fined £50.

Robbery from goods trains usually consisted of pilfering at stations and robberies from trains at sidings were relatively rare in the early days of the railways. However, in the late 1940s to early 1960s period it was a type of crime that attracted much attention as the popularity of cars and vans made it possible to steal sizable hauls. In the Wath area in 1950 thieves broke into stationary vans at signal stops and then threw goods out to waiting colleagues while the trains trundled along. In an early example of forensic testing, one of these men was caught after he left his cap behind and forensic tests matched his hair to those inside it. The reward was six months for each of the gang.

One of the main targets for thieves were the containers of tobacco that were transported from towns like Bristol and Nottingham; by 1960 the amount of tobacco stolen on BR was £220,000, well-ahead of alcohol at £35,000. In October 1947 tobacco containers were robbed between Leicester and Swindon, the police considering Banbury to be the most likely location of the crime. On 6 September 1948 a van from Nottingham was found open at Banbury and the tobacco gone. Bolt croppers had been used to force the doors, but the problem was knowing where the offence had occurred. On 17 September there was another robbery, but within hours the "receiver" was arrested in London. This should have been a warning, but on 27 September police spotted three men in the goods yard at Banbury and a "desperate struggle" ensued, during the course of which one man had his jaw broken and two escaped by jumping into the River Cherwell. When they had all been rounded up the gang were given three years in prison.

Cigarette traffic was handled at Queens Walk goods yard in Nottingham, where on 21 July 1949 a man was arrested with 1200 stolen cigarettes in his possession. However, 4000 were known to be missing and alert police soon spotted a guard leaving the site with a bulging bag. He was challenged but ran, throwing the bag into the river - but it was fished out and found to contain 390 cigarettes; another 950 were hidden in staff lockers.

Later the same year losses of cigarettes were noted on Bristol to Kingswear workings, which seemed to centre on Torre. It was believed that a porter was stealing consignments and passing them to a shopkeeper for resale; the porter became aware that he was being watched, and sent a "Do not contact me" message to the shopkeeper. Both were bound over.

One of the best known cigarette theft cases was the "Markham Loop Case" of July 1949. Cigarettes for the North were despatched from Colwick goods at Nottingham to Darlington by the 12.22am, which stopped at Markham loop for 15 minutes in the dead of night. This was an opportunity for thieves to break into the cigarette vans, but on the night of 29 July they were unlucky that another goods train went by while they were at work. The driver of the other goods saw a man with a case on his back, who dropped down as if to hide, he also saw cases labelled "Players" and a dark car standing by. Stopping his train, the driver phoned the signalman and the police were sent for. Police arrived to find the car and a man nearby, who claimed to be "poaching" - but was unable to explain how jemmies and other tools could be used to catch pheasants. Soon afterwards, a local farmer found packages of stolen tobacco hidden in his haystacks. A total of 170,700 cigarettes had been stolen, and the gang were rewarded with five years each.

Tobacco traffic between Sheffield and Mansfield, for colliery canteens, suffered from a great deal of pilfering in 1954-5 so police traced the problem to when the trains came to a standstill at Brinsley. They soon arrested Allan Marson, who lived nearby, and in his house found various stolen items - coffin fittings, a LNER signal lamp, and a case of tobacco under the floor. Marson and two miners stole goods and passed them on to a general dealer, netting about £665. Sentences of two years were handed out.

A tobacco theft case in 1958 involved £15,000 worth being stolen from railway premises in London and sold in Brighton, but this was complicated by two Brighton CID men being among the criminals. BTC police worked on the case alone because of this, eventually bringing in three sentences of five years each.

Attempts to stop tobacco thefts from wagons by fitting an "auto-locking device" were not entirely successful. On 2 January 1959 thieves at Perth smashed into a van through the roof and stole 30 cartons of cigarettes. They received a year in prison each. Thieves at Alnmouth found another route to raid a van of tobacco en route from Newcastle to Alnwick, a journey which involved an overnight stop at Alnmouth. One of the packing cases in the van contained a thief, Richard Trory, who cut his way out of the van having hidden the cigarettes in a carton to be delivered to Wilfred Street in

Alnwick. Staff must have been mystified to find a hole in the floor but two packing cases still in the van, and it did not take a lot of guile to work out there was something suspicious about any case still being there if the van had been robbed. The men were arrested when the Wilfred Street case was delivered, and 18 month sentences handed out.

The decision of Mrs Gunn of Featherstone to divorce her husband in June 1949 set running a train of events which led to the solving of another set of goods train depredations. Robert Gunn's habit of going out at night to rob the freight trains at Streethouse became the subject of local gossip and soon the police heard about it. Officers travelled on the 6.30pm Wakefield to Pontefract goods on 21 November 1949, but no robbery took place; undeterred, they continued their uncomfortable journeys until, after four nights, Gunn and an accomplice named Edward Hale were arrested at the trackside. One of Gunn's thefts was a bicycle en route from Birmingham to Pontefract, while he had sold 36 types of commodity to local people including whisky and clothing. He was given a three year sentence.

The most extensive series of depredations were practised by Leonard "Butch" Margham and his gang in 1954-5, along the east coast line between Newark and York in similar territory to the Markham Loop case. It was a common practice at the time to put slow goods trains into loops so they could be overtaken by faster trains, and this gave vigilant criminal gangs the chance to raid a van or two before they continued on their journey. Mangham's gang succeeded in robbing a number of trains, probably starting with a van load of wine between Rossington and Bawtry on 18 November 1954. On 5 January 1955 shoes were stolen from a van in Black Carr Loop near Doncaster, while on 9 February 1955 carpets and other textiles were found in a field after being abandoned following another robbery at Black Carr. A week later five men were disturbed during a raid, but escaped.

Perhaps because of this narrow escape the gang made no further attempt until 24 March when two vans were raided at Escrick near York, £700 of tobacco being stolen. On 14 April the raiders were disturbed at Dearne Junction, a police dog being knocked unconscious. A week later £226 of textiles were stolen at Carlton Loop, but a clue was gained at last - an Austin saloon car was seen near the spot. The following night tea was stolen at Mexborough Yard and five nights after that there was another raid at Bawtry loop.

After a month's rest the gang moved across to Barnetby and stole tobacco and shoes worth £600 on the night of 19 May, but by this time the police were becoming vigilant and planning how to catch the gang at work. On 28 June the police decided to observe all likely locations at Black Carr,

Bawtry, Carlton, Markham and Ranskill and had a list of seven suspects in mind. Despite this more tobacco was stolen on 19 August, probably at Carlton or Tuxford. On 26 August another train was robbed, but it was impossible to say where - it had stopped at each of the loops at Carlton, Tuxford and Markham for 8, 32 and 17 minutes respectively.

The police changed their observation points to Retford, Carlton, Markham, Tuxford and Barnetby and were at last rewarded on 9 September. That night the gang of five chose to raid the 12.05am Newark to Doncaster at Carlton, but were surprised. One of the gang ran off and was never traced but another, Hirst, was arrested in Eve's Lane. The others came to rescue him and Mangham attacked PC Norton with a rope and steel hook whilst another hit him with a truncheon. PC Metcalfe was knocked out with a heavy cane and lead. The gang escaped and Arthur Mangham went to to his home in Foundry Lane, Mexborough where he was seen to bury croppers and a steel hook. Leonard Mangham got home by stealing a girl's bike but was arrested in Conisborough whilst Hirst and Eric Bowen were also arrested.

Leonard Mangham was given twelve years penal servitude and the others eight, the gang leader having 83 previous convictions. Leonard's crimes included using threats of violence against railway guards and on one occasion taking a guard's "snap".

A similar gang of thieves operated south of Glasgow in 1960-1, managing 21 raids in a four month period that netted some £10,000 of tobacco and whisky. It is a comment on the working practices of the time that the gang used to position themselves at remote signals or alongside steep gradients so that they could force open wagons and throw the goods out for a waiting car. They once cut a hole in a truck roof to get inside, but police managed to arrest seven in February 1961.

Theft of Railway Property

Robberies of railway materials were also a problem, though also sometimes due to confusion. In April 1842 the contractors relaying the Wigan to Parkside line were arrested for "stealing" the old rails. This was a result of misunderstanding and the case was dismissed. A man named Walters was given a job as a storekeeper on the Brighton line in 1842 after being disabled while working on the track; however he was seen burying pieces of iron in his garden in order to sell them later.

When the Croydon, Merstham & Godstone Railway was dismantled, William Neal was employed to guard the materials - but instead he arranged for the rails to disappear off to Bankside foundry. However his trial in September 1842 collapsed as the indictment had omitted the word "The" from the name of the Company!

Charles Curry, the ECR policeman at Feering bridge in Essex, stole five oak "keys" from his employer in October 1843; as he had previously been a constable with Essex police this was harshly punished, with four months in prison including 28 days solitary. In 1889 switchman Huff who worked for the GWR at Chippenham was arrested for stealing paint from the company in order to decorate a small farm he ran in his spare time. He had worked for the GWR for 23 years without previous problems, and mounted a stout defence which led to acquittal at Marlborough magistrates - but despite this he was summoned to meet the GWR Board and sacked. He then sued the GWR for wrongful arrest and won £200.

William Church found his own little criminal sideline when he discovered that horsehair could be sold to furniture makers. He discovered a good source of it - the seats of GCR carriages at St John's Wood Sidings, to which he and his friends gained access from a canal towpath. He was given three months hard labour.

More dangerous were William Pearson and William White, "determined-looking fellows", who were interrupted while they were stripping lead from the roof of the LCDR's Herne Hill station in 1867. They produced a gun and threatened a porter, saying "I'll have the life out of you," but others came to help the porter. The villains were chased to a meadow where they hit the porter on the head with the gun, a stick and a brick.

In October 1939 the SR was plagued by thieves who stole the darkened "black-out" light bulbs out of their trains. A passenger between Coulsdon and Redhill was caught stealing a bulb in April 1940 because the carriage was wired "in series", and when he removed the chosen bulb all the lights went out - including in the guard's compartment; he was fined £3. The war years led to other major problems, notably the loss of huge quantities of cups and saucers. Thefts of crockery in 1938 were 38,000 - but this figure rose to 554,000 in 1941 and was still at 250,000 in 1942.[4]

Britain's railways once used huge quantities of sheeting to cover goods wagons, which proceeded to disappear at alarming rates - in 1951 the Eastern Region of BR had 10,458 missing. As ever, a pattern of losses was noticed and Police attention focussed on Padnal Sidings near Ely. On 26 August 1952 an alert officer noticed a BR sheet covering a haystack, which he discovered had been sold to the farmer by Porter Page for 10s. A garage owner at Prickwillow was using them to cover cars, but appears to have paid over the odds at £1 each. Another one covering firewood in Prickwillow had

War-time "black-out" conditions on the Southern Railway. The special bulbs
became a target for robbers – as did over half a million items of crockery in 1941.

been stolen. Fines of £5 were handed out to the offenders.

When four men were questioned about stealing couplings off
redundant wagons at Papplewick near Nottingham in 1959, they produced a
"contract" authorising them to break up the wagons. However this proved to
be a forgery, as did the National Insurance cards they showed as well. With 117
couplings stolen for their scrap value, sentences were a maximum of three years.

Railway electrification created a new source of material to be stolen,
but also created new risks for the thief although the wiring used for electric
signalling was a lot safer to remove than the overhead cables! On 15 March
1956 train services were disrupted after thieves stole two miles of copper wire
near Cornhill on Tweed and at Tweedmouth, bundling five 250yd lengths
into a car. In April the train service between Dunton Green and Westerham
had to be replaced with a bus after thieves stole half a mile of telegraph wire.
In 1957 a publican named Frank Paul, who had got into money trouble,
heard that good prices could be got for scrap copper and lead so decided to
steal some from London Transport. He tried to saw through a cable, unaware
that it carried 11,000 volts, and received severe burns as well as causing traffic
chaos. Police found him in hospital, but his fine of only £10 perhaps reflects
the fact that he'd already had one punishment.

In 1960-1 the newly electrified lines around Liverpool were plagued
with thefts. On 7 January a lorry was backed up to the line at Speke and the
one-inch power cable cut before a section was stolen. The cable end was left
trailing and this caught on carriage doors causing obstructions. The theft was

only possible as power had not yet been switched on, but the section slightly closer to Liverpool was already live and would have dealt the thieves a fatal blow.

Signalling and telegraph wires were copper and so valuable, a fact which induced three "caravan dwellers" to remove two lengths of 3800 yards and 4400 yards from the Staines branch between West Drayton and Colnbrook on 1 September 1961 and again on the 12 September; they sold the lengths to a scrap dealer for £70, having disrupted railway services. Neither of the thieves could read. In 1962 a gang used long-handled pruning shears to cut down telegraph cables at Lichfield, Walsall and between Leicester and Rugby.

When the experimental electric trains between Morecambe and Lancaster were closed down, thieves soon realised this was an opportunity. A number of thefts of copper cable occurred but a signal engineer rigged up a system that would activate warning lights if any attempts were made. In May 1968 a BTP officer caught "an old man accompanied by a blowsy old woman"; the old man, aged 61, blamed his downfall on women and drink. His "girlfriend" was 59 - using an old pram to conceal the stolen copper. They were fined and put on probation.

Copper used in wiring was a major attraction to thieves. In January 1968 a block failure at Middleton Junction was the first sign of a theft in actual progress. Transport Police were on the scene rapidly and also found that power to a nearby farm had been cut off; one of the villains was found skulking in a water-filled culvert.

Empty passenger carriages contained little of interest, but restaurant and buffet cars often had stock in drink and cigarettes. Early in 1949 people in Swansea realised the potential, and there was a spate of robberies from stabled restaurant cars. After a raid on 20 January, police found that a side door had been forced and the interior ransacked. However a fingerprint was traced to a known local criminal and a nine month sentence resulted.

Robberies on Trains and Stations

In September 1841 a man named Bryant was tried for stealing £200 from a woman in a second class train of the London & Birmingham. There was no other witness and the case was discharged.

Mrs Aspinall, an innkeeper's wife, was tried in June 1843 for theft of a suitcase on the Manchester & Leeds. Her defence was that she had picked up the case as another man had left it - there was some interest in that the case was left in a third class carriage and had contained £84. The woman escaped punishment as the trial was informed a case had been stolen from

James Burn, but his actual name was James William Burn; he got his case back, but not the money!

The crowded railway station was an attractive place for a pickpocket or petty thief to lurk, though railway policemen quickly recognised habitual offenders. Takings were often small, such as the 1s10d that Betty Cropper lost at Ardwick station in January 1845; however there were too few people around to mask the crime, and two men were seen by a witness and given into custody. The one spectacular instance where this was not the case affected the Earl and Countess of Dudley in December 1874; they were catching the 6.30pm from Paddington to Worcester at the same time as the Prince of Wales was passing through. This caused a considerable commotion during which the Countess' jewel case was left for a few moments on the platform - and £50,000 worth of diamonds were lost forever.

Criminals often worked in gangs to improve their own safety. This method was used to steal the watch of a SER clerk, on the "incline" at London Bridge in July 1868. The clerk was coming home late from a night out at the Crystal Palace and was seeing friends into an omnibus when he was surrounded by a group of men who hustled and pushed him, pulling at his waistcoat. He decided to struggle and grabbed the arm of Wright while others called the Police; a constable had already noticed Wright loitering that evening, and then he gave a false address - but the case was dismissed as the watch was not found in Wright's possession. This was a reason why gangs were safer - whoever stole the goods invariably passed it instantly to someone else. Railway police became effective in identifying people who were often seen loitering, so it could be a risky crime. Nonetheless, stations were notorious and in 1889 Ludgate Hill was described as "infested with thieves."[5] They were haunted by people like John Lawrence, who hung around at Willesden looking for people to rob the same year - unable to find anyone, he stole a cushion from a 3rd class carriage and was imprisoned for 9 months! Another typical incident for London stations was at Cannon Street in 1890, when George Brown tried a "snatch and run" theft of a gold watch - but he was caught by an official of the LCC; the punishment was six months hard labour.

Another clever approach became a problem on the LBSCR in 1875. The thieves used two large "portmanteau" cases with false bottoms, the inside of which contained "an ingenious device" for clutching at anything. They simply put the portmanteau over the top of anything they wanted to steal, and walked off with it enclosed inside.

A clever and clearly premeditated robbery occurred at Leicester in May 1913. Hatton Garden diamond merchant Abraham Brown was travelling with £2000 of jewels in a case when his bag was switched for another one - identical - during the stop at Leicester.

Criminals also discovered how to abuse the left luggage system. Louisa Holloway of Battersea had quite a successful criminal career by watching for luggage to be unloaded from trains, then waiting to see which cases were taken away for claiming later. She would then go to the luggage office and give an exact decsription of an item, which netted her over £200 in thefts from the LSWR, GWR and LBSCR. However there was a risk in repeating the crime too often.

In January 1920 another racket was uncovered - a London gang who forged cloakroom tickets in order to claim other people's luggage. Their technique was to deposit a parcel of old newspaper in order to get a ticket, then change the number in the hope of withdrawing something better. They usually hired a cab and got a porter to bring the luggage to it, but were discovered at Paddington when the rightful owner turned up at the wrong moment. Even left luggage lockers could be abused - in 1956 the lockers at Victoria had to be taken out of use after thieves discovered how to open them.

Robbing a passenger who was actually present in the train was more risky - there was little chance of escape if seen at work! In the days before carriages were lit, tunnels offered a chance to rob a person although some companies like the London & Brighton provided gas lights in their tunnels. On the London & Birmingham in July 1843 a woman returning to Leicester was robbed in Kilsby tunnel, although she did not realise it until she got off the train at Leicester. An engine was then sent forward to Derby to catch the thief, but it was found he had doubled back to Rugby where the woman succeeded in identifying him.

Under the circumstances going to sleep could be unwise, but on a long journey many gave in to the temptation. In December 1874 a train heading north from Kings Cross contained three men in a compartment - a cattle-dealer, an engineer, and an ex-resident of Wakefield gaol named H J Price. By Peterborough the two honest characters had gone to sleep so that by the time the train passed Newark Price had stolen the engineer's watch. As the train approached Tuxford Price set to work on the cattle-dealer's watch, but he woke suddenly and tried to grab him. Price leapt out of the door of the train - travelling at 60mph - and the alarm was raised when the train stopped at Retford. Meanwhile, a signalman at a level crossing near Tuxford was startled by the apparition of a man covered in blood, who said that he had fallen out of a train; the signalman telegraphed a message to Retford, where the staff soon informed him of the truth. Price was found in possession of a nine-inch dagger, false whiskers and pieces of sandpaper. He was judged to be insane.

Cattle dealer Fred McGhee went to sleep between Manchester and St Helens in 1889 and his fob watch was removed from its chain; the Leigh pawnbroker who it was taken to was suspicious and delayed the thieves until police caught them.

Where a passenger did not go to sleep voluntarily, sleep could sometimes be induced. On 24 December 1849 George Lambert travelled by train from Rotherham to Doncaster, sharing a compartment with some other men. One of them gave him a lozenge to eat and he gradually lost consciousness. Lambert was eventually dragged out of the carriage by porters, who assumed he was drunk, and charged an extra 5s for travelling beyond his booked station. However it became clear that he was unwell and it was discovered he had been robbed of £5; it took him nearly a week to recover and his eyesight was particularly affected.

A similar trick was played in October 1875 between Nuneaton and London. A passenger started chatting to another man in the compartment, and later offered him a drink from his flask; the former man then became unconscious and was woken by the ticket examiner at Willesden, by which time his money and his companion were long-gone.

Of course direct violence was also used. In order to rob a fellow passenger, John Shelton simply launched a "murderous assault" at Brooksby near Leicester whilst travelling to Peterborough. This proved to be one of several offences, but as the victim in this case went to Brussels afterwards it was impossible to pursue the prosecution. The same approach was used by Ernest Smith in March 1911 who got into a 1st class compartment between Cannon Street and Charing Cross seemingly with the intention of a robbery, picking on elderly Mrs Elizabeth Roberts who owned a cork firm. He hit her three times with his fist, so hard that her blood and teeth marks were left on his hands and two teeth were knocked out, and stole £1-5s. At Charing Cross Smith jumped out quickly and ran to the barrier but the alarm was raised and he had to jump across the line to the next platform where he was arrested. Smith pleaded guilty and admitted he needed £2-11-6 to pay a hotel bill after a pleasant stay with a young lady; it cost him 18 months hard labour.

Similar methods were used to rob Frank MacFarlane between Chessington and Wimbledon in July 1946; he was attacked with a sharp instrument causing head wounds, and was found unconscious when the train was shunted into the sidings at Wimbledon depot. £15 had been stolen from his wallet.

In 1911 a gang of railway thieves were responsible for at least two robberies every week on the Metropolitan. When "Phillips" was arrested (he refused to give his real name) for stealing the pearl out of Charles Otto's tiepin at Moorgate, he was found to have 16 previous convictions and so given 22 months hard labour.

Another audacious crime occurred at Praed Street on the Metropolitan Railway in January 1921. A gang of nine men "pushed and shoved" other passengers into the carriage, then broke up into small groups. When Arthur Phillips gave a signal with his hat, the gang surrounded an old man, forced up his arms, and robbed him. Two of the gang, including its leader, were recognised and later tried for this and a similar robbery on an omnibus. They were given three months.

Another tactic was to wait until a passenger was not watching their hand luggage. Saul Walden, a Birmingham jeweller, was robbed of a bag that he left unattended for a few minutes on his way back from London in September 1921; the bag contained 161 pearls and a diamond bracelet worth £3200 - it is perhaps surprising that he left it in the compartment at all! One trick was to wait for someone to go to the restaurant car, one man using this method on the *Cornish Riviera* in September 1953; he actually left his own meal to go and steal a radio and other items from the bags of two ladies who were also eating, then returned to finish his meal. One of the ladies was so distressed at the theft that a Navy officer had to comfort her. The villain was caught and got six months, whilst the lady and the Navy officer fell in love and got engaged.

In August 1939 a brazen attempt was made to rob a lady on the LNER's "The Highlandman" express as it passed Aberlady. Private Kingsmill grabbed a handbag containing £7 and ran off through the train. Unable to hide, he opened the door and jumped out of the moving express; his body was found at the lineside, with his hand still clutching the bag.

Passengers also tended to leave luggage unattended briefly when they were getting onto trains and saying goodbye to others. This gave an opportunity for John Maitland, who boosted his income by only selecting first class compartments on well-known trains at London stations. Over several years he stole many items valued at about £2455 until he was arrested in 1938; "It is clear you are a persistent, habitual criminal - your record is a terrible one," said Judge Beazley, sentencing him to five years.

Luggage robbery was systematically organised by a gang working the Southern Region in 1958, targeting cases loaded into the vestibules of Pullman cars. On the Victoria to Eastbourne run a case of jewellry was lost, the empty case being found in the ladies' toilet at Lewes station. On a Victoria to Bognor train goods had gone missing before it even reached Sutton, but vigilant police watched departures and spotted a man and woman team at Charing Cross. They were both arrested - and proved to have lengthy criminal records.

Three men stole a wooden jewellery case from the cloak room at Kings Cross in June 1913, valued at £3271. A reward of £500 was offered.

A confidence trickster who plied the railways in 1957 was a man named Pye, who was punished with a year in prison. In August 1957 he met a Mr Webb at Liverpool Street and introduced himself as "David Selby". After a cup of tea he persuaded Webb to lend him a camera to take a picture of a motorbike in a nearby garage, leaving his own case as "security". "Selby" did not return, and the case contained old clothes stolen from someone else. The clothes were traced to a man who had been duped out of them at Lord's, while it was also discovered "Selby" had stolen two cases from a seaman on a Southampton to Waterloo train. He was arrested at Barnehurst.

The "Golden Age" of Railway Robberies

During 1844 the number of robberies on trains became a matter of public concern, with the belief that "pocket-picking" as practiced on London omnibuses by members of the "swell mob" was spreading to the railways; a man was arrested for picking pockets in a first class carriage of the ECR and on the GWR near Cheltenham a lady lost her purse of £9-16s to a group of "well dressed men" - the standard image of the swell mob.

By the 1840s railway stations were becoming an easy target for gangs of thieves. These quickly identified that unattended luggage was a safer target than passengers' possessions. In 1844 there were a number of luggage robberies on the Grand Junction and the South Eastern, while in 1846 there were "numerous" petty robberies at Derby station organised by a porter. However, the mid-1840s also proved to be the heyday of the most famous "railway detective", Mr C Nash of the GWR's solicitors, Maples, Pearse & Stevens[6]. The railway had been the scene of "continual depredations" and in July 1845 Mr Prance was passing through Paddington with a case containing £2000, which a porter persuaded him to hand over for putting in the luggage car. This was the last he saw of it at the time, but soon afterwards he began to receive anonymous letters offering to arrange for its return in exchange for a "reward". Prance took the matter to Seymour Clarke, the Chief Superintendent at Paddington. Nash became involved in these negotiations, during which he discovered that a box of scrip supposedly worth £40,000 had been stolen from a Mr Hartley under similar circumstances at Euston six weeks earlier; this had been returned on payment of £150. Nash suggested that the police should be brought in, but it was then decided that there was a better chance of capturing the railwaymen involved by playing along with the criminals.

Negotiations were begun with Garratt, a house agent, and it became clear that the gang also included Maynard, a valet, and his mistress called Wareham. The GWR Counsel advised against pursuing a case against them, but Nash and Collard[7] got fully involved. The cloak and dagger affair included a search of the house used by Maynard and Wareham - papers relating to the Hartley robbery were found in the grate. By this time the London & Birmingham, the London & Brighton and the LSWR were also interested in the suspects. Nash was convinced that Maynard was acting as a "thief's agent" and on 5 August 1845 Maynard and Garratt were arrested, Nash advising that Maynard should be prosecuted for felony relating to accepting the money and bigamy. Miss Wareham was arrested on 20 August, but that evening a GWR director, Mills, called on the solicitors and asked for the case to be dropped - he then did the same at the solicitors handling the scrip case.

The result of this was that the gang was released, in a ridiculous attempt to protect the GWR's reputation from further disclosures. Maynard and Wareham immediately filed a suit against Nash, Collard and Prance for wrongful arrest which was clearly intended as intimidatory. The GWR already had a dreadful reputation at the time for loss of passengers' baggage, and also its own money; in 1845 £2000 in cash was stolen from a messenger and in 1847 a similar amount was lost from the GWR "cash box". The GWR Chairman did not support Mills' actions and the press criticised the company heavily.

However, Nash and Collard did not despair. "By continuous watchings, day and night, translating short hand hieroglyphics, ransacking grates and papers, and collecting together numberless incidents and isolated circumstances"[8] evidence was collected against them.

It was clear to the gang that their opportunities had come to an end, so Garratt began to liquidate his resources ready to flee to France. Nash continued to collect evidence against the gang in the hope of pressing further charges, and on 16 September Garratt was re-arrested. He offered Nash bribes and, when these were rejected, began to organise a campaign of intimidation such as threatening letters against Nash's family. Prance brought his own private case and lost.

At a hearing in November 1845 Garratt and Maynard were convicted and sentenced to 14 years transportation on both the Hartley and Prance cases; Garratt was convicted of ten robberies altogether. Nash then wrote to the Secretary of State about the threatening letters and a reward of £100 was offered; although a suspect was identified by January 1846, the authorities would not support a prosecution. Nash resigned his post with the solicitors in January 1846.

The fact that Wareham had not been convicted of any offence left Nash in an exposed legal position on the accusation of wrongful arrest. Nash was still embroiled in court actions at his own expense which meant that he could not afford to call all witnesses; Prance was cleared by the court, but Nash and Collard were found liable to pay Wareham damages for wrongful arrest - however, she was awarded only one farthing! Although this was something of a moral victory, Nash was left with legal fees of £800 and became bankrupt whereas Hartley received £150 from the London & Birmingham. Attempts to collect money for Nash merely fed his creditors. When Garratt arrived in Melbourne he managed to escape, probably by bribery.

Another to be arrested by Nash was Daniel, who was a dangerous bank robber whose crimes included stealing £20,000 in a daylight bank raid and an attack on the Belfast mail.

The other major gang active at the time was led by John Farr, alias Farmer, and included a woman named Mary Newland who received the stolen goods. Two of the gang, Williams and Dalton, were arrested in 1845 after work by Nash and were transported. In June 1846 Farr was convicted of robberies at Euston and London Bridge after further efforts of Inspector Heningham and Mr Nash. Other charges against Farr including robbing Gravesend post office and he received 21 years transportation. Miss Newland, who co-habited with Farr and ran a lodging house in Sloane Square, would have been protected under the legal system of the time if she had been married but instead was given six months hard labour. These convictions, plus those of the Williams and Dalton gang in 1845, represented the first major successes for the railway authorities in fighting organised crime at London stations.

The problems continued, though. In October 1847 a parcel of gold and silver watches disappeared at Euston. On successive days in December 1847 C Abbott and Anne Williams stole £40 worth of luggage on the GWR between Gloucester and Paddington, then a £10 portmanteau on the ECR between Chelmsford and London., then committed a similar offence on the LSWR. They were caught in May 1848.

Mail Robberies

The first major mail robbery occurred on the night of 2 January 1849 and, almost inevitably, affected the Great Western! A consignment of valuable mail was loaded into a GPO van in London and driven to Paddington in the care of guard Barrett; there it was transferred to a railway travelling post office van and Barrett accompanied it to Bristol; he travelled with the guard of the Gloucester mail as far as Swindon. At Bristol the van was positioned at the front of a Bristol to Exeter train, two clerks and the mail guard accompanying it.

At Bristol Barrett had been told of a robbery on that evening's up mail from Exeter, and looked out of the window several times on the journey in case anyone tried to climb into the mail van. However, when he checked inside at Bridgwater he found that the bags had been disturbed and their contents rifled; attempts had been made to conceal the raid, but the string used to retie and seal the bags was different to the normal type. A solicitor travelling first class, Mr Andrews, said he had seen two suspicious men get into another compartment, one having string tied to his foot!

Barrett decided the robbers must have come from the first class carriage and investigated - he found it contained Barlow, a GWR director, a youth asleep, one gentleman on his own, and another compartment with the blinds down. This contained Henry Poole, who had been a GWR guard until his dismissal. and Edward Nightingale, the son of a London bookmaker. It was noticed that Poole had string and sealing wax stuck to his heal, had a pocket book containing false moustaches and string, and had sealing wax in his pockets.

After the arrests more details of the robbery on the "up" train were revealed. Poole and Nightingale had got first class tickets from Plymouth and so positioned themselves in the compartment nearest the postal van, whose doors they managed to force open. They put all the valuables into two sacks. As the train approached Bristol they dropped off the loot for collection by others, planning to repeat the robbery on the down train before their methods were discovered. They had been seen acting suspiciously at Bristol by Mr Lee.

The first rumours were that the raid had netted £80,000, but Poole and Nightingale were eventually charged with the theft of 12 letters, three diamond rings worth £70, three other rings of the same value and six gold ring mountings worth £15. They were each sentenced to 15 years transportation although the theft of letters could have carried a life sentence.

Perhaps the most damaging aspect of the case was the poor light it again shed on the GWR. Poole, working only as a guard, had been known in Exeter as being "quite rich" and had kept a "splendid establishment" for himself until his dismissal. He had become known for "frequently appearing in the streets of Exeter in the most grotesque costume", and travelled the

GWR dressed as a gentleman or a mechanic - presumably to plot his robberies but he also ran a loans business. In late 1848 he had been disturbed in the "locker" of a luggage van, but not arrested. This was about the time that a Taunton banker had lost a parcel of £1500 gold sovereigns on the GWR between London and Bristol- the guard on that train having been a friend of Poole's, and the gold having disappeared from the compartment next to the guard.

The handling of mail bags at stations provided some opportunities for theft, though rarely by more senior railwaymen. In 1867 it was discovered that there had been a number of losses from mailbags sent via Stamford station and attention concentrated on Richard Peak, who was employed to take the letter bags between the Post Office and the station. On 20 September a special letter was made up with several marked coins inside, then put into a registered letter and enclosed in the special registered letter bag for Peterborough. Peak was responsible for looking after the letter bags at the station, but he was seen to put his hand in the neck of the Peterborough bag, cut the registered letter bag inside it, then pull out a letter. Some of the marked coins were found in his pockets and a half-sovereign picked out of the ashes of his fire. This crime was punished with five years penal servitude. Another man who succumbed to temptation was Inspector Stevens of Chatham, who in 1950-1 stole a number of items from mail bags. He was caught after claiming that an attache case containing £100 had been stolen from his office, then was found in possession of a postal order stolen from a Glasgow to Broadstairs mailbag; at home he also had a stolen frock and some nylons.

Perhaps it was just adding insult to the GWR's injuries when George Barton disguised himself in the uniform of a GWR "privileged ticket porter" to rob a mail van in Holborn in October 1849; it was suspected that the uniform had been lent to him by a genuine GWR employee, and the mail had come by GWR from South Wales. After the arrest of Barton his father, William, and Henry Hanbury were also arrested and charged with numerous parcels robberies on the GWR. An inmate of St Pancras workhouse testified that he was employed by the Bartons to make up fake parcels to cover the robberies, there being at least 22 robberies in all with a value of about £20. At the trial in October George Barton - aged only 18 - was given six months in prison, Hanbury seven years transportation and Barton senior fifteen years.

In May 1851 it was the turn of the LSWR to suffer a major robbery after a mail steamer, ironically called the *Great Western*, landed a consignment of 46 boxes of gold dust at Southampton. These were loaded for London under the watch of four guards, who got out at every station to guard the van.

Cannon Street station during the 1911 railway strike – a scene suggesting that mail bags were an easy target for theft.

Nonetheless three boxes were stolen, one of them being found near Winchester. William Pamplin was arrested and convicted at Winchester, being initially sentenced to ten years transportation but commuted to two years due to health grounds and also because he gave "valuable information" to the LSWR - presumably about the methods used in the robbery.

The most famous early train robbery was "the first great train robbery" of gold on the South Eastern. The central figure of the saga was Edward Agar, a skilled locksmith and professional criminal who was said to have made £45,000 from a raid on Rogers' Bank and lived in a comfortable but deliberately low-key style with Fanny Kay. Fanny Kay had, apparently, worked for a time at Tonbridge station[9]. Agar's accomplice was William

Pierce, who had some dislike of the SER after being sacked from its printing office which he had been using to do printing for others at the SER's expense - probably in connection with a "Westminster Bridge betting house" as a man was sacked by the SER for this in June 1852.

These two men realised they could only rob the SER bullion vans on the way from London to Folkestone with "inside" help. They recruited Burgess, a railway guard and the son of a senior SER official, and Tester - a clerk at London Bridge who arranged the guards' train roster.

Agar and Pierce observed the gold working as closely as they could without raising suspicions, finding that the gold was irregular in its shipment. Tester's job was to make sure Burgess was the guard when the robbery was taking place, but the shipments were so unpredictable that he had to work nearly every night for three months. Tester also made a cast of the keys to open the chests whilst Agar and Pierce studied what happened at the Folkestone end. Agar had to make seven trips down the line in Burgess' guard's van before he could make the key fit the locks. Each time the two principals had to go to London Bridge with carpet bags full of lead shot and more strapped around their bodies; this was to balance the weight of the gold they intended to remove.

One evening in May 1855 they at last got the signal - Burgess raised his hat and wiped his face to indicate gold on the train. The two thieves bought tickets for Ostend via Dover in front of stationmaster Weatherhead - who later became governor of Newgate gaol. A porter took their heavy bags to the van and the two went to different carriages, but as soon as Weatherhead turned away Agar slipped into Burgess' van.

At Redhill one bag of gold was handed out to Pierce and Tester joined the train. By Folkestone the safe had been loaded with lead shot and the carpet bags filled with gold; the "gold bullion" was then unloaded, while the thieves continued to Dover with their bags.

At Dover they nearly lost control when a porter became suspicious about their behaviour. Why had they arrived from London with Ostend tickets, and then not gone to Ostend? They tipped him heavily, but a year later he was able to identify Agar.

The gold was taken back to London where Pierce and Agar began the job of melting it down, which they did secretly so that Fanny had no idea what they were doing behind the whitened windows of the wash-house. Some of the gold was mostly sold via a disreputable barrister named James Saward, alias "Jim the Penman", for about £15,000 - about £750,000 in today's terms, but this was not all the goods. Burgess and Tester received about £700 each. Agar fell out with Kay, possibly over her drinking, and they

TESTER   AGAR   BURGESS

Railway clerk Tester, professional criminal Edward Agar and guard Burgess –
three of the principal characters in the celebrated "First Great Train Robbery".
It involved the daring theft of gold bullion from a South Eastern Railway mail
train in 1855.

separated - but when he set up with Emily Campbell in Kilburn he provided
£2500 for the care of Kay and their child.

Discovery of the crime was delayed until the "gold" reached France,
the weight discrepancy having been ignored. Burgess came under suspicion
as did the Folkestone stationmaster, but there was no evidence against either;
Tester got a new job with the Royal Swedish Railway, for which Samuel
Smiles wrote him a good reference.

The crime might never have been solved but for the arrest of Agar on
a separate charge in August 1855 - it seems highly likely he had been "set up"
by some enemies with a forged cheque. This was probably done by a former
lover of Emily Campbell. Sentenced to life imprisonment, Agar arranged for
Pierce to have £7000 to look after Fanny Kay and Agar's child but Kay drank
heavily and Pierce decided to keep the money for himself. Angry at not getting
the money, Kay went to the SER with her story and they sought out Agar;
seeking revenge on his old accomplice, Agar decided to tell the whole story.

Pierce received only a two year sentence as he was not a railway
servant and had not burgled a dwelling house, but this was unsatisfactory for
Herapath who said he was "the greatest rogue of the lot and, for his conduct
to the woman Kay, a blackhearted wretch"; Tester and Burgess each received
14 years transportation.

In April 1934 an attempt was made to rob the mails on the 7.55pm
Paddington to Fishguard. As the train was about to leave, two men arrived and
asked to put a large laundry basket, trunk and a small parcel in the mail van

for collection at Reading. This was the old plan of "delivering" the thieves into the mail van so they could transfer its contents into their trunk ready for all to be unloaded at Reading. The plan would have been successful had they not stopped to sort the takings near Twyford, where they were surprised by a courting couple and put in a panic, for they had got well-away from the station before the railway staff had realised there was a loss. The thieves' lorry, being driven too fast, collided with a car and there were some injuries; the police were able to arrest the thieves in a pub nearby and three were sent to prison.

In November 1950 two habitual criminals, Henry Ford and Thomas Pipe, decided to try and rob the mail compartment on a passenger train by travelling next to the guard and "looking for a chance". On 2 March 1951 they caught the 12.05am Paddington to Birkenhead and watched the guard's movements; between Oxford and Banbury he went off to the toilet, but locked the doors. Having been so careful, he was very surprised to return to see a man inside the letter mail area - for the man had a set of keys! Pipe was apprehended, and Ford picked up at Birmingham Snow Hill with bank notes and postal orders in his pockets; torn letters were found on the lineside.

After the arrests, Pipe admitted to having stolen a mail bag from a Euston train the previous night, which linked with the discovery of two bags at Tring that morning - lost from the 7.40pm Birmingham to Euston. Pipe told the whole story, and was rewarded by being merely "bound over"; for Ford, it was the start of seven years in prison but he had asked for 48 other offences to be taken into consideration, including another mail van robbery in 1943.

Pilfering from a stationary mail train required quite a lot of daring as the level of supervision was much higher than for goods trains. On 5 May 1951 PC O'Brien was on duty at Burton, watching over the Bradford to Bristol night mail which was loading, when he saw strange movements at the lineside. A quick check revealed two mail bags containing Pools envelopes had gone missing and a chase ensued. Robert Ancott was arrested, complaining that "If I hadn't slipped in some cow muck at the cattle dock he wouldn't have caught me." Ancott had travelled on the train as a passenger, got into the mails compartment, and then escaped through the "off" side door. He also confessed to robbery of the Birmingham New Street to Euston mails on 19 September 1951, stealing £300 using the same methods. He was sent to prison for ten years.

Another unsuccessful mail robber was Christopher Sullivan, who was released from Chelmsford gaol on 3 December 1960 after a five year sentence. He was given a travel warrant and some money, but spent all the money in a pub. In order to get some cash he stole two mail bags at King's

Cross, and sat on some disused steps to go through the envelopes. There he was seen by two policewomen, but while one went for support Sullivan attacked the other. He was given another ten year sentence, having enjoyed only twelve hours out of custody.

Police were also successful in catching a gang of mail train robbers on 11 November 1960. Five officers hid in the guard's compartment of the 8.45pm *Irish Mail*, which was soon broken into by a gang who got stuck into rifling the mailbags before realising they were being watched. Ronald Edwards claimed that it was the police who had cut the bags open and the evidence had been planted on him while Terence O'Malley admitted he had gone there to steal but had not actually stolen anything before being arrested. Despite this sentences of five to ten years were handed out.

Even less subtle were the thieves who stole mail bags at Euston and St Pancras in March 1962 - they simply drove up the service road in their car, grabbed a few bags lying on the ground, and drove off again.

During 1962 the Transport Police were concerned about a spate of robberies from trains, which they publicised in their *Journal*, little knowing how significant these crimes were to prove! Firstly, a gang was busy on the Brighton line, stealing mail. In August 1960 a gang had overpowered the guard on the 14.25 Brighton to Victoria and stolen £10,000 in registered mail[10], then in April 1962 five men disguised in railway caps stole £15,000 in mailbags which were being unloaded at Brighton station. Following this, in August a fire was started on a Victoria to Brighton train near Preston Park; the guard rushed off to help fight the fire, giving the thieves time to steal two mailbags.

Secondly, another source of cash on trains was the delivery of wages to railway staff and on the Western Region it was believed in criminal circles that the 9.05am from Paddington carried up to £15,000 for railway staff at Reading, Swindon and Stroud. After a practice run-through on 7 November, on 8 November 1962 four men boarded the train at Paddington with coshes of weighted hosepipe, planning to overpower the guard, cut into the strongroom to steal the cash, then pull the cord near Stockley Bridge and escape in a waiting Jaguar. However the thieves made some miscalculations - the train was only carrying £790 for a start, and they mis-timed the pulling of the cord so that they were a quarter of a mile from the car and could not get all the four chests they had stolen to it. They had also assumed that West Drayton RAF station was deserted, but were seen acting suspiciously by an RAF guard - although he was the other side of an 8ft fence and could do little. However some platelayers 30 yards away realised what was happening and joined in the chase, one of the thieves running across the tracks to a concrete works and one of the boxes being left behind. The box the thieves escaped with had the least money.

Another plan for a raid on Weybridge station, where valuable mailbags were handled under police guard, was frustrated when the thieves' garage was broken into and their Jaguar stolen. However they were also interested in shipments of bullion from Southampton to Waterloo, concluding that it could only be stolen during the journey. It was as they were considering this that the gang learnt of how valuable cash packages sent regularly between London and Glasgow, and similar consignments in reverse; the money was always in the second carriage, they were told. Buster Edwards began to look for ways of stopping the train, and heard of a gang who had made several raids on Brighton line trains by interfering with signalling - the technician here was Roger Cordrey, who promptly demanded £10,000 downpayment. Cordrey and Tommy Wisbey had completed several successful robberies having collected intelligence on the movement of money by train. Roger Cordrey at first used direct raids on the guard's van, but after a visit to Brighton library learnt enough about railway signals to be able to stop a train.

On 2 January 1963 Cordrey and his gang had turned their attention to the *Irish Mail*, which they tried to rob in a brutal attack which involved a pitched battle against some soldiers who had come to the aid of railway staff. Here again the thieves had gained little though, for the cord had been pulled by a steward and they had been unable to get their booty to waiting vehicles.

All these crimes were committed by members of the gangs who staged the best known robbery of all, the "Great Train Robbery" of 8 August 1963, which netted about £2,600,000. The gangs of Edwards and Cordrey decided to work together on the next job. The gang took over Leatherslade Farm near Linslade and 15 men went out at midnight in a number of vehicles. The first task was to cut the signal wires and also the telephone lines to nearby farmhouses. Then two of the gang climbed up onto a signal gantry so they could interfere with the signalling, communicating to another man at a ground signal nearby. Having turned the signals to red, the gang succeeded in stopping the mail train just after 3am, and then waited for one of the crew to get down to phone the signalman. The fireman did so, and was bundled into a ditch, but the driver - Mills- put up a struggle as some of the gang tried to force their way into his cab. He was coshed about the head, receiving severe injuries.

Meanwhile the train was split into two portions and the robbers attempted to move the front part forward with an elderly driver who they had brought along. He was unable to get it started due to problems with the vacuum brake, thus the blood-spattered Mills was put back into his seat and moved the train forward to a marker at Bridgegow Bridge. Then the gang hacked and smashed their way into the sorting vans at the front of the train, terrifying the sorters with threats of violence, and they soon laid hands on the piles of money in a cage by the door. With such an enormous amount available for them to steal they found the effort of shifting the sacks almost too much, and six sacks were left behind as time ran out.

One hundred and twenty sacks were taken back to Leatherslade farm for sorting and a total of £2,500,000 arrived at - half what they had been hoping for. The money was divided up between the gang members there and then.

Meanwhile the guard of the mail train had been the first to realise there were problems. After stopping at the signal he had become concerned at the vacuum gauge, and was even more surprised to find some of his train missing. After putting down detonators, he found the rest of the train a short distance along the line, rescuing the driver and his mate as well as five terrified sorters. Cheddington station immediately became a form of police incident room, while any possible witnesses were asked for statements. Roger Cordrey and Bill Boal were the first to be arrested, in Bournemouth. Over the course of the following months more arrests were made and eventually most of the gang went to gaol, six of them getting sentences of thirty years though these were interspersed with escape attempts; Ronnie Biggs escaped and remains a free man in Brazil.

Station Burglaries and "Hold-Ups"

Remote stations could often be expected to contain some cash on the premises, and even valuable goods consignments in the parcels office. In December 1841 burglars broke into Weston-super-Mare station and stole £30, trying to cover their tracks by setting fire to the station. A reward of £20 was offered. In October 1842 a day's takings at Aylesbury station were stolen - £15, whereas the locomotive department of the North Midland at Derby yielded £60 the same month.

On 2nd January 1849 an opportunistic thief picked up a wooden box on the counter at Rotherham station of the Midland Railway and made off with £1200 in bills of the Sheffield Banking Company. Though valuable, these would have been difficult to convert into cash, although the empty box was found in the river soon afterwards.

The Great Western, which already had a sour reputation as the scene for criminal depredations of the public, suffered its own losses in November 1847 in a station burglary that bore the hallmarks of "inside knowledge." The booking offices for first and second class at Paddington were parallel to each other with doors facing into the front yard, divided by folding doors between them. The doors onto the platform were fastened only by a single inside bolt, so a criminal who gained entry to the platform at night would have an easy job to break into the booking offices. Late on a Sunday night a burglar got into the second class office and robbed six tills, then broke into its first class neighbour. A safe containing cash and valuable articles was forced from the wall, the contents rumoured to be worth £1200, but the burglar missed two boxes of bullion nearby. Parts of the safe were found inside a bag in the River Colne near Hounslow. The following month another robbery took place at the same station - £82 was taken from a desk drawer.

Armed robbers broke into Acton Town station in February 1920, but in making their getaway ran into two policemen in Gunnersbury Lane. PC Kelly was shot by a man carrying a bag, but was able to blow his whistle whilst PC Cleaver was shot in the chest at Gunnersbury Park.

Some burglars relied on inside knowledge to plan their crimes. In February 1953 the National Provincial Bank sent two boxes of mixed silver via Paddington, with a value of about £1000. The boxes were left in the parcels office for the night, but at 4.15am were moved to the "High Level" parcels office. At 6.15am they were found to be missing! The parcels office door had been forced open by a man named Fishlock working in league with a porter, Williams; £258 of the silver was found hidden at the premises of an accomplice, Newman. All received two years prison.

An interesting case is of the Glasgow "lavatory bandit", George Green, in 1953. Green had discovered that a wardrobe key could be filed down so that he could extract the coins from station toilets, managing to collect 25s worth of pennies in one day at Glasgow Central. Although he always "raided" on a Sunday, he varied his approach enough to cause police difficulty in catching him and it took them two years to trap him with marked coins - he had 27s6d in pennies on him. He was given thirty days in prison.

A different type of lavatory bandit was operating at Waterloo in 1956. The stalls there were luxuriously fitted out with coat hooks, but one villain discovered you could reach over and steal a man's coat. Four offences were committed, including the theft on one occasion of a pair of trousers.

A burglary at West Hartlepool Goods station on 17 February 1956 nearly resulted in a murder charge after PC Alex Waterland was stabbed in the back. He had intercepted two men with heavy cases, arrested them, and took them to the police station but they then stabbed him and escaped. The cases contained stolen clothes. The two men were traced to a German ship and given seven years and two years in prison. A similar burglary at the LMS goods warehouse in Sheffield in August 1923 resulted in two police men being badly beaten with brake poles, crowbars and bottles.

Station "Hold-Ups" may have been common in the Wild West, but British thieves generally preferred more subtle - and less risky - methods. Thus it was relatively unusual when clerk Percy Clark of Burnage station reported that he had been the victim of an armed robbery in February 1920; in fact he had hidden the missing £6 himself and was given three months in prison. In August 1938 Thomas Warner had possibly seen too many gangster films when he walked up to a ticket clerk at Victoria Park (LMS) with something in his pocket and said, "Stick 'em up!" The clerk pulled open the cash drawer but at the same time pressed his emergency button; he then handed over two 10s notes but, with a porter's help, was able to get Warner down - and the gun proved to be a pipe! Two men in a car who held up Purley Oaks station with a revolver in October 1938 had not planned their robbery carefully enough - the clerk had just despatched the day's takings off to headquarters. However, it was possibly the same two who held up Woldingham station at gunpoint in December the same year, though their planning had hardly improved - the till contained only 7s. On this occasion they fired their gun to frighten porter Jack Ray, and the bullet lodged in the woodwork.

In May 1956 a gang tried to hold up Beckenham Hill station, attacking a porter and tying him up before taking his keys. However they were disturbed by a PC and ran off before they could complete the robbery.

An unusual style of robbery was perpetrated at Stratford locomotive depot in July 1957. Wages clerk Coles was sitting in an office with the pay envelopes when a "thunderflash" was thrown through the open window, causing shock; £150 was stolen, removed to pay for a honeymoon. The result was a six month prison sentence.

Another opportunity was to rob the station staff after they had been to the bank to collect the wages. An example of this was in September 1956 when the Goodmayes stationmaster was robbed of £1300 by a man who attacked from behind and hit him on the elbow; the porter he had taken with him for protection seems to have had little deterrent effect.

In 1961 there were 352 cases of breaking and entering stations, but few secured large sums of money. Gangs realised that certain days there were more likely to be larger amounts of money on the premises, and one of these times was at the end of a Bank Holiday. On 7 August 1962 there were several station burglaries - £300 was stolen at Hemel Hempstead & Boxmoor, £500 at Berkhamsted and at Sydenham the safe was blown open with gelignite to steal £150. However a gang that raided Greenwich had a surprise - the safe there had been blown open only seven weeks earlier and a new one had not been installed so there was no money kept at the station. In December 1962 thieves raided Greenwich, Maidstone West and Maidstone Barracks stations all in the same night - the robberies at Maidstone yielding £100 at West and a paltry £10 at Barracks.

The 1960s saw an escalation in the degree of violence that such gangs were prepared to employ, as with the robbery of Leicester Square station on 14 May 1964. Four masked men, equipped with iron bars and pick-axe handles, burst into the deep-level stationmaster's office where they surprised the stationmaster himself, his relief, and a ticket collector. After a fierce battle the gang grabbed £1200 which was made up into wage packets and leapt aboard an eastbound Piccadilly line train which was about to depart. They were never caught, though some aspects of the crime gave rise to a belief that it must have been an "inside" job to some extent - the timing was almost perfect!

Only a very foolish criminal would risk "holding-up" a buffet car on the move. On 2 September 1960 an unusual raid was made on dining car staff of the *North Briton* as they were counting the takings at the end of the run. Beer was thrown into their faces, the money grabbed and then the thief ran off with £95 - but it was an easy task to catch him. The staff locked him in the pantry but after the stops at Leeds and York he was discovered to have escaped. However one of the staff was able to pick out a man named Henry Rosney at York and he was arrested; he told the court he had done it while drunk and could remember nothing, so was perhaps fortunate to escape with a £15 fine.

Stealing a Train

Stealing part of a train was very rare. An enterprising train robbery was discovered at Farnham in March 1843, when a train of parcels arrived from Nine Elms with the rear truck missing! It was discovered that thieves had somehow got onto the train and detached the rear waggon whilst the train was in motion; they had then plundered its contents, estimated at £400. Only one of the gang, Wells, was caught and given six months in prison. A similar crime occurred during the Northumberland coal strike of 1910 at Shankhouse. Several men, women and children "held up" a train, detached two waggons and stole the contents. On another occasion several waggons were pushed from the pit head to a point near miners' houses and there were also outbreaks of hostility towards workmen filling the waggons.

In June 1846 directors of the Eastern Counties arranged a special train to take them from Colchester to Ipswich for the opening of the Eastern Union. When they arrived at Colchester station they found their train had gone - others had impersonated them and gone for a free ride!

Cases of people stealing a whole train are rare, but there were occasions when misguided individuals started a train in motion, thereby endangering the lives of others. In September 1840 the crew of a ballast train on the ECR left their train at Brentwood while they went to get their supper. An intoxicated carpenter (alternatively described as an auctioneer!) named Thorogood, who was interested in trains, climbed over the fence and onto the footplate. The driver heard a whistle and rushed out to find that Thorogood had succeeded in starting the engine, then either jumped or fell off. The train collided with a horse box and coke truck, but it could have been a major hazard as it headed off northwards - except that the line was unfinished. Thorogood was charged with setting an engine in motion and endangering life, fined £5 and given six months in prison, the jury being unconvinced by the defence that he was trying to stop the train. This case was prosecuted as a misdemeanour under common law as it was not covered by Railway Acts at the time[11].

This offence occurred very infrequently, but there was a case in September 1875. Thomas Hunt, at one time a servant to the Duke of Leeds, was drunk at Cambridge station. He got onto the footplate of the down mail train and opened its regulator so that it suddenly moved forwards and nearly killed a railwayman working on the brake. He was sent to the assizes for trial.

At a more prosaic level we might consider some youths whose ambitions only went as far as a wagon. Two lads at West Ham got 12 and 6 strokes of the birch for getting onto a truck at Silvertown and moving it onto the main running lines in August 1889.

Slightly more ambitious were three porters from the Midland Railway at Lincoln, in 1848. With three friends they decided to borrow a "manumotive" belonging to railway contractors for a day trip to Newark down the line - which we may presume had no trains on Sundays. They enjoyed a very good day out with large amounts of liquid refreshment, then tried to power the machine back again; by Collingham they had had enough, so they abandoned the manumotive and walked the rest of the way. All six were rewarded with sentences of between two and five weeks.

On 25 January 1961 the signalman at Droitwich received a telephone call from Worcester control at 2am, telling him to stop a light engine expected to reach his section shortly. He followed the instruction and tank engine no.6422 stopped smartly at the signals, then backed smoothly into a siding. Its driver then entered the signalbox and chatted pleasantly with the signalman while waiting for permission to continue, so the signalman phoned up Control to see what he should do - at which point the driver and his mate ran off into the darkness! This was the end of a curious case of train theft which began at

Stafford Road sheds in Wolverhampton, from where the train thieves negotiated a complex web of lines through Dudley managing a journey of 28 miles before some alert soul at Worcester Control began to wonder..... Whoever drove the train seemed well-versed in the rule book, but there was confusion over what charges should be brought - trespass, theft or endangering life?

Phineas Whitehouse of Wolverhampton was arrested and charged with stealing 4cwt of coal, failing to comply with a probation order, endangering the safety of persons on the railway and unlawfully driving a railway engine - he denied the third charge on the basis that he "had the right of way for most of the way."

In October 1962 a 17-year old railway fitter was charged with the theft of a 135-ton diesel engine. There was a railway strike taking place although the youth was not involved, but few staff were on duty. After the others had gone home he decided, "I just wanted to give myself a lift home." So he put his bike in the engine's cab and drove slowly round the freight loop south of Derby towards Chaddesden sidings, trying to keep to 20mph so he could watch for points ahead. However he came to grief on a curve where the points were set against him, and the engine slid over on its side, so that he had to break a window to get his bike out.

[1] L James, *The Law of the Railway*, p.296

[2] J Richards & J MacKenzie, *The Railway Station*, p.106.

[3] The theft of coal continues - in 1987 it was reported that there were regular occasions when the Cynon Valley line was blocked so that coal worth up to £10,000 could be stolen from trains.

[4] P Appleby, *A Force on the Move*, Malvern, 1992: p.106

[5] *The Railway Press*, 23 August 1889

[6] This account is based on press sources and contemporary papers on Nash's case, ref. HO/45/2370

[7] Collard was Superintendent of railway police

[8] *Herapath*, 30 October 1847

[9] BTC *Police Journal*, October 1951.

[10] This gang showed the ability to interfere with signals which was to be used in the later, famous attack.

[11] *Railway Times*, 21 November 1840

CHAPTER FIVE:
ACCIDENTS & DAMAGE

Trespass

Trespass was covered in the bye-laws of individual railways and also under standard railway regulation but, as an offence, was connected with more untoward deaths than any other railway offence - in fact more trespassers were killed most years than passengers have been murdered in the course of railway history. As early as 1843 there were 17 trespassers killed, most of them at night, a figure which had risen to 36 for the six months ending December 1847. In 1874 269 trespassers were killed on UK railways and by 1899 this had risen to 313 with a peak of 442 in 1903; after that figures fell steadily to only 91 in 1949, when 20 of the deaths were caused by contact with electrical equipment[1].

The earliest railways had their own bye-laws about trespass, for example the Plymouth & Dartmoor was advertising the penalties as early as 1824. A systematic approach was encouraged by the Railway Regulation Act of 1840 which allowed for a fine of up to £5 for criminal trespass on the railway - it was an offence only if a person refused to leave once confronted. The Acts of 1868 and 1871 extended definitions and powers, especially regarding trespass on the running lines, but many companies also introduced extra powers through their own Acts especially in the period 1899-1902.

Trespass was always a hazardous practice which is why the railways tried so hard to control it. As some examples, we may consider the fatality on 18 September 1869 of a trespasser killed while crossing the Weston Mill viaduct in Cornwall, a trespasser who was killed at Lea Bridge in March 1869 when he jumped onto the track to get his hat, and a child who drowned in a pit being dug out for a crane at Bishop's Lydeard in December 1874.

The crime of trespass on the railway was one that caused much confusion in the early days, as individuals treated the railway much as a country lane or perhaps a canal towpath. Sometimes even prominent local citizens fell foul of the regulations, such as a leading partner in a Warrington ironworks who was charged with using the Grand Junction Railway as a footpath in March 1839. He pleaded guilty, but then changed his plea to not guilty as the prosecution had a problem with a witness!

Even worse was when people rode or drove along the railway like the man at Sheffield Brightside in May 1839, who was caught riding his horse along the Sheffield & Rotherham just when a train was due; he was fined £2 plus costs. George Nile was run over by a Stockton & Darlington train while riding his horse along the line near Fighting Cocks in October 1840. John Shuter was found on the London & Croydon Railway in December 1840, "looking for his dog".

Others found it difficult to accept the regulated way in which railways worked. James Harding was anxious to catch a train at Wandsworth in April 1841 so he climbed over a gate and walked across the track, forcing entry into a carriage just as his train was starting - offering money to the guard for his ticket. This was unacceptable, so he was fined 10s for trespass.

A complex legal case arose out of a dispute at Rastrick near Brighouse, during railway construction. John Holroyd, a local surveyor of roads, took the view that the railway had blocked a right of way so he collected a gang of men together who overpowered the "constable" on duty and blocked the new line by dumping wheelbarrows full of stones onto it. They filled in the lineside ditches and chased away some men building a wall. The railway company organised a "strong force" to protect its interests, arresting Holroyd and three others; of these, one was fined £5 and the other two released, but Holroyd was sent to the Assizes. However, the Assize jury was unable to agree on a verdict after seven hours of deliberation due to the complexities of the case; although the Railway had blocked up the old road, they had allowed use of it by foot until the line opened.

This case can be compared to that of a farmer from Farthinghoe, whose land was bisected by the Buckinghamshire Railway. Although a crossing was provided he found it difficult to get his dung cart across so used his horses to pull up the rails - just before a ballast train was due. He was apprehended by some navvies.

Another dispute caused by arcane arguments over rights of way occurred in December 1842 when a gamekeeper was arrested for trespass on the Bolton & Leigh; his defence was that the Lord of the Manor, for whom he worked, had the right to "pass upon the railway." A similar case involved "gentleman" Frederick Fenner of Ilford, who was arrested on the ECR's embankment in November 1846 whilst shooting at a hare; the case was dismissed as he rented land nearby!

The climate created by Lord Seymour's Act of 1840 caused a steady increase in punishments - when Matthias Barber was fined £5 for trespass on the Manchester & Leeds at Halifax the *Railway Times* thought it was "excellent". Clause 16 covered anyone who was on the railway without permission, and punishment could be draconian - John Tennant was given a week in Glasgow Jail in December 1840 for trespassing on the Garnkirk & Glasgow even though he was "aged and frail." Even being a shareholder in the railway did not help - a North Midland Railway shareholder was fined 5s for using the line as a short cut to the station near Oakenshaw in May 1841.

When the staff at South Wingfield station on the North Midland attempted to arrest James Bramley for trespass, he brought a counter-charge of assault against them; he lost the case and had to pay £1-19-6d costs.

A foolish case indeed occurred near Leeds in 1867. Three boys decided to walk through the lengthy Bramhope tunnel - which they survived on account of it being a Sunday with few trains. On the way they destroyed a platelayer's jacket and threatened to derail trains if they were prosecuted. The NER brought a case against them and fines of 50s were imposed - or three months in prison.

Even putting up signs made no difference. W Coppleston of the *Bird in Hand* pub in Hammersmith was fined 10s for trespass on the WLR at Kensington after being seen to cross the lines just beyond the station having walked right past a "Trespassers will be prosecuted" sign - so he was, at a cost to him of 10s. The next case in the court involved a woman who had committed the same offence at the same place soon afterwards.

The GWR found itself in a costly legal battle against the residents of Neyland and Buron in west Wales after the building of New Milford station. The local people wanted a footpath across the station to give access to a ferry, and the GWR brought a civil case for trespass. The Judge observed that the Company could have built a bridge for the cost of the legal action!

There was also confusion about the status of railway stations which were, of course, private property. Many people felt they had the right to walk around a station when they did not have - the case of Barker v MR in 1856 proved that a person accompanying a passenger had no right of entry to a station. A ruling in 1879 emphasised that the railways could deny access to anyone who did not intend to travel. Anyone on a station without proper reason could be guilty of trespass. At Morecambe's MR station William Wolstenholme was prosecuted for trespass after he tried to sell toys to the crowds of

"READING BETWEEN THE LINES"

There are no known real-life examples of this unusual trespasser, although at Hebden Bridge a drunkard staggered onto the line and fell asleep. He was so close to the rails that a passing train knocked off his hat!

holidaymakers, refusing to leave when ordered to do so. He was fined 5s.

Drunks on the line were a hazard. In July 1844 a man and his wife were brought up for trespass on the Manchester & Leeds at Dukinfield, the former having been insolent, drunk and also had refused to leave the line. His wife argued that she had only been there to keep him safe, "she was wishful for him to travel on the proper road but he would not." She was excused, but he was fined 5s. The penalty for drunken trespassers could be extreme - in July 1847 on the Manchester & Bolton "a man in a state of intoxication...lay across the rails of this line and was cut in half.[2]" Drunken passengers occasionally got onto the line. At Weybridge in December 1840 a drunken passenger missed the last train, so set off on foot down the line; he was fined 50s. It seems likely that drink was involved in a case of sleeping on the track. In April 1844 a man was found at Hebden Bridge with his head only six inches from the rails; two trains had passed him, one of which had knocked his hat off. He was charged with trespass and fined 5s.

Trespass also occurred when people went onto railway property in order to steal. During the construction of the famous viaduct at Stockport in 1841 there were many problems with local people stealing tools and equipment. Young people were also climbing onto the "battlements", so the viaduct had to be fenced off. On 1 August tore down the fence and stole the wood it was made of, but were arrested by constables. One of the boys' mothers then organised a mob of 300 to rescue the miscreants, during which William Beech hit a constable in the face and snatched a boy away. One of the boys was fined 13s6d for trespass, but Beech was let off with an order to keep the peace.

Hunting caused a number of problems. In January 1841 it was reported that a pack of hounds had chased a hare along the Manchester & Leeds near Rochdale, but that the provisions of Seymour's Act were over-ruled by rights granted under the notorious Game Act. Soon after this there was a case on the GWR where hunters were nearly run over, one horse being killed[3]. The following year the London & Birmingham tried to prosecute George Elmore, who broke the locks off a gate near Harrow so that hounds could cross, and left the gate open. His father had "pulled" up at the gate, but the son was more impetuous. However, the fine of only 1s showed that the magistrates favoured the landed interest. In December 1842 the Cheltenham stag hounds tried to cross the railway near Badgeworth as a train approached, and the first hound was crushed. In 1889 three of the Duke of Rutland's hounds were killed on the GNR at Elton, near his home of Belvoir Castle.

A more recent case was in January 1961 when 37 of the West Street hounds died on the electrified line between Martin Mill and Kearsney in Kent when they plunged down a 30ft cutting in pursuit of a fox, some of the hounds even entering a tunnel. The Master of Hounds tried to drag some of the dogs off the track with his riding crop, but as he was wet he "got a nasty shock." In the end power had to be turned off so that the bodies of the animals could be removed, but the hunters were not prosecuted. The next week, and only a few miles north, eight of the Blean Beagles were killed at Seasalter while chasing a hare.

More worrying still was that trespass could be sanctioned by foolish staff. In December 1840 two LSWR guards and four young men ended up in court with the latter charged with trespass. The four arrived at Andover Road station, but missed their train, so were told to walk along the track and hold up their hats as the next train approached - a foolish venture as their route included a 600 yard tunnel! Nonetheless they succeeded in stopping the next train and paid one of the guards a nominal fare of 2s6d. They then got out at Battersea to avoid ticket collectors and again walked along the track. The LSWR men told them to say they were "contractor's men", but all were fined between £2 and £10.

In recent years the name of "Chicken" has been given to the "game" of chasing across the track in front of a train, but it is also a form of trespass of course. In March 1957 the game of "Last Across" was so prevalent between Poplar and Devons Road that engine drivers were refusing to drive along the section. Children lined up at the trackside as trains approached. Eventually police were sent out to round up some trespassers and collected six boys aged between 11 and 12; each was fined 5s for trespass and their parents bound over to ensure future good behaviour.

It should also be remembered that in the early days it was occasionally railway employees who were prosecuted for trespass when trying to make surveys; this happened in several locations such as Brentford and Macclesfield. In 1844 there were plenty of incidents as the Midland tried to survey its Syston to Peterborough line past the estate of Lord Harborough, who had an interest in a canal that would have been affected. On 13 November the surveyors entered the Park at Stapleford but were "arrested" for trespass by Harborough's men. They were then taken off by cart to see a magistrate at Cold Overton, but as none was at home they were "tipped off" the cart instead and the theodolite was confiscated.[4] There was much trouble at Saxby where on 12 April there was a skirmish involving "a number of reckless-looking ragamuffins" brought in by the MR, but the violence was limited by the presence of PCs. A fire engine was used to hose down one lot of men, while Harborough's staff built up defences on the canal towpath. It all culminated in the handing out of one month sentences for assault at Leicester on 25 March 1845 - Harborough's Steward admitted recruiting men to fight off the railway at 2s6d a day, but six railway staff were also prosecuted.

Vandalism

Vandalism of railway property was a problem from the earliest times, with throwing of objects at passing trains one of the first problems to receive notice - it was much more common than damage to carriages by passengers, for example. As early as 1824 the Plymouth & Dartmoor had the powers to arrest a person for "willfully breaking, throwing down, damaging, destroying..." its works, with a penalty of up to seven years transportation. But small boys continued to be fascinated by the possibility of throwing objects at, or dropping them onto, passing trains with the game of dropping stones down loco chimneys a persistent amusement. However, this was an area in which the 1960s again proved to be a time of change with a considerable increase in the problem to be followed in the 1980s with the new problem of spray-can graffiti.

One of the most common forms of vandalism was throwing things at a passing train. By 1840 the GWR was sufficiently annoyed about this to offer two guineas reward for names, and a lad named Simmonds duly arrived in court - where he was sentenced to a fine of £5 or six weeks in prison. The GWR was also plagued by youths at South Stoke near Oxford making a sport of it - up to forty of them were watching one night in October 1840 when a passenger was hit in the mouth by a stone; three youths were fined £5 each. In autumn 1840 a determined criminal threw various objects at GJR trains near Preston - a 30lb stone, a large block of wood and even a gate.

A young man named Hands was convicted at Abingdon in April 1841 of throwing stones at GWR trains, and sentenced to three months in prison. At Saltley in September a youth named Foxley was fined £5 for throwing a 26lb stone onto a group of platelayers. A boy of ten who threw a stone at an ECR train near Romford in 1842 was unable to pay the £5 fine, so received a month in Ilford House of Correction instead.

On the Edinburgh & Glasgow Railway near Linlithgow in January 1845 a man named Ogilvie threw a stone at a train and hit the guard on the head; the poor man, who was perched up in a good viewpoint, fell into a truck but he could just as easily have been killed. The Railway offered £2 reward and a man was soon arrested, but fined a mere 5s!

These types of offence were covered by the Offences Against the Person Act of 1861, which dealt with intent to endanger life, and the Malicious Damage Act of the same year; section 34 of the former was often used to prosecute vandalism.

In August 1956 three boys threw stones and an apple core at a goods train in Hucknall, Notts. Driver Thorne was knocked unconscious and fell to the floor and his relief driver had to stop the train. The arrested boys included two aged 9 and 10 (fined 4s and £2 each), and a 16 year old "on holiday from an approved school", also fined £2.

June 1957 brought an extraordinary crop of 22 convictions for trespass, obstruction and throwing stones at Grays in Essex, all the "convicts" being children who had made a regular practice of going on the line to throw stones. One child was fined 15s for stone throwing, but most simply had their parents "bound over" for £5 and had to pay 10s costs.

Bridges were a common problem. On the Brandling Junction Railway at Low Felling, two young men pushed a 5cwt coping stone onto the track - just missing a train. They were fined £10 and £5, but amazingly their friends paid for them. Farmer James Jackson of Rochdale dumped an old wheelbarrow over a bridge on the Manchester & Leeds in September 1843, which could have caused an accident; he paid £5 to charity to avoid being prosecuted. John Humphrey chose an unusual object to drop off a bridge onto a passing LCDR express at Bromley in 1865 - a dog. The dog crashed into the "birdcage" compartment of the train, injuring the guard who was knocked out - when he regained consciousness he found the dead dog on the floor beside him. In October 1874 a driver had to be taken off a train "insensible and bleeding from a dreadful wound in the forehead" after being hit by a stone thrown from a bridge in East Ham.

A coping stone was also pushed onto a train near Baldock in January 1862; a boy named Gentle was convicted and sentenced to nine months in gaol.

More serious still was actual shooting at a train. In October 1842 a SER train was shot at with an air rifle near Tonbridge, pellets passing through the windows. On 18 January 1867 a GNR express was shot at near Grantham, the driver picking up a bullet from the footplate; the presence of the Prince and Princess of Teck on the train was thought to be a possible reason.

There was a rash of "shooting at trains" cases at the outbreak of the Great War. In August 1914 a train was shot at near Graveney in Kent and a man was arrested at Holmes Chapel for "firing continuously" at trains. There was much talk of "spies", but this was rarely founded on any truth. Four shots were fired at the Charing Cross to Deal train near Deal in October 1946; three coaches were hit and windows broken, but there were no injuries.

In March 1961 the driver of an Adlington to Widnes goods was shot at with an airgun pellet near Ince, the pellet passing through his cap and stinging his head. The driver commented that, "I have had bedsteads, tin cans and mattresses throw at the engine when I have been driving, but this is the first time I have actually been shot at." Three boys were blamed.

In November 1963 a freight train near Keynsham was hit by a flaming arrow. This scenario out of the Wild West involved an 18 inch arrow of copper welding rod, but it was not only the railway that suffered. Staff at the local J Lyons factory complained that arrows were fired from the local school, whilst a bus had also been hit. However children were not responsible and two 4'6" bows were found in staff lockers at a radio firm. Fines totalled £172.

Occasionally the passing train supplied the missiles that were thrown or shot. For example, a workman on the LBSCR tracks between Plumpton and Cooksbridge was seriously injured in August 1884 when hit in the face by a bottle thrown out of a passing train. In September 1915 Wilfred Tebbutt, aged 18, was fined 10s with £3-3s costs after throwing a bottle out of a train window near Newton Heath; a piece of broken glass injured a railway fireman.

Damage to property also dates back to the early days of railways. At Hessle on 16 February 1841 a group of boys shot a "pipe stock gun" at the windows of the watchman's box, then pulled up his signal flag and broke it. The father of one of them had to pay 40s. In December 1847 two men were fined two guineas each for "wantonly cutting the hat straps in a carriage" of the Glasgow & Paisley Railway. The punishment for James Crawford was a much more severe nine months prison, since his offence was to remove two danger lamps from a Brighton line train in May 1851 thus endangering the lives of passengers.

In 1867 the GNR complained that most vandalism was committed by "local travellers" after one of its guards was killed on a carriage roof while trying to detect vandals in action. "You would be astonished if you knew the amount of repairs we have to do resulting from pure mischief," the Company reported.

A man who cut a strap off a GSWR carriage in 1889 was given a week in prison by Glasgow magistrates. Fortunately punishments had softened by 1954 when a passenger between Birmingham and Leamington persistently put his feet up on the seat - and was fined £2,

In 1945-6 the Southern Railway was plagued by the theft and destruction of light bulbs from its suburban trains, extending to the unscrewing of fittings to leave them in a dangerous condition. A train which was relamped at Wimbledon depot and put back into service at 4pm returned to its depot the next morning with lamps missing from each of the eight carriages. Losses were put at over 100 bulbs per day, with the theft of bulbs a continuing problem into the 1950s; later fluorescent tubes were less easy to steal.

Vandalism was sometimes the result of mental illness. In 1954 the railways of Hull were plagued with a spate of bizarre crimes - track circuit wires were cut, batteries removed from signals, telephone cables cut and speed restriction signs removed. Then an unauthorised speed restriction sign was installed! Police started "Operation Quanta" using hidden observers and dog patrols and on 22 July an observer spotted the criminal - but then fell 35ft into a quarry so the man got away. Two days later he was seen again, cutting down trees above a tunnel mouth, and was caught by a police dog.

He explained that the trees were being cut down "to help speed up the trains" and that he thought there were too many signals which was confusing for drivers, so he had decided to remove a few. He had also damaged a reservoir to make the line "soggy". All this resulted in two months prison, but one suspects proper care was required.

Probably youths were responsible for some odd incidents around Sheffield in 1956. At Brightside station signals were damaged and stones placed nearby in a pattern spelling "EOKA"; station windows were broken there on another night. In an unconnected incident the same night, wagon brakes were released in a siding at Carlton between Barnsley and Cudworth, with the result that some wagons ran down an incline and about 30 piled up in a heap.

An unusual "vandal" was an Army officer in September 1958 who badly damaged a lavatory compartment on a train at Darlington; he had intended throwing a "thunderflash" out of the window as a farewell gesture to friends, but discovered the window would not open - so he dropped it and beat a hasty retreat.

Arson has not been a problem on the railways until the end of World War Two - apart from the suffragette era. When the railways of Liverpool were hit by a spate of fires in 1954 it was unusual. One youth of 17 was responsible for a fire in the carriage sheds at Allerton on 11 June and 18 June; when arrested he told Police that "I like setting fire to things...I like to see things burn," and explained the week's gap between his attack by saying that he could only get matches at weekends. A few days before this two boys caused £18,000 damage to goods wagons at Wavertree and Edge Hill.

A case which did end in a mental institution was that of Anthony Purves in 1960. Early that year fires broke out in the leading carriage of the 10.40am Euston to Northampton and seats were slashed. Several fires occurred in carriage toilets over the next months and on 10 July a fire broke out in the leading compartment of a train near Wolverton, causing the train to stop at Hanslope SB for help. Purves was traced and incriminated himself by revealing his knowledge of where the fires had occurred, but he was considered mentally unstable.

It was probably just malice that motivated whoever broke into the signalbox at Otterspool between Warrington and Liverpool in August 1962. They set fire to cabling, smashed windows and interfered with signalling, causing a diesel train to be diverted into a loop when travelling at 50mph - the driver used the emergency brake in order to avoid hitting the points that led back onto the main-line.

It is surprising that some vandalism was actually caused by railway staff - and not only by Dr Beeching. In July 1959 signalman Geoff Abbott took over at Waterloo Colliery signalbox near Woodlesford, and reported that the up and down bells were damaged as if hit by a heavy instrument. Normal working was interrupted for several hours. In March 1960 the same signalman reported the failure of the down starting signal repeater as the wire had been severed, and also the wire to the up home had been partially cut through. On 13 May he reported that the goods line had been blocked due to vandalism, after which police began to suspect a connection between the incidents and Abbott being on duty. Eventually he admitted the damage was due to "being cheesed off at having to go on night duty" and to losing his temper; he received a nine month prison sentence.

Attempted Derailment

Attempts to derail trains by putting objects on the track were sadly very common, but quite difficult to prosecute due to the offence often taking place in remote spots away from prying eyes! It was a general view that the law on attempted derailment was too lenient, whereas in Prussia the offence carried a ten year maximum by the mid-1840s whilst Turkey made the offence punishable with death in 1891. Although partially covered through the early Regulation Acts and company bye-laws, the Offences Against the Person Act of 1861 specifically dealt with the idea of endangering life through illegal acts; section 32 specified placing items on the track or altering signals with intent to endanger life. The Malicious Damage Act of the same year allowed for up to life imprisonment for intending to disrupt, obstruct or derail a train; the powers of this Act included prosecution of people for deliberately making misleading hand signals to a train. These types of offence were a persistent problem from the early days of railways, and rose inexorably. There was an average of 22 incidents per year of endangering life in 1930-4, rising to 68 in 1956.

For example, at Stoat's Nest on the Brighton line a goods train was derailed in 1840 by two pieces of iron being put on the rails and a lad named Jenkins, who had been working nearby, was arrested. However there was not enough evidence to prove that he had placed the objects on the line.

It will be noted from this that the material used in the attempted derailment consisted of metalwork left by platelayers on the trackside. It was very common for railway materials to be used in attempted derailments. Liverpool & Manchester Railway minutes of August 1831 record problems with mile posts being removed and sleepers put on the track at Sutton[5]. In August 1840 a man named Williams was fined £10 after trying to derail a train near Bromsgrove using a railway "bar" and timber. The magistrates fined him the maximum that the law allowed at the time, but expressed the view that this was inadequate as many could have been killed. A fine of only £5 was given to a boy named Bunting, who attempted to derail a train on the North Midland line near Wingfield using an old iron chair. The boy "appeared ignorant and stupid"; magistrates blamed his father for not educating him and never taking him to church[6]. If the father was unable to pay the £5, then he himself was liable to a three month prison sentence. A sleeper was put on the track of the Chester to Birkenhead line near Sutton station in November 1842 by John Mooton; footprints were traced from the scene of the crime to his house. He was given 18 months hard labour.

A rare case of attempted derailment being morally motivated occurred in September 1841. A boy attempted to derail the mail train from Arbroath to Dundee, saying that it was "to bring them up for fleein' about that way on Sunday." A vandal near the ECR took advantage of the fact that its policeman at West Ham went to church to pile stones on the track during the hours of divine service.

It was rare for an attempted derailment to be due to a vengeful passenger, but this did occur at Seaton Bank on the Hartlepool to Sunderland line in August 1844. Two obstructions made of railway "keys" were found and the guard saw a man named Atkinson nearby; he had been put off the train for trying to ride on coal waggons. After a chase he was arrested, but found not guilty by a jury.

Two 15 year old boys employed by the NER at Hull tried fixing chains across the track to see what would happen in January 1874; they were given three months gaol. Two 15 year olds who put timber on the line between Bradford and Shipley in the same year got a month in the House of Correction and four years at Market Weighton "reformatory" as they had escaped after an earlier offence. However when Worcester magistrates gave a similar punishment in 1875 it was reversed by the Home Secretary. In 1885 a 13 year-old who tried to derail a train at Clapham Junction got a month in gaol and was "soundly whipped." In April 1882 the driver of a Caledonian Railway express saw an obstacle on the other track at Cove, and sent a warning to the signalman by writing a message and throwing it off at Cove station. The obstruction was timber placed on the line.

In August 1913 two boys put stones on the track at Polegate in Sussex, managing to derail a LBSCR engine but fortunately not the carriages. They were given six strokes of the birch each, a rather light punishment compared to earlier times. The same standard punishment was given the following month to a boy who put fishplates across the rails at Waddon Marsh.

Mental illness was a cause of some of these incidents and seems to have often been the case where adults made repeated attempts to cause disaster. Michael Flatley, a navvy working near Ince, made a whole series of attempts to derail a train in September 1867 and on one occasion managed to derail a locomotive. The LNWR put guards out on the line to try and catch the offender, but on 22 September Flatley managed to pile three sleepers across the track in front of a mail train before anyone saw him. The train hit the obstacle but no serious results occurred.

An adult offender could be severely punished. David Morgan placed iron on the Brecon & Merthyr in June 1874, being caught after a chase "of five miles or more over the hills" by a ganger and policeman. He was charged with intent to derail the train and, as there were several other offences, was given seven years penal servitude. Charles Biggs was given a year in prison for attempting to derail a NBR goods at Drumlithie viaduct on the CR in October 1884. In February 1885 Fred Andrews was given an eight year sentence for his fourth conviction, on this occasion attempting to derail a LSWR train near Farnham.

In March 1911 Frank Barker of Lambeth was charged with attempting to derail trains on the LBSCR between Coulsdon and Purley on two occasions in 1910, using a fogman's hut and a portable fireplace. In February 1911 he wrote to the LBSCR saying, "My mind is troubling me. I am afraid I shall do it again." He also wrote to the police three times, including a confession of a wrecking attempt at Exeter. He was found guilty at a trial in July 1911, appearing "in a very emaciated condition", and it was revealed he had already served a three year sentence for a similar offence. He said that "he felt he would do better in prison as he felt he must do it again", but then retracted his confession saying he only said it because he was starving. Barker was given seven years hard labour. Two others who perhaps had mental problems were arrested for trying to derail trains at Stoke Holy Cross and Beeston Regis in Norfolk in 1939; one of them said he did it because he was "fed up" with life. They were given 3 years and 18 months in prison.

A determined gang attacked the LTS line to Shoeburyness in 1957. On 19 January the 7.25pm from Fenchurch Street struck a 3cwt tree trunk wedged into the ATS apparatus near Pitsea and it was found that the trunk had been dragged half a mile to the line. On 3 February more timber was put on the line in incidents at Basildon and Vange. Four youths were seen on the line and chased, leading to sentences of 18 months each. Two boys caused £413 damage to the St Pancras to Manchester Pullman between Syston and Sileby on 14 February 1962 by leaving a tree trunk on the line; they received two weeks custody.

A definite "revenge" attack occurred between Lewknor and Aston Rowant in 1957. Four youths had met together for a "reading party" in preparation for their "A" levels and were sitting in the garden beside the railway when a train passed and blew steam over them, much to the amusement of its driver. The boys decided to get their own back by placing 80 wooden blocks and a 40lb metal chain on the line, but they were seen by a man in a nearby garden who phoned the police. It cost them a £5 fine and £10 costs.

Several fatal accidents have been caused by deliberate derailing of trains. A serious case occurred in January 1844 when the derailment of an ECR train in Essex caused the death of its driver and stoker; the accident was blamed on a piece of rail placed across the track, and the Chelmsford Coroner's verdict was "manslaughter by an unknown person." More usually cases were on the level of George Pickett, a lad who was given a month in prison for putting a stone on the GWR at Langley Marsh in July 1844.

Perhaps the most serious case was in 1851, when the 12.05pm Brighton to Lewes train was derailed by a sleeper projecting out into the track and five people were killed as the train hit a bridge parapet and fell off the embankment. First reports expected the accident to have been due to excessive speed as "trains very often shoot down these inclines at fearful speeds", but this was not the case. Running tender first, the train hit a sleeper which was one of a pile of three that had been turned to lie across the path of the train. The stoker was crushed between the loco and the wall, the driver lost both legs and died later in Brighton. Deaths occurred in the 2nd and 3rd class carriages - the "head and face of Miss Chatfield were horribly mangled and presented little trace of humanity...marks of the scalding steam were also visible."

Since the sleeper could have been moved into this position with very little effort, the obstacle could have been put there by any adult or child. Interest centred on 10 year old James Boakes, whose family had a cottage nearby and a detached potato garden which was beside the railway - and not yet separated from it by any fence. There were reports that when the train had come off the track he said, "Oh mother, what shall I do?" to his parent, but at the inquest evidence was not taken from him as he did not understand the oath.

Superintendent Acton of the railway's police questioned Boakes and later said the boy had admitted moving the sleeper, but his mother denied he had said it. There was much debate about how far the mother had been able to supervise what the boy was doing when the potato garden was 110 yards from the cottage. Sergeant Langley of the Metropolitan Police concluded that the accident was caused by the sleeper and the boy was the only known possibility. The inquest at Lewes concluded that the accident was caused by the sleeper, but criticised the LBSCR for running the train tender-first. Another inquest was necessary at Brighton as the driver had died there, and

The 12.30pm Glasgow Central to Ardrossan train derailed at Saltcoats after large stones were placed on the track. The driver, fireman and two passengers were killed.

on this occasion the boy was able to appear as he had received instruction about the oath. He made the mysterious comment that he thought people would blame him for the accident because they would think he had been "playing seesaw", but it was not clear whether this was the boy's own suggestion or someone had put the idea into his mind. The Brighton inquest decided that the sleeper had been "wilfully, feloniously and maliciously been placed across the rail...by some person or persons unknown." A year later the boy was apparently struck by lightning at the same spot![7]

Other fatal accidents attributed to deliberate attempts to derail include an accident at Saltcoats on 5 August 1939 in which three people died, and the accident at Elm Park in March 1965. At Saltcoats, the 12.30pm Glasgow Central to Ardrossan was derailed at Canal Street bridge by large stones placed on the track; this may not have been such a serious incident except for the fact that it occurred on an embankment, the engine and three carriages toppling down the slope with both footplatemen and two passengers being killed.[8] However Britain has never seen an incident as those perpetrated in its overseas Empire, with train-wrecking being a common problem in India; for example, on 12 January 1939 an express of the East India Railway was derailed at night and 21 people killed.

Derailments might also be caused by staff seeking revenge on the company or each other. On 8 December 1847 a train on the Taff Vale narrowly avoided going down a "100 foot precipice" after rails had been removed by William Scott who was jealous of stoker W Lewis. The train was running from Cardiff to Merthyr with over 50 passengers and was six miles from its destination when the engine and three carriages were derailed on a "precipice" overlooking the River Taff, but luckily the train went off the "mountain" side of the track. Investigators discovered that two rails had been removed.

The incident was soon traced to Scott, from Aberdeen, who was a navvy working on a nearby branch line and who had fallen for the charms of Eliza Williams. However Thomas Lewis had replaced Scott in her affections, with the result that he had sought a terrible vengeance. Normal railway law allowed a punishment of only two years for the offence, but the TVR Act, clause 166, conferred powers of up to seven years transportation and this is what Scott received.

Thomas Annison escaped a horrific charge in 1851 on the basis that there was no solid evidence against him. He had been working as an assistant at Reedham swing bridge on the Norfolk Railway but was sacked for dishonesty. A few weeks later a train drew onto the bridge and then suddenly there was a strange noise and "great oscillation" of the engine. Iron wrenches had been deliberately placed across the track in an attempt to plunge the train into the river. Annison was seen nearby and arrested, but there was no other evidence against him.

At Worcester in July 1868 Samuel Jenkins was charged with maliciously placing iron on GWR tracks near Churchill station, close to Kidderminster. He had been a guard on the GWR for 15 years but had left for reasons of his own, yet returned in April 1868 to place four "serious obstructions" on one track and one on the other. He was given penal servitude for life, perhaps reflecting his previous job.

Another motive for staff was to attract attention to themselves to win promotion. In 1882 signalman Thomas Rivett of the LNWR found an object on the line between Attleborough and Rugby which was believed to be an attempt to derail the *Irish Mail*. He later confessed that he had put it there himself to increase his chance of promotion. A similar story has been told about the stationmaster at Black Bank on the GER in about 1900, though on this occasion he told the porter of his plan - and the porter reported him. The porter laced the stationmaster's tea with castor oil so that he was confined to bed and could not put his dastardly plan into action until the District Inspector could get there.[9] It was the porter who got the promotion.

More bizarre still was Albert Pearce, aged 17, a porter at Wallington, who was charged in 1911 with putting an iron bar on the track at Carshalton. He told the police that "I did it because I was in a temper, for fun."

It was thought that an attempt to derail a NLR train near Richmond in 1874 was due to seeking revenge. A train passing the Lower Mortlake Road bridge hit a sleeper and metal levers embedded in the ballast, the levers penetrating the engine's firebox. Men were sent to the scene from Kew Gardens station, but by the time they arrived another sleeper had been placed there.

Accidents

Accidents were covered by laws on negligence and manslaughter, but after 1840 were covered by many aspects of Seymour's Act which affected behaviour of railway staff and also the 1842 Act which dealt with the concept of recklessness[10]. This law allowed a railway employee to be punished by magistrates with up to £200 in fines or 3 months in prison for misconduct. However, if the case was referred to the Quarter Sessions punishment might be up to two years in prison. The 1861 Offences against the Person Act provided some additional legal framework where injury was caused by negligence. However, even in Victorian times it was very difficult to secure a guilty verdict on a charge of manslaughter; "the Judges made it repeatedly clear that they were not going to hold employers and superior employees vicariously liable in criminal law for the deaths of employees in accidents[11]," a view which also applied to superior employees when passengers were killed. There is no known instance of a murder being committed by deliberate neglect. A large number of cases, some of which are described below, have established the groundwork for prosecutions of railway workers in a style which has continued up to the present. The prosecution of Benge after the Staplehurst disaster showed that the foreman who had not allowed time to replace the rails was guilty of negligence, but not his superior the inspector. The prosecution of a driver named Hilton in 1938 established that if a man left his engine and it was then used by someone else to cause death, the driver was not guilty of negligence. Those who went to prison tended to be the lower orders of the workforce.

In the early days there were many instances of ignorant working practices among newly-recruited staff. For example, Joseph Barrow and Samuel Dexter were fined £10 and £1 each for running their engine on the wrong line at Normanton on Soar - the driver receiving the severest punishment.

Lord Seymour's Act made it a criminal offence to be negligent on railway duty and introduced custodial sentences, mostly of up to two months. Under these regulations the London & Birmingham Railway prosecuted a policeman for neglect of duty after an accident at Rugby in

October 1840, for which he was given two weeks Hard Labour. The same month a guard on the ECR was found to be drunk on duty but it took five constables to restrain him; he received the same sentence, but was told that he could have had up to two months in prison. This maximum sentence was given to Joseph Jobling, who drove a L&BR engine down the wrong track at Camden Town whilst very drunk, nearly colliding with a mail train. A similar sentence was handed out to platelayer Babbington of the Manchester & Leeds in December 1840, who removed a rail and then failed to warn an approaching train, yet a Midland Counties driver who derailed his train at Thurmaston due to excessive speed was only fined £5.

Some companies dismissed men rather than taking them to court. Stephen Hasler was meant to be in charge of the points at Southampton in January 1841, but went to sleep in his box; he was sacked, but could have gone to prison.

By 1841 prison sentences were becoming commonplace after accidents. In January three men were directed to take a horse-drawn crane along the Manchester & Leeds from Leeds to Summit Tunnel. By the time they got to Elland the horses were tired out, but against orders they set out on the line again - only to be run into by a luggage train near Sowerby Bridge. The leading man, Mr Nutter, was given two months in prison. Another problem on the same line occurred a year later in 1842 when four platelayers got drunk at Luddenden Foot and decided to use a "truck" to get to Sowerby Bridge. They were soon hit by a train and two were injured; the uninjured pair were fined £10 and £5 for wilfully obstructing the railway.

The same line saw a strange incident in May 1845 when a Manchester-bound goods train ran out of water at Littleborough - the driver and fireman decided to run it back downhill to the nearest supply, using the wrong track, and collided with the following train. Perhaps surprisingly, the driver was fined only £5 and the fireman sacked. Two employees of the NSR were charged at Macclesfield in 1867 for neglect of duty after a passenger train collided with two trucks at North Rode Junction; the pointsman and breaksman were fined £10 or two months prison.

The drinking habits of railway workers have become one of the most circumscribed of any workforce, to the extent that white-collar staff are now liable for dismissal for drinking at lunchtimes even though they have no operational duties. The 1840 Railway Regulation Act began this trend which means, as L James has put it, that "the drunkeness of a railway servant can constitute a criminal offence which is peculiar to railway service and quite outside the general law of dealing with drunkeness in public places."[12]

Magistrates fined Crossley, a London & Croydon guard, only 10s for being drunk on duty and assaulting his superintendent, having taken into account that he had already been sacked from his job. In contrast, a GWR policeman who went to sleep while on tunnel duty near Bath was given a month's hard labour the same month.

The punishment of John Adamson, a driver on the Stockton & Darlington, seems rather kind: in February 1841 he left his engine *Dispatch* on the line while he went to a nearby hostelry and got drunk; he was fined £1. A drunk driver of a Leeds-Brighouse train in March received the maximum sentence as did another Manchester & Leeds driver for being drunk at Brighouse in October 1841. Drink was believed to be behind a remarkable accident at Nine Elms in May 1843, when a luggage train arrived at 2am but failed to stop - it ploughed through a group of waggons, crossed Nine Elms Road, and ran into a warehouse yard causing £300 damage. Both men on the footplate said they had thought they were two miles from Nine Elms, but others suggested that had dozed off under the influence of alcohol.

Railway policemen seem to have been as susceptible to drinking on duty as anyone. James Painter, a policeman at Longsight in May 1841, was so drunk on duty that he fell across the lines just as a locomotive was backing towards him; the driver braked and a couple rescued him, but he was fined 40s.

In the early 1840s engine drivers were in short supply, and it took some really bad behaviour to get the sack at a time when colleagues were earning as much as £5 a week[13]. In the summer of 1843 George Turner of the Manchester & Leeds held onto his job when he hit the buffers, but was sacked when he turned up to drive an evening train when drunk; he was ordered off the footplate but refused and had to be removed by force. He claimed to have only drunk 4d of whisky, but was fined 50s and sacked.

It seems likely that the rapid expansion of railways contributed to there being a number of poor quality drivers and therefore a high number of accidents. After an accident at Stratford on the ECR in July 1846 the driver and stoker of *Firefly* were sent for trial for reckless driving, but the coroner's jury observed it was the task of management to ensure drivers obeyed the rules. Two Brighton line drivers were given a month and two months in prison in October 1846 "for not attending to signals at Reigate."

On 17 August 1957 driver John Metcalfe booked on to work the 9pm Carlisle to Newcastle DMU. As he walked along the train to the cab some passengers were worried that he appeared to stagger, and were even more concerned when they noticed him slumped over the controls only two miles out of Carlisle. Unable to contact the guard, a passenger pulled the

Nervous Party. " The train seems to be travelling at a fearful pace, ma'am."

Elderly Female. " Yus, ain't it ? My Bill's a-drivin' of the ingin, an' 'e *can* make 'er go when 'e's got a drop o' drink in 'im ! "

Drunken train drivers were certainly no joke – except in the pages of *Punch*.

communication cord near Durran Hill Junction. The driver would not get out, so a signalman sent for a relief driver.

Metcalfe was charged under the 1840 Act with much of the evidence coming from a 12 year old enthusiast, Keith Haselhurst,[14] who pointed out the driving errors that had been made. Metcalfe's defence was that he had contracted an infectious disease while in the Army, this caused a wasting of the nerves and the loss of control of muscles in the lower part of the body. A doctor defending him confirmed this would give Metcalfe the appearance of staggering, but a BTC police officer said "His eyes were glassy, his face flushed and he smelled strongly of beer."

Another driver with a drink problem was Kenneth Ferington, driver of a Leeds to Heysham DMU on 10 March 1967. The guard noticed sudden variations in speed but the driver told him it was because two engines were "out", although all six blue lights were showing correctly. Near Apperley Bridge station the train stopped though signals were at clear, then moved slowly forward and stopped in a tunnel. A Train Controller was also travelling and observed that the driver was trying to move the train forwards even though the brakes were on. The driver was removed from his position and the Controller moved the train forward to Thackley Junction signalbox and then to Shipley. Police met the train at Bingley Junction and found the driver sprawled in a seat, having drunk the equivalent of nine whiskies. He was found guilty of endangering life and given a three month sentence.

Another type of railway worker prone to prosecution were signalmen, and their "ancestors" policemen and pointsmen. Beech was a "pointsman" at Blisworth on the Northampton & Peterborough in 1846; he was so busily engaged in making a mousetrap that he forgot to attend to the points and an engine derailed and overturned. He received two months in prison. John Latto, a pointsman on the NBR at Esbank Junction, left the points wrongly set on 31 July 1856 causing injury to eight people; he was given two years in prison. In 1865 signalman Edward Jackson, on the GNR's Lincoln to Boston line, was given a month in prison for "failure to show a green flag."

Manslaughter

Excessive negligence could lead to a charge of manslaughter, a charge often levelled against signalmen and drivers after accidents. In December 1840 a small truck or "lurry" was left on the line of the Birmingham & Derby Junction at Coleshill by two trackworkers. It was hit by a train and one passenger killed, the coroner's court deciding the cause of death was manslaughter by King and Barber. Both were acquitted in the subsequent trial.

A North Midland driver was charged with manslaughter in January 1843 after an accident at Barnsley, when he was driving a luggage train that was four hours late. At his trial, Edward Jenkins was found not guilty as the speed of 15mph was not considered reckless and commentators wondered why the prosecution had not called his stoker as a witness.

On 5 June 1847 seven people were killed on the LNWR at Wolverton when the down Liverpool mail train, of 19 carriages, was signalled into the station but then diverted into a siding full of coal trucks by a careless "policeman", Fossey. All the fatalities were in the sixth carriage. Fossey was arrested and found guilty of manslaughter, the Judge, Baron Alderson, summing up:

"The prisoner has been most properly convicted by the jury of carelessness in the discharge of his duty. He ought to have exercised more caution and care in distinguishing between a goods train and one carrying passengers."

The jury had their own view, observing "We find the prisoner guilty, but we blame the company for not keeping two men at the points." Fossey was given two years hard labour.

In May 1853 a coroner's jury took the view that LSWR chairman Francis Scott and his traffic manager, J H Beattie, were guilty of manslaughter after one of the workmen on the Farnham to Alton line was run over. The two men had organised a train to inspect the new line but had given no notice that it was running.

A manslaughter verdict was returned by a Yorkshire coroner's jury against Thompson, the chairman of the York & North Midland, in July 1853 after an engine was derailed and its two crew killed. However Judge Earle rejected the case, saying that it could only be manslaughter if the directors had knowingly used an improper engine, knew the railway was in a poor state, or had issued regulations forcing improper speeds. More senior railway officials were almost always exonerated - even the Superintendent of the Line of the notorious ECR was found not guilty after a disaster at Thetford in 1854.

Two people were killed on a foggy night at Barkston Junction on 10 January 1874 when the 6pm from Boston failed to stop at signals and collided with a "Scotch 3rd class train." The driver of the Boston train was arrested and charged with manslaughter but the case was dismissed as the weather had been so bad it would have been difficult to prove his negligence. In September of the same year there was a terrible disaster near Norwich Thorpe station on the GER which was the result of negligent working of a single-line railway; Inspector Cooper was found guilty of manslaughter, but was given only an eight month sentence for an accident in which nearly 30 people died.

After the Rutherglen accident on 24 January 1880, the driver of the

Graphic depictions of the worst single-line collision in the history of British railways. Shoddy operating at Thorpe, near Norwich, on the night of September 10th, 1874, led to the deaths of 25 passengers – and the criminal conviction of station inspector Cooper.

5.15am Carlisle to Glasgow was gaoled for manslaughter. His union, the ASRS, called in railway expert C E Stretton to argue that the main cause of the driver's error was in fact the failure of the Clark & Webb brake to operate properly. Because of this, Lord Coleridge in 1880 and Baron Pollock in 1885 ruled that an error of judgment should not be considered criminal; from then onwards, a signalman or driver who made a mistake, but was not negligent, was not to be regarded as criminal.

A famous case of a signalman being prosecuted was that of James Holmes, a signalman at Manor House box between Thirsk and Northallerton on the NER in 1892. After working a shift from 6pm to 6am,

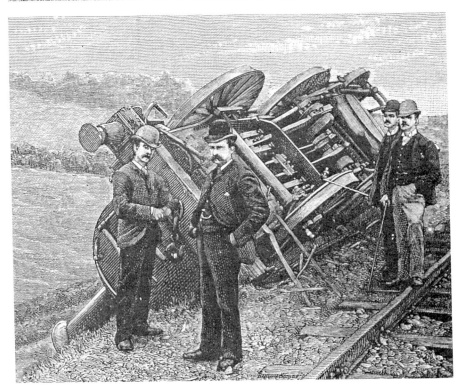

Holmes had to attend to the problem of his child being seriously ill - he had to walk to Northallerton to fetch a doctor, but the man was out on another case and could not be found. When he returned home the child was dead and his wife was distraught, yet Holmes was also due to return to work without having slept. He went to his nearest station, Otterington, to report himself unfit to work, but the NER was unable to provide a relief signalman. He had to begin his night duty, but at 4.30am become overcome with exhaustion and forgot about the position of a goods train; an express hit the guard's van of the goods and eight people died as well as the guard. Holmes was arrested and charged with manslaughter, it being argued that his carelessness had caused the deaths; he was found guilty, but the Judge ruled he be discharged with no further punishment. This ruling was greeted with "prolonged cheering" in the court, and led to substantial changes in working practices.

A famous accident that resulted in prosecutions was the Armagh disaster in 1889, when a heavy passenger train become stuck on a gradient and was divided into two. Half of the train rolled back and collided with another, with eighty deaths[15]. The Coroner's jury found some of the railway staff guilty of culpable negligence and it was decided to prosecute them for manslaughter. *The Railway Press* was incensed about this and set up a fund to defend the men, who were not in a trade union, as well as campaigning against the trial being held in Armagh itself. Attention mainly centred on James Elliott who, as superintendent of the train, was responsible for giving orders to the others.

Elliott was tried in August 1889 for the felonious killing of one of the passengers but the jury was unable to agree and he had to suffer a retrial in October. He was acquitted at this hearing and as all the others had acted under his orders this meant they were acquitted too. The railway company was heavily criticised for failing to provide proper brakes on the train, but employed a detective to check for fraudulent compensation claims. The accident influenced the Regulation of Railways Act, 1889, after which the Board of Trade could impose block signalling and, most significantly, continuous brakes on all passenger trains.

John Smith, an assistant guard on the MR, was charged with the manslaughter of Levi Flint on 7 November 1891 at Pinxton. The train had restarted too quickly as Flint was getting out, and he had fallen between the

Aftermath of Ireland's worst railway accident in 1889, when 80 people – many of them young children – were killed in a runaway train. It is one of the most famous occasions when criminal charges for manslaughter and "felonious killing" were brought against railway staff.

platform edge and the train. The prosecution argued that Smith had been negligent in showing the "green" of the lamp too soon, but it was demonstrated that green could have appeared accidentally as the guard turned his lamp.

Another who escaped a manslaughter charge was West Hampstead signalman William Hollis who was on duty when three passengers were killed in an accident on 26 October 1907. This occurred on one of the terribly foggy days which plagued London's railways at the time, and Hollis forgot about a Neasden train in the fog - allowing a Willesden one to run into the back of it. He said to the inspector, "This was my fault. The disc broke down and I could not see the train because the fog was so thick." The signalling disc still showed "Line Clear" according to Hollis. The coroner's jury returned a verdict of manslaughter by culpable negligence against him.

The trial revealed quite a muddled situation for a densely used suburban line in foggy conditions. Hollis had been late for work and he cut corners in his signalling routines - he wrote the arrival and departure of the Willesden train in his book at the same time to save returning to it, then forgot about it still being there. The treadle beyond the station should have indicated when it had left, but Hollis ignored it as it did not work properly, and the driver of this train should have whistled after being left standing for several minutes. A signal engineer tested the treadle for the next two weeks and found, on one occasion, that it failed in a "clear" position. At the end of the trial the Judge advised that for manslaughter it had to be "gross and culpable negligence" but he thought that Hollis had been mainly careless; the jury returned a not guilty verdict in line with the Coleridge and Pollock rulings.

Even when a famous accident did lead to a conviction, there was still some public sympathy for the convicted criminal. After the terrible accident at Ais Gill in 1913, driver Samuel Caudell was indicted on a charge of the manslaughter of Sir Arthur Douglas by the coroner's court. However, the Prosecutor decided not to bring a manslughter case even though Caudell had passed three signals and in October 1913 Caudell was convicted on a lesser charge, the defence being that he had been distracted by the need to oil the engine and maintain steam. When he was released from prison in November he was met by a cheering crowd of over 100 people and it was reported by the *Railway Gazette* that the Midland Railway intended to find him another job.

Manslaughter charges could also affect non-railway people. On 1

The fatal consequences of a collision between a train and a lorry on a level crossing at Hilgay, Cambridgeshire, in June 1939. The lorry driver survived – only to be arrested and charged with manslaughter.

June 1939 there was a terrible accident on an occupational level crossing near Hilgay in Cambridgeshire which resulted in four deaths. The 11.02am, Hunstanton to Liverpool Street, hauled by no.8783 which was often used for Royal trains, hit a lorry carrying straw at about 60mph; derailed coaches collided with trucks in a siding and their sides were torn off, all the dead being in the second carriage. The lorry driver, Reuben Height of Downham Market, was arrested and charged with manslaughter whilst some lesser charges were brought against his "mate", Arthur Pearse. The two men had broken one of the most clear procedures for the use of such crossings - Pearse had opened the nearside gate first, allowing the lorry to pull onto the tracks before the far gate had been opened - even though a train was signalled and a nearby public crossing had already been closed to traffic.

Height's defence was that the gates had to be "held" to remain open, therefore they had to cross the line in the manner he had used, although the Inspecting Officer's report concluded that the accident was "solely attributable to Height's failure to exercise reasonable precaution." Height was tried at Norfolk Assizes, but on the second day of the trial the Prosecutor offered no evidence and the Judge directed the jury to return a Not Guilty verdict.

A case that attracted a lot of attention because of its wartime circumstances occurred at Bletchley on 13 October 1939. The "Night Scot" was running in two portions, but even so the first portion had to stop at Bletchley for additional carriages to be added to the rear by an 0-8-0 locomotive on shunting duties. Whilst this was taking place, the shunting engine was hit from the rear by the second portion of the express - which was double-headed, and had passed no less than six signals. The shunting engine was forced up onto the station platform, killing its driver and three railway staff. The driver of the pilot engine on the second portion was charged with manslaughter but the defence argued that the blackout had made it difficult to pinpoint the location and judge speed. There was no evidence of excessive speed. The driver was acquitted.

In January 1959 a PW gang foreman, Albert Roberts, was brought to court on a charge of manslaughter after one of his gang was killed at Hadley Wood. The Prosecution then decided to offer no evidence and he was discharged. The use of manslaughter charges has continued up to the present and was much-discussed after the Southall accident; although there was again a pattern of a driver ignoring signals, he never appeared in court. Yet the rate of convictions has continued to be very low in the last fifty years. After the Lewisham accident in 1957 the driver was prosecuted but the jury failed to reach a verdict and a retrial was dropped due to the mental condition of the accused driver. After the death of four people in a rear-end collision at Eastbourne in 1958 a driver was prosecuted for manslaughter, but acquitted after the Judge advised against conviction. The Connington derailment in 1967 resulted in a signalman being charged with manslaughter under the Offences Against the Person Act; he was acquitted of this, but sentenced to two years for unlawfully operating the signals, by changing the points as the train was passing over them. However a driver who disconnected his AWS and allowed an unqualified second man to drive in 1973 was convicted of endangering the safety of persons.

In Scotland a charge of culpable homicide could result. James Boyd, a driver on the Dundee & Arbroath, was charged with this after a person was killed crossing the line near Westhaven on 11 October 1841. The prosecution alleged Boyd was driving at excessive speed - 30mph - but evidence was given that the victim was infirm and deaf. James Cooper, a "switchman" on the Edinburgh & Glasgow, was sentenced to ten months prison for culpable homicide of Mr McLeod in September 1842. Mr Paton, superintendent of engines at Cowlairs, was seen as legally liable for an accident and given 17 months in prison; when he came out in November 1846 he was rewarded with £400, a dinner and a watch from his former workmen - on top of £150 already subscribed by the directors of the Edinburgh & Glasgow. Twelve people were killed at Kirtlebridge on the Caledonian Railway on 2 October 1872 after an express from Euston collided with a goods train; the stationmaster was tried for culpable homicide but acquitted.

Driver George Gourlay was also charged with culpable homicide after an accident at Elliot Junction near Arbroath on 28 December 1906 when 22 people died after his NBR express collided with a local train - fatalities including the MP for Banffshire[16]. Gourlay was described as "experienced and trusted" by the NBR's locomotive superintendent, and was used to drive the royal trains; he had 47 years of service.

After the accident Gourlay was arrested at his house in Edinburgh, where he appeared with his head in bandages. He was taken to Dundee in custody but the cab broke down and he had to walk the last part of his journey. There he was charged that he drove the train recklessly whilst intoxicated and against the warning of the Arbroath stationmaster - which he denied - amounting to culpable homicide. The substance of this was that the block system had failed in a severe snowstorm, he had been told to proceed with caution yet had passed two danger signals.

The defence argued that Gourlay did not see the signals as they were obliterated by snow, and that fog signals were only installed on the line after

Criminal prosecution of railway staff followed Britain's worst-ever railway accident at Quintinshill, north of Carlisle, in May 1915. Jail sentences were imposed on signalmen Meakin and Tinsley

the accident. Added to this he had had to run tender first as the turntable had been inoperable. In the jury's view Gourlay was still guilty, though they found that exceptional weather and the lax state of affairs at Elliot also contributed; his five month sentence was the shortest permitted. However even this caused concern and a petition of 70,000 signatures was gathered before Richard Bell of the ASRS went to see the Secretary of State for Scotland, who reduced the sentence to three months.

The worst railway accident ever in Britain was at Quintinshill, north of Carlisle, in 1915. On 29 May signalman James Tinsley, who had admitted to the enquiry that he "forgot all about the local train", was arrested and taken to Sheriff Campion at Dumfries. At the hearing "he was bordering on collapse and wept bitterly", having to be removed to a motor ambulance.

Tinsley was charged with culpable homicide of the driver and fireman of the troop train and three of the officers who were passengers. Charges were also brought against fireman Hutchinson, and the other signalman - Meakin. However the Lord Advocate dropped the charges against Hutchinson after evidence from the drivers of the express train and pilot engine.

The Lord Advocate criticised the two signalmen for their

"clandestine arrangement" which compromised safety so they could have an extra half hour in bed. Meakin was negligent in beginning the shunting movement and not putting the signal collar on so he received 18 months in prison, Tinsley being sentenced to three years penal servitude.

Accidental Damage

Early railways were involved in several complex cases where the rule of deodand came into play[17]. This allowed the item causing death or injury to be seized and its value "given unto God" for charitable purposes, normally via the Lord of the Manor of wherever the incident occurred. One of the earliest known incidents was in February 1838 when a man was knocked over by a horse-drawn train on the Redruth & Chasewater Railway, dying a couple of days later; a deodand of 5s was placed on the horses and wagons. In May 1839 Thomas Hogg, a GJR driver, was killed in a collision at Perry Barr involving the locomotive *Mermaid*. The main cause of the accident was felt to be bad management by the GJR - "The Company so unskillfully and negligently managed the business of the railway" as to cause an accident[18]. However, "the inquisition then absolved the two engines from blame and declared the value of the engine which had been the cause moving to the death." This was seen by the courts as an award of deodand against the *Mermaid*, but the GJR appealed - and lost the case. For the next few years deodand became a feature of some compensation cases.

On 19 October 1839 a waggoner named Thomas Gray and three of his horses were killed at Guisborough Lane crossing, Stockton. Driver Matthew Appleton was found guilty of manslaughter by a Coroner's jury and taken off to the cells of York castle, while a deodand of £1400 was set on his locomotive. In contrast, a deodand of only £500 in all was levied after an accident on the ECR in 1840 in which four were killed; due to arcane legal ritual the deodand was payable to the Lord of Weald Hall, who used it for the benefit of the sufferers in the accident.

In August 1840 a fatal accident on the Hull & Selby Railway at Howden was caused by an iron casting on a goods vehicle derailing passenger coaches and a £50 deodand was awarded against the railway company; this was the first accident reported on by a Railway Inspector. In November 1840 Henry Pattinson was killed in an accident on the York & North Midland, after which a deodand of £500 was levied on the locomotive *Zetland*. In the view of the *Railway Times* this was a genuine accident and it was unfair that the railway company should be penalised.

On 12 November 1840 driver Joseph Simpson and fireman William

Dawson were killed in an accident on the London & Birmingham at Harrow. Driver Bradburn was in charge of engine no.15 which was delayed by a blocked line at Woodcock Hill, so he went off to the *Queens' Arms* to get some supper. While he was there, Simpson drove into his engine. The accident was caused by Simpson's dangerous driving, so the coroner's jury returned a verdict that Dawson was murdered by Simpson, who committed "felo de se" himself. They then imposed a deodand of £2000 on the engine and its tender. The *Railway Times* felt the jury had been unduly influenced by Simpson having been fined £1 in an earlier case; he had been described as a "hasty, impetuous, reckless driver....who neglected every caution".

On 24 December 1841 a Paddington to Bristol mixed train hauled by *Hecla* ran into a landslip in Sonning Cutting. Two 2nd class carriages at the front of the train were crushed against the engine by the heavy goods trucks behind with eight people dying on the spot and another one later. The Coroner's Jury, meeting at a nearby public house, laid a deodand of £1000 on *Hecla*, which was payable to the Lord of the Manor of Sonning. The Board of Trade, though, felt that no blame should be attached to the GWR and the deodand amount was reduced on appeal to a nominal sum.

In December 1841 a seven year old boy was run over by the engine *Amazon* near Haydock Colliery in Lancashire. The boy may have been attempting to ride on the train, or he may have been one of the many local people who used the railway line as a footpath; a deodand of £1 was imposed on the engine.

In October 1844 a deodand of £300 was declared on a locomotive of the Brandling Junction Railway after the deaths of John Brown and Joseph Burrell. A locomotive was involved in a collision at New Harton Colliery, then ran back down the gradient to South Shields where it hit the mail train. The *Railway Times* reported that the deodand should have been declared on *Nelson*, but it had been quickly sent off for repair so the other engine had been victimised instead.

An unusually precise reading of the rule was made by an Oxfordshire Coroner's court after Fanny Gosling was killed at Abingdon Road station in 1845[19]. Having got off one train, she was attempting to cross the line behind it when she was struck by another travelling in the opposite direction. A deodand was imposed of one shilling on the actual buffer that hit her, rather than the engine, and the GWR was told to improve the arrangements at the station.

Lord Campbell's Act of 1846, properly known as the Fatal Accidents Act, improved the legal situation by giving dependants of those killed the right to claim compensation. Until this time the law had given few rights to dependants but now that it was clarified the law of deodand was abolished on 1 September 1846.

Railways were involved in many civil claims for damages after accidents, it being proved quite early on that goods and property could be claimed for. For example, Mr Palmer won £170 from the Grand Junction in March 1839 after his horses were injured in a collison while travelling from Liverpool to Birmingham. These sorts of compensation cases replaced the law of deodand.

Thomas Dean was killed at Dean Lane station in Lancashire after his LYR train started without warning and knocked him off the platform. Damages were £1000.

However there were regular problems with fraudulent accident compensation claims. Between 1906 and 1911 a London gang made many successful claims by the simple method of always keeping their demands modest. When two of the gang were finally put on trial, the cases cited included £7 from the LNWR and £6 from Thomas Tilling & Co. The two arrested got a year's hard labour each for obtaining money under false pretences.

Crossing the Line

Level crossings were the subject of clauses in many Acts of Parliament, notably the Highways Act of 1839 which said that crossings over highways and turnpikes had to be guarded by "good and proper persons." Acts of 1842, 1845 and 1863 also regulated crossings.

Crossing keepers also got involved in negligency cases, such as Hughes of Kelvedon in 1843 who forgot to open the gates for the mail train! He was fined 10s by magistrates and sacked.

None of this was proof against human nature, though this hardly excuses the appalling behaviour of T Cronk, proprietor of the Beckenham stagecoach in June 1839. Cronk arrived at the Penge level crossing to find the gates closed against the road, and started lashing out with a pole to force the gates open. When a Constable intervened, Cronk got down from the stagecoach and whipped him, then struck him with his fists. Witnesses agreed there would have been an accident if the stagecoach had crossed onto the line. Cronk was fortunate to escape with a £10 fine.

A bizarre incident on the Stockton & Darlington Railway occurred at a level crossing in June 1840. A waggoner named Prest arrived at a crossing to find the gates closed, the woman and boy in charge refusing to let him cross although there were several minutes before the next train. Prest forced the gates

Level crossing at Gomshall, Surrey. It is easy to imagine that the staff at lonely crossings could be intimidated by angry travellers. On other occasions, altercations gave rise to prosecutions.

open and attempted to cross, but his waggon was hit by a train - three horses were killed and the train damaged. The magistrates gave a decision for Prest as they felt there had been time for him to cross *before* the gates should have been closed, and that the woman and boy were "not fit and proper persons to manage a station of so much responsibility." Only men would do, apparently!

In November 1840 a Mr Redwell was fined 40s for driving a flock of sheep across the line on the London & Croydon Railway - with predictably chaotic results.

Railway companies were expected to maintain crossings in safe condition. In January 1920 a man who was knocked down on the crossing at Slade Green, SECR, sued for damages on the grounds that the pedestrian wicket gate should have been fastened if a train was due; he won £550 plus costs.

Occupation crossings were a cause of many problems and were governed by strict rules that were often difficult to enforce. Under the 1845 the user was responsible for crossing the line in a correct manner and could be fined 40s for failure to do so. On 16 December 1840 James Wright, a farmer at Winwick near Warrington, left a gate open whilst carting manure across the line with the result that cows got onto the railway; he was fined £2. At Welton on Hull & Selby, a farmer drove a waggon and four onto the

PRIVILEGES OF HIGH RANK

Railway Gatesman. " It's agin the rules, my lady, openin' o' the gate like this; but it ain't for the likes o' me to keep yer *ladyship* a waitin'."

Noble Countess. " Why is it against the rules, my good man ? "

Railway Gatesman. " Well, my lady, the 5.17 down express has been doo these ten minutes ! "

The cartoonist's point about the breaking of rules may have been emphasised unintentionally by the fundamental error of allowing the carriage onto the line before opening the far gate!

line without stopping or looking - despite the train whistling to get his attention. He was fined £5 in March 1842. Of course the accident at Hilgay (see above) was on an occupation crossing.

Dangerous Goods

Railways were generally obliged to carry any goods that were submitted to them, and this caused some problems in the early days until the Railway Clauses Consolidation Act of 1845 gave railways the right to refuse dangerous consignments and ensured that those sending them had to take certain steps in advance, such as having the packages clearly labelled.

The Act clarified practices that were already becoming well-established before this date. For example, in 1841 a Greenock shipowner took barrels of gunpowder on a passenger train after which the gunpowder

EFFECTS OF THE GUNPOWDER EXPLOSION ON THE LANCASTER AND CARLISLE RAILWAY AT YANWATH BRIDGE, NEAR PENRITH.

It was not without good reason that the carriage of dangerous goods by rail was tightly controlled. This was the appalling spectacle at Yanwath Bridge, near Penrith, in 1867, when a van of gunpowder derailed and was hit by a goods train travelling in the opposite direction. Two men were killed in the subsequent explosion.

was seized by magistrates as no prior warning had been given. Directors on the London & Birmingham imposed a £20 fine on anyone who did not give advance warning that a consignment was dangerous.

On 20 August 1841 a party of Liverpool sportsmen were returning home from Castleton and intended to go by train from Stockport. They wanted to take three shotguns with them, but porters said this was not permitted - especially as there were sixty people travelling in the carriage. However another porter put the guns under a seat in the 2nd class carriage where one went off - hitting the porter and a sportsman. The latter died a few days later, but the Coroner ruled that the cause of death was actually delirium tremens - but still reprimanded the owner of the loaded gun.

In September 1844 Thomas Jack was charged with sending "combustibles" - a consignment of lucifer matches - on the Brighton line. They were packed into a tea chest but the smell of phosphorus alerted railway staff. Jack's defence was that they were meant to have gone by Horne's waggon to Brighton, so the case was dismissed.

Fireworks caused the death of Mrs Isabella Bartrope in November 1847, who had the misfortune to live near to Bricklayers Arms goods depot in London. A box of fireworks had been delivered to the station for shipment to Margate, but as it was illegal to carry them they had been put aside to be destroyed. For some unknown reason the place they were put was Mrs Bartrope's wash-house yard, following which sparks ignited a rocket; Mrs

Bartrope fled into the wash-house but seems to have been trapped by the burning fireworks and burnt to death.

In May 1913 Leon Serne was charged with sending explosives by LSWR without giving the statutory 48 hours notice, pleading guilty. On 1 March he had sent a package to Devonport which exploded when it arrived there, injuring a porter and causing much damage. Serne was a regular offender having made a habit of sending undeclared explosives and on one occasion a parcel had exploded and injured his own nephew. His trade was in making "toy" pistols which were fired by explosive corks, but having been convicted for an explosives offence the previous year he was not allowed to make them himself. He was now fined £50-15s for an act which had saved him 5s!

Dangerous goods covered more than just explosives. A civil law case of 1868, Rylands v Fletcher, had ruled that occupiers of property had a duty of care towards their neighbours if they brought anything dangerous onto their own land. This had obvious applications for a railway company. As an example, the GWR was sued in 1926 for leaving an oil tank wagon at Stoke Gifford, which leaked into a brook and damaged the property downstream. Although the Judge ruled that the main blame lay with the owners of the defectively constructed tanker, the GWR also shared some responsibility.

Live animals could also prove to be dangerous, and railways were responsible for keeping them under control. In 1923 a consignment of bullocks sent from Tipperary to Dublin was unaccountably unloaded at the passenger terminus rather than the goods station. As there was no proper fencing available it was inevitable that some of the bullocks should escape into the street, where they caused mayhem. The railway company was found to be negligent.

Fires

Railways were liable to civil actions if they caused fire damage to neighbouring properties, and damages could be substantial. A Kent farmer named Hamerson won £895 from the SER in April 1845 after losing haystacks and farm buildings due to sparks from an engine.

A ruling in the case of Aldridge v GWR found that the railway company still had to pay damages even when the farmer had chosen to put his haystack within 11 yards of the railway, an immediate result being that the ECR had to pay for a field of barley at Witham in 1850. The situation was covered by Parliament in the Railway Fires Act of 1905, which provided for a structure of compensation up to £100 in agricultural cases where there had been a problem with fraudulent claims.

Finally an offence which is hard to categorise as it occurred in an age

when the concept of a railway was rather different. The Stockton &
Darlington Railway was unique in that it allowed local "waggoners" to use
the line almost as a public highway, and various rules were needed to make
this a safe practice. Waggoners were meant to allow for passenger trains, but
four West Auckland men took their waggons in front of a first class train in
December 1840 delaying it by eight minutes; they were fined 2s6d. The
following month William Thomas was fined 6s for taking his waggon on the
line after sunset with no signal light.

1 Annual accident reports furnish many statistics and examples; the 1998
figures were 251 - but including both trespass and suicide.
2 *Herapath's Railway Magazine*, 17 July 1847
3 *Railway Times*, 24 December 1842.
4 G Body, *Great Railway Battles*, Peterborough, 1994
5 BTC *Police Journal*, October 1954
6 *Railway Times*, 26 September 1840
7 BTC *Police Journal*, October 1958, p.20.
8 It has been claimed that three were killed, but the fireman died afterwards.
9 This colourful tale comes from the *East Anglian Magazine*, 1973, but
includes no names or precise dates.
10 L James, *The Law of the Railway*
11 B Phillips, *Crime & Authority in Victorian England*
12 L James, *The Law of the Railway*, London, 1980: p,72
13 *Railway Times*, 31 September 1843
14 Keith's age was given as 12 by *The Times* and 15 by the BTC *Police
Journal*; who should we believe?
15 *The Railway Press*, 13 September 1889
16 The widow of Alexander Black later sued the NBR for £20,000 damages.
17 *Jnl of the RCHS*: a short article on deodands in March 1998 produced a
number of examples in subsequent correspondence.
18 *Railway Times*, 1 June 1839
19 *Oxfordshire Chronicle*, 20 November 1845, given in *Journal of the RCHS*,
March 1999

CHAPTER SIX:
FRAUD & EMBEZZLEMENT

Financial Frauds

During the Railway Mania there were many companies which existed purely as a means to enrich their promoters at the expense of credulous investors, often publishing inflated prospectuses to lure the unwary. One such "bubble" company was the Great European Railways, whose shares were only ever quoted in the *Iron Times* and whose advert in the *Railway Gazette* was never paid for. This became a matter for concern in the City of London and its directors were summoned to appear before the Lord Mayor at the magistrates court in December 1845. The Lord Mayor asked who the Secretary was and, being told that it was Edmund Smith, asked where he came from; "No-one knows", Counsel commented, but then Smith turned up at the court and handed in the names of the provisional committee which impressed his Lordship. The case was dismissed, but it would seem the *Iron Times* was in on the act, for it was quoting shares at a premium for a company no-one else had heard of!

However a whole crop of cases began to come to court - Lambeth "railway promoter" Benjamin Brown was charged with defrauding Charles Jacobs of £45, and as the bottom fell out of the boom cases began to come up of people who had failed to pay calls on their shares as they realised the error of their investment. Woolmer v Toby in April 1846 involved non-payment on Exeter & Plymouth shares, and Tootal v Jolnston involved £2106 defaulted on Huddersfield & Sheffield shares; these were civil cases settled with damages. In 1850 barrister Mr Webster had to pay £1000 to the Cheshire Junction Railway after he had defaulted on a call of £10 on his 200 shares.

The first two convictions for forgery of shares were in 1845, in cases brought by Mr Nash the famous "detective". The wholesale enthusiasm for shares also created the chance for forgeries to enter the market, and Bentham Fabian became notorious as a forger of scrip shares in railways. In May 1846 he and John Faulkner were accused of forging up to 18,000 scrip shares in the

Buckinghamshire, Oxfordshire & Bletchley Junction as well as three other railways. When arrested, Fabian had cash of £5693 in his pockets and Faulkner had £1025. They were bailed at £500 each in July and another associate, Captain Richards, was committed for trial for forging a £5000 cheque on Coutts Bank. Fabian absconded the day before the trial in December 1846.

Faulkner was tried but acquitted, although he was then imprisoned in Whitecross Street prison for debt. He and Fabian had made £4000, but they spent £1000 of this "rigging" shares in the Kentish Coast Railway. A Maidstone jeweller, Mr Solomon, brought a case against another of the gang, Edward Richards, who he said had sold him £480 of forged scrip shares in the Buckinghamshire Railway. Forged certificates in the South Yorkshire, Doncaster & Goole were also doing the rounds.

Later in 1846 the investors began to fight back with a group of cases aimed at unfair practices by share dealers and others. One of the problems, though, was identifying the persons to prosecute - attempts to bring cases against the Manchester & Chester Direct after forged adverts in the railway press had been "concocted for stock jobbing purposes" were frustrated by unscrupulous promoters who "borrowed" the names of real people to "puff" their company. Some investors tried to prosecute "directors" for conspiracy to defraud; for example, in September 1846 a case was being organised against the Trinidad Great Western & Eastern Railway for which 25,000 shares had been issued but only 600 had been properly paid up.

To press a case involved risking financial loss, though there were successes; solicitor Mr Wontner succeeded in his case against Shairpe of the Direct London & Exeter, where the deposits he had paid on his shares to cover the Parliamentary deposits had been spirited away although no Bill had ever been prepared.

A notable early forgery case was of Horatio Nelson West and his accomplice William Farmery in April 1847 who forged scrip certificates of the LSWR and tried to sell them through the New Money Market. He forged about £2500 of shares, but drew suspicion on himself by overpaying a cheque to the bankers. Both were convicted in June at York, but were found guilty of only a misdemeanour rather than felony due to legal doubts about whether forgery laws applied to scrip cases. West was sentenced to three months, but had already been in custody for eight, and Farmery received 15 months for uttering forged scrip. A York clerk received seven years transportation the same year as his offence was classified as a felony rather than a misdemeanour.

Of course to denounce financial criminals was to risk being sued as these cases rarely succeeded. *Herapath's Railway Magazine* accused the deputy chairman of the Richmond Railway, William Chadwick, of "misapplication of funds", for which he claimed £5000 of damages. The jury clearly had a low opinion of him as he was awarded only £50. One director who was brought low was Mr Weiss of the London & Birmingham Extension; a bankruptcy warrant was issued against him but he evaded arrest - "he must now be regarded as an outlaw," *Herapath* commented dramatically in July 1847. In October 1847 a Sunderland "sharedealer" fled after forging £1800 of shares.

Another "Mania" case which did not reach the courts until May 1848 concerned Thomas Fuller, the promoter of a "bubble" company called the Great Southern of Madras Railway. Fuller was really the entire company on his own, but persuaded people to invest by giving a false set of names for its directors and failed to register its directorate correctly; the fine for this was £10, but its effectiveness was increased by fining Fuller £10 for *each* case.

In October 1849 a stockbroker, Nairne, became a spectacular bankrupt to the tune of £35,000. In order to meet some of his debts he had systematically robbed some of his clients, one man losing £4500 in GWR shares and another claiming losses of £2000. The following month Nairne was arrested in Paris and brought back to London.

"King" of them all was George Hudson, who for a time was a master at exploiting the inadequate financial controls of the period. After shares in the Great North of England Railway had been sold at an advantageous price in 1849, Robert Prance noted that "someone has received great benefit by selling them at this extravagant price."[1] It was also claimed that Hudson received deliveries to his house at Newby Place of hay, corn and straw by rail at no cost. It is likely that Hudson broke company law of the time through his price fixing machinations and he was suspected of many "expenses" frauds. In May 1849 it was alleged that bribes were offered to speed Bills through Parliament, that accounts of the ECR were falsified, Hudson had raked off a huge sum on a rails contract, that the York & North Midland had been defrauded through the sale of shares in Sunderland Docks, and that the same company paid off landowners via Hudson's own account with the inference that he always took a percentage.

Hudson agreed to repay £100,000 to the YNMR in order to avoid a court case though his liabilities were estimated at £750,000; however, as an MP, Hudson could not be arrested for debt. In January 1853 the YNMR began a suit against him under the Companies Act, alleging misappropriation of shares which culminated in Hudson being ordered to pay £54,000 into court. Hudson lost his seat as an MP in 1859 and then stayed abroad for six years to avoid arrest but in 1865 was adopted as Tory candidate for Whitby. On 9 July he was arrested for debt as there was a fear an election might again put him beyond the

George Hudson, who for a time exploited the inadequate financial controls of his age with brilliant success. This illustration dates from 1844, when it was noted that "he enjoys unbounded popularity in his own district".

reach of the law, and he was incarcerated in the York county gaol where he stayed for three months. On 10 July he was released after a debt was paid for him, but on 15 June 1866 he was again arrested - this time for a debt of £13,000 to a Mr Bartlett. After three weeks he was released - and fled to France. However from the start of 1870 imprisonment for debt was abolished and so Hudson returned to England, but he died in 1871 with many of the issues unresolved.

A contemporary of Hudson was John Sadleir, Chairman of the London & County Bank, who poisoned himself on Hampstead Heath in February 1856. Although principally a banker he was also Chairman of the Royal Swedish Railway and had issued false shares to the value of £150,000 - pocketing the proceeds himself; in some ways he resembles the infamous Redpath. As he led a fairly simple lifestyle it was not understood why he should ruin everything in this way, so there were persistent rumours that the poisoned corpse was not Sadleir at all - he had fled to America with the money. This was, unsurprisingly, never proved.

Such cases of depredation became rarer as the law was tightened and the market became more sophisticated. Even so cases were still occurring as late as 1889, when a Miss Browne sued the Golden Valley Railway on the grounds that she had been induced to invest £500 by false statements. She said that it had not been made clear that the railway was being part-financed by the contractor taking some of his payment in shares - a practice which tended to reduce the value of other people's holdings.

Cases of bribery were rare, but in November 1846 the *Sunday Times* reported that a £25,000 bribe had been offered to a "senior railway official" so that he could buy a landed estate and retire. This was soon revealed to be Mr C Saunders, Secretary of the GWR, but he denied having been offered money by the LNWR which was then embroiled in a territorial battle. It was alleged that the money was offered by Boyes of Banbury using the assumed name of Cobb[2]. However, the press then began to speculate that the money had been proferred by GWR shareholders who were anxious for an agreement with the London & Birmingham and saw Saunders - a dedicated Broad Gauge man - as an obstacle. As he was on a handsome salary of £2500 a year it clearly needed a sizable sum to dislodge him!

Staff Conspiracies

Where small sums of money were involved, and accounting techniques poor, railway staff stood to make regular small sums of extra income. Occasionally, such practices were organised by groups of staff conspiring together.

On the Grand Junction Railway in 1840, six railway guards were arrested for conspiracy to defraud after evidence was collected by Cottam, the GJR's Inspector of Police. The group allowed passengers to travel without a ticket in exchange for a "douceur", or alternatively allowed them to travel further than their ticket authorised, then met in Liverpool beerhouses to share their takings. The railway company announced that it had "secret" plans to prevent similar occurrences in future, but the prosecution failed as there was only Cottam's evidence.

Allegations that railway staff cheated passengers were rife in the early days, but not all reports were true. An ECR clerk and policeman sued the *Chelmsford Chronicle* after it suggested they systematically cheated innocent young ladies, winning 40s damages in December 1840.

Railway staff more often cheated their own company than they cheated passengers. Ticket fraud was a matter of having an organised group, such as the clerks on the Manchester & Leeds in 1842. Robert Lloyd collected tickets at

Manchester and sent them to Harris Sloane at Normanton, who then altered and reissued them so that cash takings could be pocketed. The pair had then "indulged in expensive habits", but in July 1842 were sentenced to six months in prison.

J Hayes, a clerk at Newcastle station on the York, Newcastle & Berwick in 1848, was attempting to set himself up in the shipping business using money obtained dishonestly from his employers. He was one of a group of four - including a guard and two ticket collectors - who managed to pocket cash by issuing tickets then collecting them back in without them going through the proper collection system. The ticket collector at Newcastle noticed that the number of tickets being issued each day appeared to be too low and an investigation began. Hayes was found with 41 issued tickets in his possession, and the guard in the group had £411 cash on him! At this stage Hayes had already made enough to buy a half share in two vessels.

In August 1875 two GWR clerks were shown to have worked out a system between their respective stations in Oxford and Birmingham. They simply sent tickets to each other and redated them, pocketing the subsequent cash sale. The scheme was uncovered when Mills, the Oxford clerk, gave a parcel containing tickets to a guard to deliver to his friend; the guard mistakenly took it home where he noticed the paper coming off and of course the contents were revealed. An escape attempt by Mills got him no further than Didcot.

In 1960 Ganger Draper was the leader in a conspiracy by a number of labourers to defraud British Railways. Draper was in charge of casual labourers on the Bletchley to Northampton stretch of line, regularly booking men on as present when they were not - and splitting the unearned wages between himself and the invisible men! In September 1960 all sixteen in the gang were interviewed by police using the ladies waiting room at Castlethorpe station, and 28 offences were identified. Draper was fined £60 and the others £50 in total.

Restaurant cars gave opportunities for pilfering too, as it was possible to pocket small sums of money and adjust stock figures. Improved accounting made this more difficult, but some staff still found ways of altering receipts or stock figures. In 1951 the 7.15am Hook of Holland express did a roaring business in breakfasts, but the staff ran a racket of reissuing bills so that 108 people bought breakfast but official figures showed only 81. This left a sizable amount of cash to be pocketed, but the problem remained of how to satisfy 108 people whilst serving enough food for only 81. This was done by providing small portions, but the dishonesty began to reveal itself when letters appeared in both the *The Times* and the *Amsterdam Telegraaf* complaining of the size of meals. Police travelled incognito on the train and calculated gains of £11-8-0 were made in three days - which could have amounted to £600 a year. Initially they were puzzled by the strange practice of serving soup at breakfast, until it was realised that this was a food that could easily be watered down to serve more people! Five people were sent to prison for up to 20 months.

In April 1957 Fred Hartree was fined £20 by Stockport magistrates for falsifying accounts on the Manchester to London restaurant cars; he had reissued bills 16 times in order to pocket the cash for himself, but had been caught by a group of six police travelling in the guise of ordinary passengers. Hartree was perhaps fortunate, as two men who embezzled the takings on the *Brighton Belle* the same year were sent to prison for six months; after their arrest takings rose by 2.5%.

In 1964 two restaurant staff on *The Talisman* express train were sent to prison for false accounting and in January 1976 it was reported in court that restaurant car workers on the same east coast line had defrauded BR of £66,724 in one year by using a bogus rubber stamp to defeat the accounting system at Kings Cross. Another common practice was for staff to sell their own stock rather than the railway company's.

Even worse, perhaps, was Charles King who tried to defraud his work colleagues. King was one of a pools syndicate among dining car staff of the *North Briton* between Leeds and Glasgow in 1961. He organised the coupon and money, and for two years the group did very badly. Then they had a set of good results and expected a bonanza, but King said that he thought he'd put a match down wrongly. After a few days he turned up with some money and a handwritten letter, supposedly from Littlewoods. The other staff complained to the police and it was found he should have paid them £33 each; King got three months prison.

Goods Frauds

In the early days of railways it was quite common for goods to be lost or damaged. Insurance could be arranged, and this opened up a whole new territory for enterprising criminals. In February 1841 a conspiracy to defraud the Midland Counties was uncovered when £225 was claimed for "money parcels" lost between Leicester and Derby, a scam which clearly needed an insider to help lose them. The parcels contained nothing but old paper cut into a convenient size, and the gang was arrested - it included "two leading Chartists." Thomas Richards, the leader, was given six months hard labour.

In February 1849 a gang of three were arrested for defrauding the LNWR, ECR and the Cricket Steamboat Company by claiming for non-existent injuries and lost luggage to the value of £150. John Coles claimed £47 from the LSWR for the loss of two bags between Portsmouth and Waterloo in 1907 - but the claim was a fraud and Coles a convicted horse-stealer who had been discharged from the army; he was given a three month sentence.

Carters on the Liverpool & Manchester Railway collected goods around Manchester and took payments from the consignees. This gave the chance to embezzle small sums systematically, and a number were arrested in September 1841. Although there were many cases against two of them there was a lack of firm evidence and they were discharged.

Many goods staff were employed on a casual basis for much of the Victorian era, and this opened up opportunity for other types of fraud. Mr Salt, the LNWR goods manager at Manchester, was sacked in 1856 after being closely observed by Superintendent Beresford. It was alleged that Salt had used the casual labourers - paid by the LNWR - for his own private business purposes and rumours circulated that he had defrauded the company of £34,000. This enormous figure seems to have been mythical but the LNWR refused to justify its actions and Salt was reduced to printing a pamphlet to deny the rumours.

Betting

An unusual case of two men betting on when a railway would open ended up in a Bath court. £30 was staked on the opening of the Great Western, but the loser refused to pay and so was sued by his erstwhile friend!

Other Frauds and Embezzlement

Problems with fraud and embezzlement were sufficiently rife in the early days of railways for many officials to require "guarantors" who stood to lose if they fled with the cash. For example, when the stationmaster at Ormskirk, John Johnson, embezzled £29 and absconded in December 1856 his debt was met by the British Guarantee Society. There was a constant problem with staff defrauding companies by rackets with tickets and pilfering of cash, but the most spectacular cases involved large-scale financial chicanery usually in the companies' senior offices.

The Secretary of the Sheffield & Manchester Railway made a high-profile court appearance in August 1841 on a charge of defrauding his own company. Charles Thomson altered a receipt in September 1839 to create a £100 opportunity for himself as a result of getting into debt by share speculation. He was sentenced to life transportation, then "sank down in a fit and was removed with difficulty."

Office staff often had the opportunity to adjust paperwork to their own benefit, and this temptation led to the downfall of William Eicke who worked in the LSWR treasurer's office in 1849. His job was the registering of debentures - and he issued a £2000 debenture to himself without having paid in any cash, after which he received regular interest from the LSWR which he used to set up a chemical factory at Battersea Fields.

Edward Antey, a clerk on the Leeds, Bradford & Halifax Junction in January 1857, gained £40 by forging the signatures of directors on the company's dividend warrants whilst GNR accounts clerk William Snell embezzled £1000.

1856 was the *annus horibilis* of white-collar fraud for the railways. Redpath's frauds on the GNR amounted to about £250,000[3], whilst there were also frauds on the Nord in France (which had many British investors) of about £200,000, the GSWR of Ireland of about £40,000 and from the Crystal Palace Company about £28,000.

In the latter case, the registrar - William Robson - issued shares to himself; he was convicted on 1 November 1856 and sentenced to twenty years transportation. He had used the money to "satisfy his strong desires and vitiated tastes including gambling and women;" he supported a wife and two mistresses with the money he claimed to have made on the stock market. Interestingly, he had worked previously for the GNR and knew Redpath, then changed to the West End of London & Crystal Palace Railway and finally the Crystal Palace Company where he maintained a false record of shareholders.

The Nord case involved £200,000 of shares belonging to the Rothschilds and left in the keeping of the Company, which had been resold to members of the public - though bizarrely dividends were paid on both lots of shares.

But the most famous case was that of Leopold Redpath, of 27 Chester Terrace, Regent's Park, whose exact profits were never proven. Redpath was first a clerk with P & O, then had failed as a wine merchant and become bankrupt in 1840, then was dismissed from a post with a shipping company for embezzlement; when he joined the GNR in 1846 he had gained some experience after working as a clerk in the registration departments of the Brighton & Chichester and London & Brighton railways. Redpath was paid a modest £130 a year from 1846, rising to £250 per year by 1854 when he was Chief Clerk to the Registrar, yet moved into a luxurious property[4] which cost £400 a year, rented his own box at the opera and participated in society in ways such as being a governor of Christ's Hospital. He became Registrar himself, employed over a dozen servants, including one man who looked after his boat and fishing tackle. He outbid Napoleon III in an auction for the painting "Leda and the Swan". However all was not well at home for his wife did not live with him but with an elderly lady. Not content with his Regent's Park house, he bought a country home in Weybridge. All this was explained away as the fruits of some speculation on the Stock Exchange.

Redpath exploited a system whereby individuals often held stock registered in other people's names[5] - it was said that GNR director Graham Hutchinson held £100,000 of stock in this way[6]. For eight years Redpath exploited this weakness by creating and selling fictitious stock, transferring it between apparent stockholders using real names - John Morris of Manningtree being one and his own godson another. It was also claimed that he used the simple trick of adding a "1" in front of the transfer amounts, keeping the difference for himself[7]. In March 1854 Turner Townshend complained to a GNR director that he had been sent a dividend warrant for £1250 when he had no GNR stock at all - this was one of the names being used by Redpath, whose system invariably used real people and never fictitious names. The chief clerk, Kent, acted as witness for some of the fraudulent transfers. Redpath achieved some form of bizarre completion to his financial chicanery in lending back to the GNR at a rate of 4.5% some of the capital he had appropriated from it.

The overpaying of dividends was brought to the attention of the accountant Reynolds by some GNR clerks in 1854, he already knew something of Redpath's past and had borrowed money from him, but so tardy were GNR affairs that it took Redpath two years to respond with an admission that it may have been true. Dennison, Chairman of the GNR, was talking to a lord at a railway station one day when Redpath was nearby; he was surprised at the intimacy between his official and the noble aristocrat, who told him that Redpath gave "sumptuous dinners and capital balls.[8]" When pressed for an explanation of his dealings in September 1856 he offered his resignation, which was not accepted.

In November 1856 Redpath suddenly fled from the GNR offices as evidence grew of irregularities in the issue of GNR stock - it had become apparent that the company was paying dividends on considerably more stock than its audited accounts suggested existed. Redpath had time to plan his departure, but not all went well - he sent a porter to get his house title deeds, but the man took them back to the GNR offices from where Redpath had already dashed away. His chief clerk, William Comyns Kent, was arrested.

After sending a telegram to alert the GNR, Redpath made his own way back from Paris and was arrested at 4 Ulster Place, New Road, London. His trial came at a bad time for the railways, as it occurred in the same sessions as the SER gold robbery gang. On 3 January 1857 *The Times* reported that he was to be charged with "enormous frauds" including the transfer of £1000 stock to his adopted son; to be charged with him were William Kent, his chief clerk, and a stockbroker's clerk named Thomas Hogben. Redpath appeared in court looking "healthy but sullen", and there can have been no surprise when he was found guilty; he was sentenced to life transportation. Kent was acquitted.

The LNWR found itself embroiled in a case due to its own carelessness in the face of the corruption of others. In 1870 the wealthy Samuel Barton died, leaving £40,000 in stock and appointing as trustees his son Thomas and his wife. £12,000 of the stock was in LNWR shares, but between 1872 and 1878 Thomas Barton committed systematic frauds which were discovered after the appointment of a new trustee in 1886. The transfer of stock required the signatures of both trustees, but Barton forged his wife's signature in order to transfer LNWR stock to his own enrichment. After the discovery of the crime, the new trustees sued the LNWR for failing to check the signatures adequately - causing a loss of £12,000. The LNWR lost the case, causing problems for the LBSCR and NSR as well.

William Tapson was secretary and treasurer of the Metropolitan Railway Provident Savings Bank in 1874, proving to be very improvident when he ran off to America with £10,000. He was pursued by Chief Inspector Gosden of the Metropolitan Railway's police, who arrested him in Philadelphia.

Another senior official to "do a Redpath" was the Treasurer of the LYR, D Asquith. He earned a comfortable £800 a year in 1883-4, but forged two cheques for about £1000 and tried to cover it up in the books - but was found out by the improved accounting methods of the later 1800s. He fled to London, sending a letter to his son saying he had got into trouble and feared the shame of exposure. It was believed he was likely to commit suicide as a telegram to his son said that he had a choice of gaol or water; arriving in Guernsey, he sent a telegram to his son saying "Your Papa is dead" and then killed himself. Losses of £2000 were insured through his guarantee company.

A common problem was that staff were entrusted with large sums of cash, and occasionally succumbed to the temptation this offered. On 4 June 1841 John Booth, a police inspector on the London & Birmingham, was entrusted with collecting £96 but he then absconded. He went to America for a time but was arrested when he returned the following year. William Naylor's job for the LNWR involved collecting the money from farmers who rented out the slopes of the railway embankments for hay; he was meant to collect this in then pay it as a lump sum to the chief engineer with accounts, but the district inspector failed to check the accounts and Naylor collected £300 for himself before being discovered. He was sentenced to twelve months hard labour.

Unsound accounting practices made this sort of problem common, and after a case involving the GNR in December 1855 magistrates criticised that company's lax practices. William Dixon was the booking clerk at Boston and one of his duties was looking after the cash payments, so that on 29 November £60-6-3 was sent from the goods depot to his house in a leather bag. This arrived at 7.50pm but Dixon did not count it until the next day, when he found a discrepancy of 19s6d. The fact that his 14 year-old servant, Elizabeth

Beecham, had bought a posh silk bonnet for precisely that amount excited suspicion and she was duly sentenced to three months prison. It was a matter of some concern that the GNR sent bags of cash about the town and to people's private houses with no seal on them.

Stationmaster George Gooch of Biddenden on the Kent & East Sussex Railway was charged with embezzling £8 in 1921. A factor in this case seems to be that Gooch became very muddled through overwork and poor accounting, paying the station's postage out of his own pocket but not keeping a proper record of money paid in. He lost his job and was fined £25.

Perhaps a more typical example of the level of the problem was ticket collector Henry Adrian, who was charged with having embezzled 1s7d at Willesden Junction in 1956. Adrian had to collect small sums charged on excess fares and during busy periods he put the money into his pocket - 7d, 8d and 4d. He would then be able to make out the tickets later without delaying all the passengers at the barrier. Magistrates criticised the system and dismissed the case against him.

At the end of 1841 a clerk on the Manchester, Bolton & Bury ran off with £14 from Bolton station and this prompted the company to make a check on its books. When clerk Samuel Heywood heard of this he ran off to Liverpool and booked a passage to Philadelphia, but the ship was delayed by adverse winds and this gave time for him to be arrested. Heywood's job was to collect the tolls on the canal that the MBB also owned, and over a period of about five years had systematically defrauded the company by entering tonnages in the books below the actual amounts - keeping the balance for himself. This amounted to about £1400, for which he pleaded guilty and was sentenced to ten years transportation. Of course most sums were much smaller than this and the typical case was of regular embezzlement of small sums of cash - for example, by ticket collector Williams of the LSWR at Richmond in 1849. Clerk Broadbent of the East Lancashire Railway was found not guilty of embezzlement in another 1849 case involving the princely sum of 3s.

The London & Brighton was embarrassed in 1842 when its Secretary Nicholas Wood absconded without the directors having taken any guarantors, and then a Brighton station clerk named Frederick Ball also ran off. Ball stole £300 and was traced to a brothel in St Martin's Lane, where he only had a few sovereigns left; most of the rest had been lost at Ascot. He was "a young man of fashionable habits" whose income of 30s a week was inadequate for his tastes. The L&BR must have been mortified by the revelations that it only checked his accounts once a month and that no-one had bothered to collect the surety from his two guarantors. However, friends settled his debts.

Robert Anderson, a railway policeman at Stratford-le-Bow, was given three months prison in June 1843 for embezzling £8 which he had been entrusted to deliver to ECR offices; his defence was that he caught a bus to the West End and the money was stolen from his pocket, after which he panicked and fled to Birmingham.

More serious was the allegation that a railway company encouraged its staff to defraud customers. In the 1879 book *Memories of A Stationmaster*, which described the early days on the GWR, an account was given of what was called a "bunce", whereby a ticket clerk delayed opening for business until a queue had built up and then served the customers rapidly as they waited impatiently for the train - defrauding each one of 1s change. Controversially, author H A Simmons alleged that GWR directors were quite aware of this practice.

In 1849 the death of Wilson, cashier at Waterloo, brought to light the "considerable extent" of embezzlement in which he had been involved. Just after this Edward Cole, a clerk on the Bristol & Exeter, absconded with £900 in cash.

In 1951 a junior clerk at Largs station, aged 15, met an older woman from St Albans who had come to the town on holiday. She had such an impression on him that he ran off to St Albans with £541 from the station till.

The introduction of National Insurance opened another opportunity for fraud. In 1956 an inspector from the Ministry of Pensions & National Insurance discovered something suspicious about national insurance payments from the staff at Smithfield goods station, following which clerk John Thwaites was sent to prison for a year after defrauding the government of £895.

A guard who succumbed to the temptations of his job was George Barlow. The first problem that came to light was the loss of the cash bag for Staithes station on 10 February 1956, containing about £57. The cash bags contained wages for stations on the Middlesbrough to Whitby line and were made up by the bank at Loftus, where Barlow was required to sign for them. Before the train left Loftus Barlow raised the alarm that a bag was missing and there were some doubts over how many bags he had signed for. A month later the empty cash bag was found beneath the viaduct near Whitby's West Cliff station. Barlow was arrested but his defence that he had not been given the correct number of bags held firm and he was acquitted.

Foolishly, Barlow then stole £2 from the shopping bag of a woman on the train between Middlesbrough and Scarborough; he was caught with the money in his pockets. Meanwhile he had been arrested for stealing £5 from a house in Whitby, for which he was fined £5, and then he was sent to prison for three months for the railway theft.

Railways had relatively little to do with counterfeit coinage, except stations were a favourite place to "pass" such coins. However, the people of Ayr discovered in 1841 that a train was a good way of flattening a 4d coin into the size of a 6d! This might have turned into a profitable trade except that profits were eaten into through a tendency of some coins to stick to the passing wheel!

A well-publicised case of passing forged coin embarrassed the Metropolitan Railway in 1875, when a booking clerk was arrested for issuing false coin. The general manager of the company, Myles Fenton, had to defend his railway's actions by arguing that the arrest could have taken place much earlier if the Inland Revenue officers had told him of their concerns. Instead they had tried to enter the booking offices and had been rightly refused entry by the clerk in charge. However other commentators thought the railways placed too much on the clerks: "Badly paid and overworked men have the means of acquiring great wealth thrust hourly before their eyes" but could also be fined if their accounts did not tally at the end of the day.

Railways in Court

Railways occasionally found themselves in court for debt due to civil disputes over payments to be made, and occasionally due to financial problems. One can assume that the LNWR had failed to pay St Pancras poor rates of £1000 in October 1851 due to a dispute over the sum, but it must still have been embarrassed on 3 October when a parochial official turned up to take possession of Euston station to meet the debt!

More problematic were the affairs of the Preston & Longridge Railway in June 1852, which was forced to close after the enforced sale of its locomotive and tender under warrant.

[1] B Bailey, *George Hudson*, Stroud, 1995
[2] *Herapath's Railway Magazine*, 21 November 1846.
[3] The exact amount can never be proved and there were many different estimates at the time; £137,000 excess stock was registered in the books. Bogus dividends had also been paid out. Wrottesley's estimate is £220,000.
[4] He left his previous home at Dartmouth Terrace, Blackheath, as he could not pay the rent!
[5] A system shown to full effect in Emile Zola's novel about French finance in the 1860s, *Money.*
[6] *The Times*, 17 January 1857.
[7] D M Evans, *Facts, Failures & Frauds*, 1859
[8] Evans, *ibid*

CHAPTER SEVEN:
BAD
RELATIONS

Relations between a Company and its employees were governed by the Master-Servant Act which prevented workers going off to seek a better job, but also placed some controls on the employer. For example, in 1847 a worker on the LSWR left without notice and was prosecuted by the company - he received 3 weeks hard labour[1].

This Act was used to control trade union activity, especially strikes; in 1836 a strike broke out among drivers on the Liverpool & Manchester after a driver was sacked for saying he intended to strike. Four strikers with written contracts were sent to Kirkdale prison for a month for breach of contract; there they spent several hours a day on the treadmill, though the prison chaplain acted to secure their early release. In the NER strike of 1867 there were several cases as with John Binns, a driver, who returned from Ilkley to Leeds then "pulled the fire out of his engine" and went home; he had left work without notice so was convicted of breach of contract, but magistrates reserved judgment. A further six cases against NER men at Carlisle were then withdrawn. However the NER continued with several cases at York in May 1867 after the men had been on strike for three weeks, though after discussions the Company agreed not to press the cases so far that the men would have been sent to prison - they had already lost their wages. In April 1875 the LSWR found itself in court charged with breaking the Master Servant Act. George Hughes complained to Wandsworth magistrates that he was owed a week's wages of 22s. The LSWR argued that the men were engaged by the day but only paid by the week, presumably as a mechanism for treating them as casual labourers whilst also being able to control whether they turned up for work. The LSWR was ordered to pay its men as proper "weekly servants".

However there has now also been almost a century and a half of gradually increasing "health & safety" legislation which has meant that railway companies have increasing statutory duties with regard to the safety of their employees. The most important law here was the Railway Employment (Prevention of Accidents) Act of 1900, which compelled railways to introduce many safety reforms; however, prosecutions were rare.

Disciplinary Matters

Many disciplinary matters were covered by bye-laws within each company, but regularised by the Railway Disciplinary Procedures introduced in 1912 which allowed staff to ask for formal hearings; criminal offences were covered by legal processes, of course.

Poor working attitudes became criminalised by the early railway regulations, at least as far as staff who had clear responsibility for human safety were concerned. Railways also tended to gather large numbers of men in one place with occasional bouts of unruly behaviour. In 1839 the ECR engine sheds at Romford gained a bad reputation as the men were "rather wild fellows" who tended to get drunk in the town and turn round all the road signs. The ECR later moved most of its operations to Stratford so that "the calm of Romford was restored", although the town did not in fact have a good reputation at the time![2]

Clearly a worker with a grudge, a GWR driver named John Leonard found himself before the magistrates at the *Crown Inn*, Slough, in October 1840. Given the task of driving the *Leopard* back to Paddington after Princess Augusta's funeral at Windsor, Leonard arranged to give four friends a lift on the tender. He was discovered, and retaliated sulkily by driving at a funeral pace back to London - taking two hours. He was fined 40s.

In August 1850 there was a strike among drivers on the ECR caused by fines being handed out for minor accidents as part of a drive for greater efficiency by a new locomotive superintendent, which the company responded to with dismissals; it was suggested that the ECR sacked its senior drivers so it could employ cheaper men![3] The ECR's Secretary, Cusack Roney, reported deliberate damage to some of the engines by strikers and the company issued a "black list" which it sent to other railways. However, the replacement men lacked experience and caused damage to at least three more engines!

In July 1946 1500 porters and carters at Bishopsgate goods station went on strike over 6d worth of tomatoes. This was because two of their colleagues had been arrested for stealing the tomatoes. The men hoped that their strike would force the LNER to drop the case. The strike spread to Liverpool Street but was ended after talks between the LNER and the NUR; it was agreed to drop the case but to suspend the two miscreants for a period.

A case involving a disgruntled employee occurred at Bricklayers Arms in 1954. A youth named Rainey had been taken on for training at the Firing School, but had failed his tests. He wanted to be sacked immediately so that he could claim unemployment benefit, but instead was given a week's notice. So he collected together some old oily rags and set fire to the cleaners' lobby at the depot in the hope of getting the sack there and then. Instead he got sent to court!

Another worker with a grudge was travelling ticket collector Edward White of Rugby. It had been discovered that White had diabetes and so he was to be taken off the trains and given an office job, but White resented this and harboured a grudge as he worked out his last few days. On 11 to 14 June 1957, he sought revenge by repeatedly pulling the communication cord on the Euston trains he was working. On 11 June the cord was pulled seven times on one working, a pattern repeated the next two days. On 14 June police were watching White, and duly noted that the cord had been pulled in an empty 1st class compartment! He was fined £3 with 5 guineas costs.

Industrial Disputes

As detailed above, there were "industrial disputes" from the early days of the railways, the first usually involving drivers. These men had a big advantage in the 1840s of being in short supply - two of the L&MR strikers soon got new jobs with the London & Birmingham[4]. More unusual was a strike by some labourers working on the GWR in 1838 - some Horse Guards were sent from Windsor to "restore order." There were periods of strike action in 1848-50, 1866-7, in the 1890s and in the significant strikes just before the Great War.

Rail workers were not in the vanguard of the union movement, but railways got dragged into other people's affairs on occasions in the earlier period of their growth. In January 1870 a strike among miners in south Yorkshire led to a serious riot which damaged the station at Westwood and some nearby houses; Barnsley police had to intervene with cutlasses.

There was a major strike in Scotland starting on 22 December 1890, its object being to achieve the Ten-Hour Day, and involving over 9000 men. The GSWR tried to prosecute its strikers under the 1875 Conspiracy & Protection of Property Act. As many of the men lived in tied houses belonging to their employers, eviction was one tactic used to force compliance by the Caledonian; this led to rioting in Motherwell after attempted evictions from Hope Street. The Sheriff had the legal duty to evict from ten sites, but a large crowd prevented this from 2 January onwards. On 5 January 1891 the 13th Hussars were used to cordon the street off but a turbulent crowd of 20,000, including miners and iron workers, fought back, smashing the station roof and

Westwood station, near Sheffield, was damaged by rioting miners in 1870.
Barnsley police had to intervene with cutlasses.

wrecking a signalbox. The NBR reached a settlement on 29 January and the CR on 31 January.

In 1892 there was a strike among the drivers at Ebbw Vale with a lot of bad feeling as senior employees continued to drive trains. Suspecting there would be attempts at sabotage, extra watchmen were stationed along the line and a sacked stoker Jeremiah Hayes was caught putting iron chairs and stones on the track. Charged with intent to endanger life, he was sentenced to a considerable seven years of penal servitude.

In June 1892 the Witnesses (Public Inquiries) Protection Act was passed which provided for a £100 fine or three months in prison if a witness to a Parliamentary inquiry was pressurised or intimidated. This was a direct response to the bullying behaviour of the Cambrian Railway, who had persecuted John Hood after he had been a witness on railway conditions.

The Taff Vale Case is by far the most significant trade union issue to have involved criminal prosecutions but also to have changed the face of British politics and the law of trade unions. It began when Ammon Beasley was appointed general manager of the Taff Vale in 1891, setting out a pronounced anti-union agenda from the start. By 1893 there were already protests at arbitrary dismissals and in 1895 10% of the workforce were sacked whilst 20% of the remainder were working over sixty hours a week. In February 1900 several

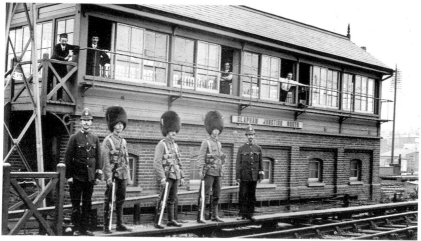

Soldiers and police "on guard" at Clapham Junction during the 1911 strike.
(NRM 381/68)

other Welsh railways agreed pay rises, but the TVR did not and picked out a union signalman as a scapegoat. On 20 August 1900 many of the workers went on strike, organised by the ASRS. Beasley arranged for help from the National Free Labour Association, which brought in non-union men, but the union paid them to go home again. The ASRS was unable to control the passions of the men and legal boundaries were crossed. On the 1 in 40 climb between Quaker's Yard and Abercynon men greased the rails so that trains would stall; when they did so, wagons at the rear were uncoupled. If the drivers got down to investigate, the engines were tampered with.

On 21 August a non-striking driver had to be rescued by police and two days later eggs and stones were thrown. Beasley wanted to prosecute men for "watching and besetting" of the non-strikers at the stations and their houses which had been ruled illegal by the Lyons v Wilkins case of 1896-8. He succeeded in bringing a case against the ASRS for damages, which almost bankrupted the union and forced a halt to many strikes until the law was changed by the Trade Disputes Act after the election of a Liberal government in 1906; the case is seen as having given an early impetus to the Labour Party.

In August 1911 a serious railway strike broke out in Liverpool, particularly involving the delivery drivers or "carmen". Fearing rioting, the 2nd Warwickshire Regiment was sent to the area and stationed at Seaforth Town Hall on 10 August. The same day a contingent of police arrived at Lime Street from Leeds, being "hooted" by thousands of strikers. When the Birmingham

A crowd inspects a Great Central Railway signal box in Lincoln, damaged by rioting around the city's railway stations in 1911. Extra police had to cycle from Grimsby due to the lack of trains!

police arrived they were followed by a mob to Hatton Garden police station and mounted police had to charge them. Throughout the day there were attacks on delivery lorries still operating from Lime Street and Central stations. Eventually LNWR drivers stopped work as they felt it was too dangerous to move trains in the prevailing conditions, but they were not on strike.

In London some railway delivery drivers joined the strike and troops at Aldershot, Shorncliffe, York and Rhayader were mobilised to go to Liverpool or London. On 11 August the railway companies in Liverpool met and decided to try and reopen stations at Edgehill and Brunswick if the authorities could provide adequate protection - this meant that 33 carts of perishable food could be moved from the latter station, with 100 soldiers protecting the carts. In London the same day police guards were necessary to escort vans from Kings Cross goods to Covent Garden and to protect the GWR wharf at Acton. At Paddington men tried to cut the horses loose and the parcels depot was guarded by railwaymen from outside the metropolis. The LBSCR was affected by 500 men going on strike at Willow Walk goods depot. Such was the tension that special trains were kept ready overnight at Aldershot in case the situation in Liverpool escalated - there was much fear of socialist revolution.

On 13 August the National Federation of Transport Workers declared the strike over in London, but a meeting at St George's Hall in Liverpool ended in rioting. The Riot Act had to be read and there were a number of baton

Confrontation at Llanelly, South Wales, when soldiers fired on an angry crowd during the railway strike of 1911.

charges so that Lime Street station "presented the appearance of an hospital." The riot started when a man climbed up on the Lime Street Hotel and was ordered down by police - there was much dislike of "foreign" police, and stones were thrown as well as a battle being fought against the Warwicks Regiment in Christian Street. Some of the crowd tried to force open the iron gates of Lime Street station so that the fire hoses had to be used to keep the rioters out, while the superintendent of the Birmingham police was hit with a stolen truncheon. The platforms "presented a terrible appearance, blood lying in pools in all directions" with estimated persons injured being about 200.

Over the next couple of days the strike began to spread to Manchester and Glasgow, where trams were derailed. On 15 August MR signalmen at Sheffield joined the strike and a LNWR dray was the centre of a riot. In Liverpool, vans taking arrested rioters to Walton gaol were attacked by a crowd of 3000 and troops opened fire: carter Michael Prendergast was shot dead and another man died later.

By 16 August Liverpool gaols were so full that prisoners had to be sent to Knutsford and the situation in London remained tense. Plans were developed to move more soldiers to London from Farnborough using hand signals, and to run the London to Paris services using the Royal Engineers. The fruit of this was seen on 17 August when large numbers of troops were moved from Bordon and North Camp stations to London, camping in the Parks and at Hackney Marshes, but the Grenadier Guards had to march from Pirbright to Waterloo - where they camped on platform 5!

Signalling was clearly seen as the main factor in control of the network, so that in Birmingham all signalboxes around New Street were guarded. Some attempts were made to sabotage traffic on 16 August - GWR signal wires were cut, and an attempt to remove rails at Sheffield on the MR was prevented by the arrival of police on a light engine.

By 18 August the strike affected many far-flung corners of the railway empire, with many offences being committed. The Fishguard to Paddington boat train got one furlong towards its destination before it found the track blocked by strikers; a detachment of police then got down from the engine and more arrived by light engine from Goodwick. Any soldiers on leave who were on the train were rounded up and supplied with rifles from the Territorial Army in Fishguard. After reading the Riot Act and fixing bayonets, the train was able to proceed.

Aftermath of the ugly scenes at Llanelly, showing the results of the militant crowd setting fire to trucks – including one that contained gunpowder, carbide and gelatine. Also shown is the wall, on which troops shot dead the alleged ringleader of the riot.

The same day strikers tried to uncouple carriages at Nantybwlch and Port Talbot, while a Blaenavon to Port Talbot train hit stones placed on the track - only one passenger had been brave enough to travel by it. In Llanelly a crowd tried to "hold" a level crossing against a train of 120 soldiers. The MR signal box at Holmes Lane, Rotherham, was stoned and the police had to launch a baton charge while in Leeds a MR milk float was attacked. At Maidstone strikers tried to pull drivers off their footplates and in Birkenhead magistrates closed pubs to cool tempers, but the men replied by stealing three barrels of beer from a van.

All main London stations and important signalboxes were guarded by soldiers with bayonets on 18 and 19 August while at Birmingham New Street 100 men who were still working were provided with beds at the station. Meat deliveries from Lawley Street were attacked. A Colne to Blackpool train was stopped at Blackburn by a crowd who "occupied" a level crossing and on the line between Nottingham and Mansfield coal-miners assisted their brothers in the holding up of trains.

Other places affected included York, where points were jammed with coal and stones and Goose Hill Junction on the LYR where the signalbox was besieged by a crowd of about 1000 strikers. Normanton station remained open but the signalman had to be protected by thirty soldiers. At Newton, near Stafford, a chanting crowd surrounded the signalbox for two hours before attacking it; the Chief Constable closed seven pubs in Stafford to help cool tempers.

On 19 August the trouble in Llanelly flared up again. At 2.30pm a train approached from Llandilo Junction and was stopped near Union Bridge, where a crowd attacked and badly injured the driver; they then damped down the fire and damaged the engine. The Worcestershire Regiment was stationed at the station, so they ran up the tracks to the beleagured train and a riot broke out. The Riot Act was read and a shot fired in the air - but the crowd only laughed. The troops opened fire and a man on a wall was shot - it was later said that he owned the garden wall and was only a spectator, but in the army's view he was the ringleader of the riot. One soldier, Harold Spiers, had been ordered to shoot him but had refused and deserted - walking 100 miles home to New Radnor, living on nuts and berries. He was courtmartialled.

The crowd began to discuss vengeance and returned to the "dead" train near the Llandilo station - the police and soldiers were based at the GWR station. The captured train had a load including a fatal combination of drink and ammunition, so it was ransacked and then set on fire. The crowd marched off to attack some magistrates including the home of Thomas Jones at Brynmair.

They then returned to deal with the GWR station, attacking its goods depot. Beer and whisky were stolen, then they set fire to the goods shed and trucks in the sidings. Sadly one truck contained cylinders of gunpowder, carbide and gelatine which exploded, killing four people immediately with one dying later so that the death toll in the riots at Llanelly was six, and 19 injured. Even after this it was necessary to have another bayonet charge by the soldiers.

Other events in South Wales that day included an attempt to wreck a TVR mail train near Cardiff, and strikers at Pontypool Road attacked a Bristol to Cardiff train, trying to uncouple its engine until chased away by the fireman with the hot water pipe.

Also on 19 August there was an attempt to wreck the MR station at Chesterfield after two men had been arrested and the crowd had become frustrated at being unable to rescue them. The cabmen's shelter was demolished and its wood used to make weapons, but police and non-strikers fought back unti. there were 20 people unconscious in the booking hall. At 1am soldiers arrived and the Riot Act was read belatedly.

At Lincoln the same day trouble initially focussed on the High Street level crossings, where the signalmen were in an exposed position and where crowds could try to block the tracks. As night fell both stations were attacked and the GCR box at Pelham Street Junction was wrecked. Extra police summoned from Grimsby had to cycle due to the lack of trains, and arrived exhausted at 1am just as the riot was in full swing. Soldiers left the stations and marched up the High Street with fixed bayonets.One man was seriously injured in an attack on the signalbox at Portishead near Bristol, also on 19 August.

The strike was settled late in the evening of the 19 August, but this did not prevent some trouble the next day. Langley Green signalbox on the GWR near Birmingham was attacked by a mob at 3am and Fusiliers had to come from Birmingham. However the NER men did not return to work until 24 August, so in the intervening period there were attacks on signalboxes at Durham and West Hartlepool. At New Shildon a driver was dragged from his engine and stoned, and the contents of his mineral train emptied onto the track.

Bad feelings continued after the strike was over - at Alfreton the house of a non-striking signalman had every window broken. In the signalbox at Post Office station on the Central London Railway there was friction between two signalmen as W Neal had continued to work whilst Ernest Hands had gone on strike. When they were on duty together Hands attacked Neal, striking him in the face, and only stopping when a train arrived; as soon as the train had left he renewed his assault. Hands was fined £3.

In the railway strike of October 1919 soldiers were again sent out to protect key stations and installations. There was the curious sight of Woking station surrounded with machine guns and barbed wire, while in Glasgow naval

ratings protected the main terminii. The Midland main-line was covered by a new Government radio system[5].

The most famous incident of the 1926 General Strike was an attempt between Annitsford and Cramlington, on 10 May, to derail the *Flying Scotsman* by removing a rail of the LNER main-line. The group of miners had removed one rail from the down track and had started to work on others when the train appeared. The engine no.2565 and four carriages were derailed near milepost 9; although there were 270 passengers, there were no injuries, because the LNER had been aware of a possible attempt and the train had been instructed to travel at moderate speed.

Disruption of the press meant that full details of the incident took some time to reach public attention. In the House of Commons on 3 June, the Home Secretary was asked "if he thought there was foul play" in the derailment. Mr Joynson Hicks replied, "I am like a parrot. I may think a good deal and not say much." A normal accident enquiry was conducted by Colonel Pringle, one of the key witnesses being Mr Martin of the LNER who had been patrolling the track between Benton Quarry and Plessey. He reported that he had been attacked near Annitsford station by people from "Dudley Council Houses", armed with stones and clods. When he reached an old signalbox between Dam Dykes crossing and Cramlington, which was being used as a PW store, he was again attacked and there was evidence that attempts had been made to steal tools from the box.

Fearing an attack on the railway, Martin had flagged down the down "Flying Scotsman" at Cramlington, and warned the driver to expect trouble; he then got into one of the carriages. After the derailment a number of passengers and staff chased some men across the nearby fields, but no-one was caught.

Colonel Pringle's conclusion was that the fishplates had been removed and a rail toppled out of the chairs, so a criminal investigation was pursued. Eight were arrested and all found guilty - sentences ranging from eight to four years. An appeal against the sentences was dismissed.

Two other incidents which occurred on 11 May from the General Strike will illustrate that this tactic was spread geographically wide, but was not common - most strikers were worried about the chance of endangering life. Near Stafford a fireman and a platelayer removed rails, fishplates and keys from the LMSR at Bishton and tried to get others to join them. Patrols found the rails removed and,

The wreck of the "Flying Scotsman" during the General Strike of 1926. This famous incident occurred when miners removed a rail from the down main line between Annitsford and Cramlington, near Morpeth. *(NRM 147/81 – top)*

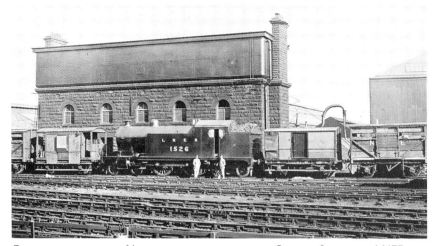

Expecting trouble in Northumberland during the General Strike, the LNER prepared its own armoured train. Quite whether it created fear and terror in all around is open to doubt! *(NRM 31/00)*

although detonators had been placed, this was not enough to serve as sufficient warning. Both men were given five years for endangering life. In Scotland, nineteen young miners blocked the railway between Auchinleck and Cumnock and threw stones at a train; twelve were given sentences of three months.

However the NUR sought to "maintain perfect order" and there was much less violence than in 1911. On 8 February a member of the NUR in Croydon attacked three volunteer platelayers with a hammer and was given two months hard labour while at Shipley a man was given a month inside for throwing a stone at a "blackleg" train. Out of 400,000 NUR members, only 174 were arrested and only 88 received convictions[6]. The LMSR reported that "on the whole the conduct of the railway strikers was quite orderly."[7]

[1] F McKenna, *The Railway Workers*, London, 1980: p.34
[2] F McKenna, *The Railway Workers*, London, 1980: p.30
[3] *Railway Times*, 14 September 1850
[4] P S Bagwell, *The Railwaymen*, p.29
[5] Bagwell, p.389.
[6] Bagwell, p.480
[7] *Railway Gazette*, 11 June 1926

CHAPTER EIGHT:
THE SUFFRAGETTE CAMPAIGN

When the impact of terrorism or war on Britain's railways is discussed, interest usually focusses on Nazi bombers or the work of the IRA. Yet there was a sustained and damaging attack on railway property much earlier in the century, when the miltant supporters of votes for women attacked many railway installations as part of their campaign to force government concessions.

There had been a campaign for female suffrage through most of the Victorian era, but this began to gather momentum after 1869 when a Bill was presented to Parliament - and repeated every subsequent year. When a Liberal Government took office in 1906 the "Suffragists" (who were supported by many men) expected rapid success, but they became victims of wider political considerations. As a response to this the "Suffragettes" began a more violent campaign which became more intense after the scandal over the force-feeding of suffragette prisoners and the subsequent "Cat & Mouse Act" of 1913.

The major period of the onslaught on railway property was between December 1912 and May 1914; the Suffragette campaign ended later that year with the start of the Great War. There were some minor incidents before this, one of the first occurring on 25 June 1912 when six compartments of a LBSCR Tunbridge Wells to Victoria train were vandalised by some people who alighted at Clapham Junction. Papers pasted in the windows read, "We wish the release of Mr Petherick Lawrence and women's rights."

One of the first protesters to be caught was Hugh Franklin, a 23-

year old member of the Men's Political Union for Women's Enfranchisement. This apparently wealthy young man was seen leaving a GCR train at Harrow on 25 October 1912, from a first class compartment which had been set on fire with parafin-soaked canvas. Franklin was arrested and remanded in custody by Wealdstone magistrates and at a hearing on 26 February 1913 claimed that he "did not recognise men-made laws." In March he was sent to prison for nine months and charged costs, it having been revealed that he had already been in prison for an assault on Winston Churchill (then a Liberal) and had been force-fed eighteen times.

These two cases both show one of the favoured Suffragette techniques of vandalising railway carriages. However, more destructive were the attacks on empty stock left unattended in isolated sidings. On 26 June 1913 an attempt was made to set fire to a rake of carriages at Teddington (LSWR), though only one was damaged; postcards to Prime Minister Asquith were found nearby. At midnight on 15 March 1914 a rake of Midland Railway suburban carriages was found to be on fire in a siding at King's Norton, Birmingham. The Fire Brigade was of only limited use as the nearest water supply was half a mile away, so six carriages were destroyed and three others badly damaged before a locomotive was able to pull the other stock clear. A Suffragette newspaper was found nearby.

Railway signals were prone to attack during the early part of the campaign, which could have led to prosecutions for endangering life. At 10pm on 24 December 1912 the GNR signalman at Potters Bar found that a signal failed to respond to his efforts with the lever and he went out to investigate; he found that it had been tied up with a window sash cord and a note left advising that, "The only way to stop this trouble is to remove the cause by giving votes to women." In February 1913 a signal wire was cut on the GWR at Llantarnam near Newport and a "Votes for Women" note left. A week later the same thing happened at Nantyderry near Monmouth, with a note reading "This will stop when we get the vote." These two attacks seem to have been by the same person or group, who probably had a car - reflecting the popularity of the Suffragette cause among some more wealthy people.

A common Suffragette technique was setting fire to buildings. On the night of 9-10 March 1913 the station buildings at Saunderton (GWR) and Croxley (LNWR) were both destroyed by fire, at the former causing delays to night goods workings but the latter was unusual in that no evidence had been left by the Suffragettes. At Croxley two "well dressed women" were seen nearby and it was believed the same people had started the Saunderton fire - again suggesting wealthy people with a car. The Croxley stationmaster

All that was left of the station at Kenton, near Newcastle, after an attack by Suffragette arsonists in September 1913.

received another surprise a few days later - a copy of a Suffragette newspaper with a note saying "Afraid copy left got burnt."

The most destructive attack was at Leuchars Junction in Scotland on 30 June 1913, where the station was almost totally destroyed in a fire causing £2000 damage. Suffragette literature was left behind. Another heavy loser was the NER, whose Kenton station was destroyed on 13 September - a luggage label was left saying "Asquith is responsible for militancy. Apply to him for the damage."

In April 1914 an attempt was made to burn down the station at Bangor, County Down, where a watchman found a lighted candle, cotton wool and a pile of inflammable material by a wooden staircase. Suffragette slogans were fastened to the signalbox.

Given the level of technology available to the Suffragettes at the time - and the accuracy of reporting - it is often hard to distinguish between an incendiary device and an actual bomb. However, several serious attempts were made to use explosive devices, though fortunately there was no loss of life. An example of this confusion relates to an explosion in an LNWR carriage at a siding between Cheadle and Davenport in April 1913; a carriage was wrecked and its door thrown 30 yards, but this may have been due to paraffin igniting quickly rather than any explosives being used.

Nonetheless April 1913 did mark a more violent approach by the Suffragettes and this included one of the most intriguing incidents where the identity of the "bomber" has become known only fairly recently. An attempt was made to blow up the gents' toilets at Oxted station in Surrey, though only minor damage was caused. A clock timed to go off at 3am, a two-gallon can of petrol and a revolver with one cartridge were found by a postman, who picked up the gun - which promptly went off! The police were able to follow the trail of two men, one of whom had left a hat behind, but they never discovered that one of the "terrorists" was Harold Laski, later to become Professor of Political Philosophy at the London School of Economics. Laski escaped to Dover and spent several weeks hiding in France.

Two weeks after this an unexploded quarter pound bomb was found at Aberdeen station and in May 1913 a bomb was left in a waiting room at Liverpool Street - it consisted of gunpowder, nuts, bolts and a note saying "Votes for Women." On 15 May a porter at Aylesbury (GWR) found a bomb after being alerted by a ticking noise - and dumped it into a bucket of water. The next night a bomb on the GWR at Westbourne Park "went out" and there was an attempt by two men to place a bomb on the viaduct at Whalley in Lancashire. A bomb left at Haslemere in July 1913 did not go off - its ingredients of clock, battery, guncotton, fuse and message to Haslemere District Council somehow failing to ignite.

In a rash of bomb attacks there were also some hoaxes - the boys of Tiffin School near Wimbledon got themselves into trouble, whilst "bombs" at Eastbourne and Forest Hill proved to be no more than an old clock and two bananas in the first case and coal dust and bicycle parts in the second.

A potentially very serious incident occurred at Reading on 27 May when a bomb was thrown from the non-stop 11am Paddington to Bristol train as it passed through the station. Something was seen being thrown out of the train, then there was "a loud report and two puffs of smoke." No-one was hurt, and no-one arrested. In May 1914 a goods train at Wellingborough was found to have a bomb in one of its trucks, supposedly dropped from an overbridge. The bomb contained a potentially lethal mixture of gunpowder, gelatine and iron bolts.

Most of the bomb attacks and arson attempts were timed to cause damage at night, as it was the stated intention of the Suffragettes not to cause injury or death. One of the most unusual events was therefore the warning sent to the Midland Railway in May 1913 of an attempt to derail an "express". Police in Northamptonshire watched all bridges but eventually concluded that it was an hoax.

A study of the pattern of attacks will make it clear that the majority of them were the work of only a handful of people. Notable is the cluster of attacks in the Birmingham area, which could easily have all been carried out by one or two people with access to a car - needed to move around at night. This early form of political terrorism seems to have gained little support within the wider suffragist movement and perhaps even helped to delay the granting of votes to women. More sustained than the attacks by Irish nationalists, it is fortunate indeed that there were no fatal injuries.[1]

[1] A full list of known incidents is given at the end of the author's article in *Backtrack*, August 1995, p. 424.

CHAPTER NINE:
TERROR & POLITICS

Irish Nationalism

Outbreaks of Irish terrorism on mainland Britain have been little discussed with the exception of the various "Fenian" incidents of the later 1860s such as the abortive raid on Chester Castle on 11 February 1867 when it was planned to steal arms from the garrison and then hijack a train to get back to Holyhead. However informers had given the secret mission away to the British authorities, with the result that one of the leaders - John McCafferty - was late arriving as his train was put in a siding while emergency troop trains were rushed through to Chester. Fenians attacked railways in Ireland in March 1867 and one of their leaders, Godfrey Massey, was arrested at Limerick Junction station on 4 March.

Railways became a focal part of the activity of nationalists from about 1880, both as a target and as a means of transporting the "infernal machines" about the country; in addition, they eventually became a central feature of the struggle for control of Ireland itself.

The first known "terrorist" attempt on an English railway was near Bushey on the LNWR on the night of 12 September 1880. The fishplates on the down fast line were removed, a hole dug beneath the loosened sleeper and then a brown paper parcel packed into it. The parcel contained 27 cartridges full of dynamite, tied together with twine, and some piping as part of a mechansim to set it off. The fishplate was then reconnected. Perhaps because the night was very wet the device failed and it was found by a platelayer at 7.10am the next morning.

Some "dynamite machines" were captured at Liverpool in 1881 smuggled inside cement barrels, but the most serious phase of terrorism

Bushey, on the London & North Western main line, where the first known terrorist attempt on an English railway was made in 1880. A parcel containing 27 cartridges full of dynamite failed to explode.

began in 1883 at a time when many of the more extreme Irish nationalists had lost patience with the "Home Rule" party. The Irish were strong in Glasgow and this may explain the choice of that city to open the campaign of violence, for which a group began preparing in July 1882 under the tutelage of an American named Timothy Featherstone (or Johnstone). On 20 January 1883 a gasworks, a bridge on the Forth & Clyde Canal, and a coal shed at the Caledonian Railway's Buchanan Street station were all attacked. The canal bridge bomb was in a small tin box and was picked up by a soldier; he found some sand inside so put his hand in - whereupon it exploded. The gasworks attack caused a nearby house to be blown in and a man's clothes were set on fire. One of the gang involved, J E Kearney, had been a signalling worker at the station but escaped from Glasgow after the explosions.

The campaign in England was launched with a large dynamite explosion outside Local Government Board offices in London on 15 March 1883, where there was "an immense destruction of glass" but little significant damage. The same evening there was an attempt to attack the offices of *The*

Home to a terrorist? The railway hotel at Charing Cross was used by Dr.
Thomas Gallagher in 1883 to plot dynamite attacks in London .

Times in Playhouse Yard but this was a failure "by the providential accident of
the vessel containing the explosive falling over." A reward of £1000 was offered.

This attack produced a much heightened awareness of explosives
and the chemical processes involved in making bombs. Sergeant Price of the
Birmingham police heard of reports of chemicals being delivered to a rented
shop in Ledsam Street, supposedly used as a paint mixing shop by George
Whitehead whose tenancy began on 6 February. Once there had been a small
explosion and Whitehead had emerged choking from the smoke. The astute
Price visited the shop in the guise of a painter and noticed some carboys of
acid. The Chief Constable was alerted and, at 2am on 2 April, the premises
were searched; nitric and sulphuric acid, key ingredients of nitro-glycerine,
were discovered. It was found that a man named William Lynch carried the
bombs to London.

Whitehead, Lynch, Henry Wilson and several others were arrested
on 5 April 1883. The leader of the group was Dr Thomas Gallagher, who had
stayed in the Charing Cross Hotel to organise the London activities, whilst
his brother Bernard was arrested in a Glasgow pub the following day. These

two and William Ansburgh had arrived from America on the *Parthia* on 26 March 1883 but had been active since at least November 1882. However many of their activities had been infiltrated by police and Sergeant William Melville had managed to rent a hotel room next to John Curtin's (or Kent's) and even shared a breakfast table with him on 7 April before his arrest.

On 11 April Bernard Gallagher offered to turn witness and was taken to London. William Lynch, alias Norman, also turned evidence and described how Thomas Gallagher had given him a box in New York on 8 March and had told him to take it to London. This Gallagher, Whitehead, Wilson and Curtin were all found guilty and sentenced to penal servitude for life in June 1883.

A cell of terrorists was based in Liverpool as well, purchasing chemicals and sending them to the Glasgow group via the Clyde Shipping Co.; a box of chemicals traced to Dennis Deasey was found on 6 March. Those arrested in May 1883 for possession of explosives with intent were Deasey, who had brought chemicals from Cork, Henry Dalton who kept a pocket book containing notes about mixing chemicals, Patrick Flanagan, Timothy Featherstone and Daniel O'Herlihy. A green document found with them labelled "Cure for Gout" turned out to be the mixture for making incendiaries! The whole group had been spied on by police since at least 24 March, soon after the Local Government Board explosion.

In early August a large tin box of dynamite was found at the Cupar factory of Honeyman & Co., linen manufacturers. This was similar to the Playhouse Yard bomb and its packing included a letter written in French, suggesting a suppy route via France. However this attempt on a factory was at variance with the usual type of operation.

On 4 September 1883 nine Irishmen were arrested in Glasgow, including one who had been employed at the Irvine chemical works, and charged with conspiracy to levy war against the Queen in connection with the explosions on 20 January. A key figure, J E Kearney, escaped, but others charged included Dalton and Featherstone who had already been convicted of the explosives charges at Liverpool; explosives were similar to those traced to Deasey. All were members of the Irish National Land League and had been meeting since July 1882, although it was Featherstone who had come from America to teach them about explosions. Five of those arrested were found guilty on the most serious charge and given penal servitude for life - Devaney, Callaghan, McCann, and McCullagh; five others were considered to have not been fully aware of the situation and received seven years.

Before the Glasgow cases could come to trial, two potentially highly

dangerous explosions occurred on underground railways on 30 October 1883 that fortunately cost no lives; however the events show that the nationalists had been able to get another operational group into place in England very soon after the arrests of April and May 1883. The first of these was at about 7.51pm when explosives were dropped from the window of a carriage near Praed Street station (now Paddington), probably by being dangled out on a piece of string which was then cut; the bomb exploded and passengers in the last three carriages of the train were injured by glass. 32 people received hospital treatment due to cuts. Security was clearly lax at Praed Street as members of the public were allowed to "go into the tunnels" between trains, which were about every ten minutes.

At 8.05pm another bomb exploded between Charing Cross and Westminster stations plunging both into darkness as the gas lights went out. "Volumes of black dust came pouting out of the tunnels to add to the confusion." The roofing over the tracks was blown loose. On 4 November the LCDR stationmaster at Holborn Viaduct received a threat to blow up the Snow Hill tunnels.

The Police received intelligence that there was to be an attack on the Midland Railway on 3 January 1884. It was believed that St Pancras was to be bombed and the whole line north to Leicester was placed under secret surveillance; men sent out to watch the line were not given their orders until in position, and this state of readiness maintained for several days.

On 17 January five bags of explosives were found in Primrose Hill tunnel of the LNWR, having probably been dropped out of a moving train. There was no fuse or detonator with the explosives so it seems unlikely an actual explosion was intended, though much was made of the information that the Prince of Wales was using the Euston route to go to Hatton. The pattern of this event, though, suggests it was the work of the same gang as the October bombs. The North Eastern Railway announced on 17 February that an attempt had been made to destroy its goods station at Hull, but produced no evidence to show that this could have been the work of Irish nationalists.

At 1.03am on 26 February 1884 the West End of London was rocked by a large explosion at Victoria where "the booking-office, waiting rooms and luggage depository...were blown into the air" with a noise "like

Irish nationalists were active in London in October1883, when two explosions occurred on the underground. One was between Charing Cross and Westminster stations – "volumes of black dust came pouring out of the tunnels to add to the confusion".

The booking office, waiting rooms and luggage depository at London's Victoria station were "blown into the air" when an explosion occurred in February 1884.

that of heavy artillery." The gas pipes ignited and the LBSCR offices caught fire - the wood and glass station buildings having little resistance to blast or fire. Two men were injured and a photographer was also hurt when he fell into one of the holes made. Government explosives experts sifted the debris and then had it loaded onto trucks, which took it all to Cold Blow siding for examination.

　　　　The explosion at Victoria led to a search of other London stations with bombs being found at Charing Cross and Paddington. However it was a week before the curiosity of a cloakroom attendant led to the discovery of an unexploded device at Ludgate Hill, which had been there since 25 February. The discoveries of these unexploded devices yielded many clues as to the bombers and their materials which confirmed Police information that the bombers were Irish-Americans who had arrived from New York. The bags all seemed to have been left at the stations in the early evening of 25 February, so it was believed the bombers had then caught boat trains to France. The bombs were fired by an alarm clock connected to a pocket pistol, but the Charing Cross bomb had misfired and thus, crucially, the contents of the trunk in which it was hidden were not destroyed. These included a

Details of the bombs used to attack Paddington and Victoria stations in 1884. The sketches show:- 1. The firing mechanism – an alarm clock connected to a pocket pistol; 2. Cake of dynamite, with holes in which the detonators were placed; 3. Combined cap and cartridge for pistol; 4. Detonator containing Fulminate of Mercury; 5. Fused main spring, found at Victoria after the explosion; 6. Cash box containing firing mechanism and dynamite; 7. Leather valise, holding cash box wrapped in cloth and a large quantity of dynamite.

coat with unusual quartz buttons which was used to convict one of the nationalists, Burton.

On 9 April a passenger on a northbound Midland Railway train from Bristol gave the guard a small package to look after which burst into flames near Charfield, "singeing" the guard. The box contained various chemicals and attempts were made to follow the man to Liverpool.

Two days later a man named John Daley was arrested at Birkenhead railway station whilst buying a ticket to Wolverhampton - having been under surveillance since December during which time he had made regular trips between Birmingham and Liverpool by train. He was carrying four parcels, three of which were made up as bombs and the fourth of which contained various useful chemicals. Daley had been born in Limerick in 1846 and had, whilst still in Ireland, attempted to disrupt a meeting held by Isaac Butt following which he had been acquitted of a riot charge. He had gained a reputation for being well-off, yet had no visible means of support, and was distrusted amongst the nationalist fraternity as a possible informer - he had not been trusted whilst in New York and had spent two years between 1880 and 1882 working at a lunatic asylum in Sussex.

Other arrests followed in Birmingham, where Daley had lived with James Egan at Grafton Road, Sparkbrook. On 15 April the police found a can of documents buried in the garden, including "The Constitution of the Irish Republic" and "Rules for the Irish Republican Brotherhood South of

England Division", but most of them dated from the era of activity in 1875. Daley received a life sentence and Egan twenty years, though the tin in the latter's garden was described even by Daley as the "fossil remains of the IRB"; William McDonnell was bound over. The thought of Irishmen travelling up and down the country by train, carrying explosives, was almost as terrifying as the deliberate explosions themselves.

The next round of explosions at just after 9pm on 30 May included a spectacular success against Scotland Yard itself and two explosions in Carlton Square which damaged the Junior Carlton Club and the Military Education Department, the latter causing most serious damage to Sir Watkin Wynne's house; 27 people were injured. A fourth bomb would have brought down Nelson's Column but failed to explode and was picked up by a boy at 9.35pm; it yielded crucial evidence and was similar to the railway station bombs of February. The Scotland Yard bomb caused heavy damage to the *Rising Sun* pub, but this was made up for by the trade from thirsty sightseers.

On 22 July a box labelled "A Perry" exploded in a Regent Street doorway. More dramatic, but no more destructive, was a bomb attempt on the actual London Bridge on 12 December 1884. Two men had hired a boat from Greenhithe Stairs and simply hung the bomb on some iron grilles at the side of the bridge - ironically the grilles had been installed to prevent bombers hiding a bomb inside the bridge structure itself! However this time the nitro-glycerine was not American-made, this being seen as a triumph for the close watch of the ports. A "clockwork apparatus" was found amidst the wreckage after a serious fire at Windsor GWR station on 19 December, but this proved to be the remains of a parcel of fishing tackle. On 28 December the Police found a store of explosives at the *Black Horse* in Evelyn Street, Lewisham, but failed to make any arrests.

A Metropolitan Railway train was the next target on 2 January 1885, when a bomb exploded near Gower Street (now Euston Square) station. The train was the 8.57pm from Aldgate to Hammersmith and the bomb went off in the tunnel beside the train at 9.14pm when it was near Charlton Street signalbox, damaging the rear carriages and the signalbox. The train and signalbox were plunged into darkness as all the gas lights were blown out, and some people above in Euston Road were blown over but injuries were few.

Saturday 24 January 1885 brought the three most brazen bomb attacks of all at Westminster Hall, the House of Commons and the Tower of London - but security measures at the latter managed to trap one of the bombers, James Cunningham, before he could escape. The bomb went off and injured three people before Cunningham could make his getaway, and the

Tower's primitive security measure of sounding a bugle to close the gates meant that he could not get out. He was found to be wearing a hat made in New York and then gave a false address before his real one was discovered and searched.

A black bag containing a bomb was left at Westminster Hall, and this began "smoking"; it was picked up by PC Cole who brought it out to near the entrance of the crypt, where he dropped it due to its heat. It then exploded, injuring Cole seriously, and there was almost immediately another explosion in the House of Commons. The Commons Chamber was "a complete wreck" and the government benches were torn up with the Prime Minister's seat badly damaged; the attack had been possible as the public were permitted to walk around the Chamber on a Saturday.

The arrest of Cunningham and his associate Harry Burton was a major breakthrough - they were also charged with the Victoria and Gower Street explosions, but not the explosions of 30 May. Cunningham had been in London since 23 December and latterly lived at Scarborough Street, where a detonator had been found hidden in his socks; another address he kept, 30 Great Praed Street, was watched and this led to the unfortunate arrest of his defence counsel who had called to collect some things! Burton was arrested at 90 Turner's Road, Bow on 3 February.

Cunningham was identified by the guard as having been on the Metropolitan Railway train between Kings Cross and Gower Street. The guard was certain that he had seen him in the "spare" guard's compartment at the front of the train, with three other men and a "toolbag"; he also saw him when the train was cleared of passengers at Gower Street. Burton was implicated by having worn a coat with unusual quartz buttons when he arrived at Southampton on 20 February 1884, and this had subsequently been found in the Charing Cross trunk. His movements were well-charted by the security services, who knew that he had travelled on to London, then to Le Havre and back to New York, where he had arrived on 13 March. Burton was back in London, lodging at Limehouse, between May and September, then went back to America and returned to London by 25 December.

Both Cunningham and Gower were found guilty, a decision which took the jury only 15 minutes, and sent to prison for life. This brought the total of Irish or Irish-American bombers in prison to 24.

An isolated incident occurred in a compartment of the LNWR between Whitchurch and Chester. An American traveller joined two other gentlemen and started denouncing Earl Powis, whose lands they were passing, for oppressing the Irish people. The American said he was a Fenian and would shoot the Earl for 2d, which Mr Sandfield objected to. The

Fenian then produced a revolver, put it to Sandfield's head, and said "if he repeated his sentiments he would blow him to the infernal regions." The man ran off at Chester and was not caught.

Railways in Ireland

During the early 1920s there were many incidents in Ireland itself in which railways were involved, especially in 1921 when the struggle for independence from the United Kingdom was reaching its peak. Britain used the railways to help it control the country and they were therefore a political target, though Britain viewed all such attacks within the normal criminal law. For example, a Derry to Burtonport troop train was ambushed near Burtonport in January 1921. A large boulder was placed on the line which derailed the train and then it was "riddled with bullets", but there were no casualties.

A fierce gun battle broke out at Mallow station on night of 31 January. Captain King of the RIC was returning from the Royal Hotel with his wife when they were ambushed and Mrs King killed. The assailants had taken cover behind rolling stock in the railway yard, so police rushed into the station and began firing. Unfortunately innocent railwaymen were caught up in the firing and two of them were shot by police as they ran along the track - a signalman and a cleaner. The wounded were taken by train to Cork, but some twenty railwaymen were rounded up by the police on the platform and made to put their hands up. The men were marched away and further shooting was heard and one of the railwaymen died; the police took the view that the railwaymen had allowed the armed men to make the ambush. Another report suggested that some of the railwaymen got away by escaping on a light engine. Later that night the station refreshment rooms were looted.

Such was the publicity about the incident that a Court of Inquiry was set up in March to investigate the shooting of a railwayman after the ambush. The Inquiry was told that the party of arrested men, including the railway staff, came under fire from rebels and the RIC responded with the result that three were hit. Allegations included that the railway men were shot deliberately, and that others were beaten up at Mallow barracks. The railway men were represented by officials of the NUR and ASLEF and had to counter accusations about why so many of them were still at the station; it was argued that the men who organised the ambush must have had a very good knowledge of the station and that the second attack on the arrested party came from close to the South signalbox. The President of the Inquiry was himself killed by the IRA on 5 March.

On 12 February there was another incident at Mallow when the 6.30pm troop train to Killarney was hijacked by two armed men as it prepared to leave. The hijackers stopped the train in a cutting 1.5 miles out of Mallow, where a light was shone as a signal. Then heavy shooting began from both sides of the line, aimed at the troop carriage. One soldier was killed and six injured, after which the train continued on its way though two women passengers were detained for having shouted "Up the rebels."

On 15 February fifty rebels attacked a train at Upton & Innishannon station, 15 miles SW of Cork. The train was carrying soldiers with their ammunition, but also civilians, and the soldiers had adopted a new tactic of scattering themselves around the train rather than being an easy target in one carriage. On this occasion the rebels took over the station ten minutes before the train arrived, taking the stationmaster prisoner, but the new tactics gave the soldiers time to start shooting back with a machine gun. In the ensuing bloodbath nine men, including a signalman and a railway checker, and a woman were killed.

A cunning plan to divert the rails of the Castelnagore to Gweedore line in Donegal into a lake failed because it was discovered before a train came along, then in mid-March a train was machine-gunned at Tubbrid station near Tralee, killing a police cadet and wounding the train's driver and fireman. On 17 March Richhill station in Armagh was held up, signal wires cut, and the buildings set on fire.

On 20 March there were two serious incidents. A group of about 100 rebels took over Headford station, ejecting the stationmaster and his wife from their house, and moving the wagons in the sidings to get the best sightings. When the troop train arrived from Kenmare, it was allowed to stand for a minute, and shooting only began when Lt Adams got out and was shot through the heart. Led by their sergeant some of the soldiers managed to get out and start shooting back before receiving support from another train which brought 14 extra men from Mallow; the officer on this had heard the shooting and stopped the train outside the area so as to surprise the rebels. Seven soldiers were killed and one passenger, plus the body of one rebel was found - but there may have been others. It was suggested that a senior IRA man had been killed and that some of the passengers on the train had produced revolvers and joined in. Also that day two police were shot at Portarlington station.

On 31 March three armed men called at the signal house at Castledowson in Derry and told the signalman's wife to explain how to operate the signals as they were planning to hold up the mail train. While delaying them with talking, she managed to get her daughter to set the signals to "all clear" with the result that the train was able to steam past while the men shot at it futilely.

In May there was a series of outrages in the North which included attempts to set fire to High Westwood station and also a bridge over the line at Blackhill, County Down. In late May the Bantry to Cork mail train was held up at Durrus Road, near Bantry, by twelve armed men using cars. The following month the action moved to the mainland with attacks on the railways there, as described above, but there were further incidents in Ireland itself again in July. A train was held up near Oola and two wagons of military stores set on fire. Then a police patrol came up along the railway and a fierce battle took place, with two police killed. At about the same time an army patrol came across a group laying landmines on the track of the GSR near Celbridge as part of a plan to blow up a troop train; there was a gunfight before the rebels ran off.

On about 6 July a goods train was stopped near Donaghmore by removing a rail from the track, then it was surrounded by about 100 men. The wagons at the rear, one of which contained horses, were uncoupled and set rolling down the incline while the rest of the train was set on fire. On 8 July a passenger train with soldiers on board was shot at between Clondalkin and Inchicore and several passengers were wounded. An attempt to blow up a bridge in County Limerick failed. On 7 November two armed men robbed a train on the line south-east of Dublin at Milltown, having carefully selected the working that collected the weekend takings - though this occurred after the truce of July 1921 had restored some semblance of normality.

Terrorism in the Twentieth Century

During the height of the Irish campaign for independence in 1921, the methods being used in Ireland itself were used on selected railway targets in England. On the night of 16 June raiders attacked signalboxes around London at Clapton, Barking, Plaistow, Walthamstow, Bromley, Bounds Green, Northolt, Hanwell, Barnes and Carshalton. The raiders were well-organised and used cars to attack a variety of targets; they were masked and armed. One group in a car was challenged by a PC in Burnt Ash Lane, Bromley, shooting and wounding him. At 11pm signalman Batley at Walthamstow Marshes box on the GER answered a knock at the door and was shot in the face, though he was not seriously wounded. The Bounds Green signalman was tied up by three armed men. At Barking six men tied up the signalman and set the box on fire whilst the box at Barnes was also burnt down.

A new campaign of violence by the IRA in 1939 led to the destruction of the left luggage office at Leicester Square underground station. The incident caused the Special Branch annual dinner scheduled for the following evening to be cancelled!

    The attacks were clearly well co-ordinated - for example, the Bromley and Northolt raids started at the exact same time. In the latter case five men cut signal wires, firing at the signalman and his assistant, then set the box on fire; at Northolt Junction a porter was shot at and tied up, the attackers getting away on cycles. Also on the GWR, wires were cut between Hanwell and Southall, signalman James Culley had something thrown in his eyes and was then gagged and tied up; an attempt made to burn down his box, but Culley managed to crawl across four tracks to summon help from the locomotive shed.

    Petrol was carried to the Clapton attack in a hot-water bottle, but a tin of burning petrol placed under Carshalton signalbox was spotted by workmen and knocked away. An attempt to cut signal wires in Dartford was spotted by police, the men getting away on cycles again.

    On the night of 18 June the attacks moved to the Manchester district. That night Edward Axon was on his lonely duty in a MR cabin near Marple when, at 00.10, he was suddenly shot in the groin. He was able to put the lights out, but the attackers opened fire again and he was wounded in the shoulder. Axon was able to phone for help and his screams awoke Mr

King's Cross cloakroom after the explosion of a sulphuric acid bomb on 26th July, 1939. An Edinburgh doctor was killed and four others injured.

Galleymore who lived nearby at Aqueduct Cottage, and who arrived to assist with a shotgun.

Slightly earlier that night, the signalbox at Woodlands on the LYR electric line to Bury was set on fire, but there was no man on duty at that time. Yew Tree Lane box on the GCR near Fallowfield was also set on fire, but it was dowsed down with water from an engine. The following night there was more trouble in London with fires at Limehouse and West India Docks station, though a pile of sleepers set on fire in the LBSCR loco yard at Battersea with a scratched message may have been a hoax.

The independence of the Irish Republic did not bring a final end to the conflict as the issue of partition gradually came to be the focus of a new wave of terrorism. The IRA began a new campaign in Britain on 16 January 1939, which first affected railway targets on 3 February. In what was to become a feature of terrorist attacks in the latter half of the century, the bombs exploded in the left luggage offices at Tottenham Court Road and

Leicester Square underground stations in the early morning - causing the cancellation of the Special Branch annual dinner scheduled for the following evening. At the former station a ticket collector noticed a red glow in the luggage office before the explosion occurred - his leg was broken by the flying door. The bombs were believed to be alarm clock bombs.

The next attacks came at the unlikely site of the coal bays at Kings Cross goods depot, where two bombs caused little damage. However police found brown paper parcels containing hot water bottles and rubber pipes which they put in the back of their car with rather more damaging effects. On 4 March a Metropolitan Railway worker stopped some men who were carrying boxes from their car onto the embankment at Park Avenue Bridge near Willesden Green. A fight began and one of the Irishmen yelled, "Shoot, Paddy," but the bullet missed and the bombers ran off. Three days later an alarm clock bomb was found at Acton Lane bridge on the LMS at Willesden.

Early on 5 April a bomb exploded close to the GWR station at Snow Hill, Birmingham and then on 2 July there were seven explosions at LMS stations in the Midlands. At Leicester London Road a ticket collector's booth was blown up and one man injured and at Leamington Spa (Milverton) the booking and parcels offices were wrecked. Damage was mostly at the cloak rooms in the explosions at Birmingham New Street, Derby, Stafford, Nottingham Midland and Coventry. The Derby explosion nearly claimed the life of the cloakroom attendant, who was drinking tea when he saw a blue flame "playing about" a suitcase - he just had time to escape before the blast.

On 26 July a bomb exploded at Kings Cross cloakroom at lunchtime, killing an Edinburgh man, Dr Donald Campbell, and injuring four others; this was a sulphuric acid bomb. That evening an alarm clock bomb struck the Brighton side of Victoria, damaging a train in platform 15 and causing panic in the News Theatre - five people were taken to hospital. However outbreak of the war against Germany caused a re-evaluation of the situation and the only other incidents were two occasions when mailbags caught fire on northbound trains out of Euston on 4 November; this was assumed to be IRA work.

The prevalance of bomb threats in this century has also given rise to the curse of the hoax bomb which was not just a phenomenon of the 1970s, but had been a problem earlier. For example, there were several incidents of this in 1956 - in August a buffet at Waterloo had to be closed after an anonymous warning and on 9 November *The Talisman* was stopped at New Barnet and everyone had to get off the train after another anonymous phone call. There was no bomb on either occasion. However, on the occasion a live hand grenade was found on a seat in the 6.03am Raynes Park to Waterloo at Christmas that year there was no warning!

A rather more substantial "fake" was found by a ganger between the rails at Tempsford north of Hitchin in August 1957. The ganger had bent to pick up a crowbar that he had seen lying near the track, and was surprised to hear a ticking sound. He then saw wires leading to a large tin buried in the ballast, so he flagged down an approaching engine and the alarm was raised. Trains were diverted via Cambridge while police came to remove the "bomb", which proved to contain only a clock mechanism. Brighton line services were disrupted on 23 January 1962 after a bomb scare affecting the 10.45pm Victoria to Hove, which had to be searched at East Croydon.

Of course attacks were renewed in more recent times, notably in 1976 when there was an explosion on an empty stock train at Cannon Street on 9 March and on a London Transport train on 15 March. There were further attacks between 1991 and 1994. The first in this phase occurred at Paddington and Victoria on 18 February 1991, the last being at Victoria again on 11 October 1994; though the technology had changed slightly, the methods and targets remained almost identical to those a hundred years before.

CHAPTER TEN:
MAINTAINING
LAW & ORDER

The railways contributed to the improvement of law and order in Victorian times in two ways - by providing the means to transport police or soldiers quickly to the scene of an emergency, or through use of the electric telegraph to catch villains. However, the converse could also be true - London gangs were known to have used the railways to make burglary raids into country districts.

One of the earliest known emergency uses of the railway was for a Chartist meeting in Coventry in July 1839, when a corps of riflemen were sent from Birmingham at just under 60mph![1] Sir Richard Jackson devised a plan to use the railways that year as a result of which the depot at Weedon was set up close to the London & Birmingham.

It was soon realised that railways could help police too to control districts and in April 1841 Derbyshire Sessions suggested having a "central barracks" near Derby station "for the preservation of the peace of the county in the event of any popular commotion."[2]

One of the first major uses of railways to assist law and order occurred in August 1842, with a spate of disturbances in industrial districts. General Napier was controlling the northern districts and had already used the Liverpool & Manchester to send men from Manchester to Ireland. A policy of concentrating troops at key points on the railway system was used, and the advantages of the good connections from London to the provinces became apparent - it took eight hours to move troops from London to Leeds, whereas it had formerly taken fourteen days! The position of Weedon Barracks also became important, with access to the London & Birmingham.The following troops were sent north from Euston:

13 August	Morning	600 men, 56 horses, 2 cannon
14 August	Morning	45 men, 23 horses, 2 "guns"
14 August	Afternoon	600 men
16 August	Morning	215 men, 63 women, 44 children, Ammunition
18 August	Morning	650 men, 4 horses
18 August	Afternoon	2 tons ammunition
19 August		650 men, 6 horses

Further detachments were sent the following week.

This activity reflects the findings of the historian F C Mather, who wrote:

"The British railway network raised markedly the efficiency of the military force which was maintained on home service, by making the troops stationed in the southern part of England more readily available for the restoration of order in the manufacturing districts of the North."[3]

The railways could also be used to carry police, and the Railways Act of 1844 allowed Metropolitan police on duty to travel at a reduced rate - though they continued to pay full rate until an alert official noticed that money was being wasted after several months.[4] Soldiers were to be carried at a fixed charge of 1d a mile, and 2d for officers. This was because the Quartermaster General reported to Parliament that he was now able to send a battalion to Manchester in nine hours instead of 17 days, saving the extra 1s1d a day soldiers had to be paid when on the march! In fact he calculated it was 3d cheaper to send them by train to Birmingham than to march them there.

However the importance of the railways in this respect was only to last for a decade or two; by the late 1850s virtually every district of the country had an efficient local police force and the army's role was much reduced.

Railways were also used to capture fugitives. In May 1841 George Comley of Nibley in Gloucestershire left Gloucester with his family of seven, bound for Birmingham and America. Just after he left it was discovered that he had defrauded W Gillmonger of £40 as well as his landlord. For the payment of £10 an engine was got ready at Gloucester and managed to catch up with the Birmingham train at Spetchley station. Comley was arrested and locked up in Birmingham.

In November 1842 a runaway girl was apprehended at Euston, having arrived from Tunstall with no ticket. She said that her collier father beat her, but she was sent back home.

Railways were also important for the transport of prisoners, though this was not always popular with other passengers. This was a common traffic between Halifax and the gaol at Wakefield, and in March 1841 a burglar tried to escape by leaping from the speeding train. He fractured his skull and broke both legs. Soon after the first lines of the SER were opened in Kent it began to be used for carrying prisoners between Bromley and the county gaol at Maidstone.

The *Railway Times* received complaints about this happening on the Grand Junction and the LSWR in 1843. The latter conveyed prisoners from London to Portsmouth for transportation, usually in chains or handcuffs; at Nine Elms "there was one of the most forbidding looking females accompanying them to see them off" and the *Railway Times* thought it unacceptable that the prisoners were placed close to decent ladies travelling in second class.

Rail passengers disliked meeting criminals on the trains, and many stories were told about dangerous escape attempts. In December 1864 a lunatic was being taken by Police to Devizes when he suddenly accused them of shooting at him with a revolver and tried to get out through the window. A furious fight followed until the guard in the next compartment stopped the train.

In February 1862 the Chief Constable of Fife, Mr Bell, was escorting the former publisher of the *Fifeshire Journal*, Samuel Robinson, back to Scotland to face charges of forgery at Cupar. They took first class seats on the 9.15am from Kings Cross with Robinson in manacles locked to Bell's wrist. Despite this, Robinson managed to slip off his shackles near Northallerton and tried to dive out of the window, but Bell managed to catch hold of him by the foot. For thirty minutes the train sped along with Robinson dangling out of the window, seemingly determined on suicide. Eventually Bell tired and let go. At Darlington the alarm was raised and an engine sent down the line to look for the body - but none was found. The last that was heard of Robinson was a report of a man with a bloody face seen near Northallerton.

In July 1926 a prisoner in handcuffs escaped from two warders at Fenchurch Street station and was seen running down Aldgate, still in his cuffs.

The most famous case of a prisoner being taken by train was of Charlie Peace, the notorious robber and murderer. Charged with the murder of an admirer's husband at Banner Cross[5], Peace was being taken from Kings Cross back to Sheffield by express train in January 1879 when he leapt out of the window head first. His leg was caught in the window and a prison warder clung to his foot; Peace dangled out head first as the train rattled along for two miles, until the cord was pulled. Then he managed to slip out of his shoe, but was injured as he fell and was soon recaptured - before being put back into the guard's van. There was some discussion that he intended suicide as the spot he chose was close to where he said he wanted to be buried - "Bury me at Darnall", he had written. He was hung in February 1879.

Another who tried to escape this way was a seaman who had been arrested in Canterbury and was being returned to Sheerness in 1891; when the train was going "at a smart pace" he jumped head first out of the window near Sittingbourne. No doubt he had intended to roll down the embankment, but his head collided with an iron signal post - bending the lever - and his injuries were such that "no hopes are entertained of his recovery."

In May 1957 five Dartmoor prisoners were being conveyed by express from Tavistock North to Waterloo when a loaded revolver was found on the train by a woman passenger. A message was sent from Andover and police watched the train as it arrived at Waterloo, but nothing untoward happened. On 8 July 1961 a prisoner being taken from North Wales to Carlisle jumped out of the train near Lancaster and was killed.

Use of the Electric Telegraph

The telegraph was used to catch a Portsmouth pay sergeant in 1845 who robbed a captain and then absconded. A message was sent to Nine Elms and the man was arrested as he got off the train.

One of the most famous early cases involved a murder committed by John Towell, who killed a woman at Salt Hill near Slough in 1845. His victim was poisoned by some cyanide he had slipped into her drink before leaving, but this was not an instant death and it gave time to send out an alert. He caught the 7.42pm from Slough and must have thought he was safe, but his description was sent by telegraph to Paddington:

" A murder has just been committed at Salt Hill and the suspect has been seen to take a 1st class ticket to Paddington on the 7.42pm. He is dressed as a Quaker with a long overcoat down to his ankles. He is sitting in the second 1st class carriage."

From Paddington he was shadowed by a member of the GWR police to the Jerusalem coffee house in Cannon Street where he was arrested.

In November 1847 a telegraph message was sent from Newton Abbot to Exeter about a woman thief; a GWR man was busily hunting for her when she stopped him to ask for directions!

The 1840s were also the heyday of using the electric telegraph to intercept eloping couples. Just after the MR branch was opened to Lincoln its telegraph was used to stop a couple who had eloped by train and in February 1847 the following message was received at the ECR's Bishopsgate station:

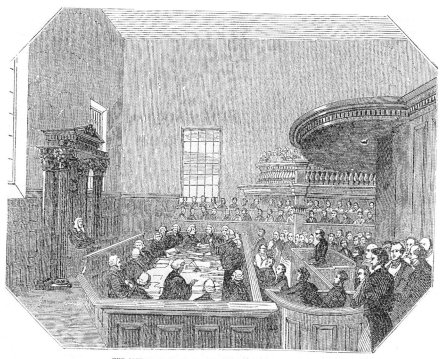

THE COURT-HOUSE AT AYLESBURY.—TRIAL OF JOHN TAWELL.

The trial at Aylesbury in 1845 of John Tawell – the first murderer to be caught by the use of the railway telegraph.

"Detain a man in the three o'clock up train from Yarmouth. He is attired in a flannel jacket, fustian trousers and blue cap; has small whiskers and is accompanied by a female named Read. She is dressed in a dark gown and Tuscan bonnet, and has with her a child."

The couple were detained by police at the station and then another message arrived, saying the man in the cap had "run away with £30 and the prosecutor's wife" explained it all - adding that the wronged husband was following on the next train. He did not arrive and, as £30 could not be found on the couple, they were released - to the chagrin of the constable from Whittlesea who arrived a few hours later. Two years a later a young lady who had eloped first class with a student from Cambridge was "captured" at the same station.

Railways and the electric telegraph were instrumental in the response to two serious incidents about fish. On 22 February 1851 there was a serious riot in Great Yarmouth after a dispute broke out between fishermen and the trawler-owners. A huge crowd gathered outside the police station planning to rescue imprisoned colleagues and a desperate telegraph message had to be sent from the railway station to Norwich for help from the 11th Hussars. The Norfolk Railway was able to get the men on their way within two hours of receiving the message but the mob assembled at Yarmouth station and threatened to pull up the rails as well as disconnect the telegraph. The Hussars got off the train outside the station and soon quelled the riot.

A particular dispute arose when the police sought to use the electric telegraph when a railway company did not wish them to - as in the case of the prize-fight at Wadhurst in December 1863 when the police were refused permission to send emergency messages from Wadhurst and Etchingham stations as the telegraph was "too busy" - yet there was time to send the result of the fight back to London! The SER was summoned to appear before Sussex Eastern Sessions, where they said that they had changed the instructions to stationmasters so that police messages could be given priority. In 1869 the telegraph system was bought out by the Post Office and there ceased to be a problem.

The May 1881 "fish riot" was actually caused by the Highland Railway's decision to start loading fish on a Sunday at Strome Ferry, a strongly sabbatarian town. Fifty people "armed with clubs and bludgeons", arrived to prevent it, overpowering the railway officials. A telegraph message was sent to Inverness and the HR sent out a "special", which picked up some police at Dingwall but military help was refused. They arrived at Strome Ferry to be confronted by 150 men and had no effect on the situation until the stroke of midnight when the men went home - by which time the fish was "past its best" for sending to London!

On 15 September 1891 a race special left Sheffield for Ayr but it was then discovered that 31 tickets had been stolen from Sheffield station. The telegraph was used to wire ahead to Carlisle, where 12 men with unstamped tickets were arrested. The men refused to say how they had all got the tickets and so were convicted of receiving, being fined between £1 and £10 each.

The Railway Police

The origins of the railway police were the "specials" sworn in by JPs to assist with maintaining law and order when railways were being built - until the 1850s organised police forces were rare in the counties and totally inadequate in many districts. The modern force was effectively formed by the British Transport Commission Act of 1949, but the BTC police were not a "force" as defined in

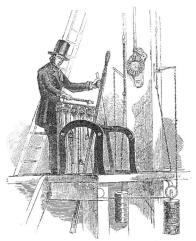

JUNCTION SIGNAL-MAN AT WORK.

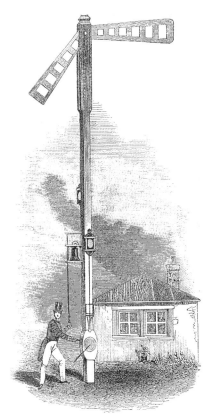

STATION POST SIGNAL—" CAUTION AND DANGER."

Railway Police at work in the 1840s. At this date their duties were indistinguishable from those of the "signalman".

STARTLING!

Constable (to nervous passenger, arrived by the Ramsgate train). " I've got yer "—(" *Ger-acious Heavens!*" *thinks little Skeery with a thrill of horror.* " *Takes me for somebody that's 'wanted'!*")—" a cab, sir."

The Railway Police could seem frightening to a nervous traveller. At first they were not altogether welcomed – in the 1830s and 1840s a broad spectrum of society was still opposed to the idea of police in general.

the Police Act of 1964 and so were not answerable to the Home Secretary.

At first the policeman's duties were indistinguishable from those of the "signalman", although words such as "pointsman" were more common at first. Thus the GWR Rule Book of 1841 defined a "policeman's" duties as:

"The duties of the Police may be stated generally to consist in the preservation of order in all the stations and on the line of railway. They are to give and receive signals; to keep the line free from casual or wilful obstructions; to assist in cases of accidents; to caution strangers of danger on the railway; to remove intruders of all descriptions..."

The LSWR police wore "swallow-tailed, chocolate-coloured coats, dark trousers and tall leather-crowned hats."[6] Their GWR colleagues had a truncheon decorated with a golden crown with the letters "GWR" picked out in gilt script and lined in red, white and green.

The police were one of the most tightly disciplined of the railway working groups and it will be noted from cases above that railway police who

Huge crowds attended race meetings by train, and these gatherings offered rich pickings for criminals. In this lively scene at Doncaster in 1875, at least one likely character is "having his collar felt".

committed crimes tended to be harshly punished. Railway companies could also sack a man for poor behaviour even when not at work and this was confirmed by a ruling in Tomlinson v LMS in 1944; here a railway policeman had attended a meeting on railway premises but not in his working hours, where he had assaulted a fellow LMS employee. The LMS had sacked him and the legal ruling underlined their right to do so.

One of the problems with the railway police was how far the officers were the direct responsibility of the railway company. In the case of Lambert v. GER in 1909, it was ruled that the railway company was liable to damages in a case of false arrest by two railway police and this remained the law until it was overturned in 1930.[7]

The first railway police to use dogs was the NER force in 1910[8]. Railway police were also an additional support to the normal police since they could keep watch at stations and on trains for wanted criminals. For example, in April 1951 BTC Police arrested a man at London Road station

"I'M AWFULLY SORRY TO GET YOU FELLOWS OUT ON A NIGHT LIKE THIS"

Transport Police also patrolled railway sidings in the dockyards, as this 1950s cartoon shows.

who was wanted in connection with a murder at Tyldesley.

Police also helped their colleagues when railway luggage lockers were abused - in November 1938 a man was arrested after a complete safe-breaking kit, including gelignite, was found in a locker at Uxbridge Road station. Railway police watched for ten days until the man came to collect his equipment, also collecting a five year sentence.

Railways and Prize Fights

An area where railway interests came into direct conflict with law and order was in the traffic that railways carried to illegal prize fights at remote spots in the countryside. In the period from about 1839 to 1867 the railway companies actively encouraged the illegal, bare-knuckle sport, which survived because it enjoyed support from the aristocracy and the lower classes alike.

Although small-scale fights took place all around the country, any "big" fight had to involve London's "sporting fraternity", amongst whom were many titled gentlemen - rumours even included Lord Palmerston. However fights could not be held in London because of police activity, so the prize-fighters soon organised excursions down the Thames by steamer - usually to some desolate piece of Kent or Essex marshland.

The first known use of a train to get "pugilists" and the supporters to a fight was the contest between Ward and Bailey in October 1839. The spot chosen was Ditton Marsh, up-river from London, and a large crowd packed into a LSWR train at Nine Elms - imagine then their horror when they saw the Surrey magistrates getting into a 1st class carriage of the same train! However the magistrates all got out for their sessions at Kingston and the other passengers got out at Ditton station to go to the "ring". Police soon arrived on the scene, so the "fraternity" returned to Ditton station and caught the next train to Woking - a barren and desolate place at the time.

On 2 February 1841 Caunt was in action again, this time against Ward. An LSWR train ran to Andover, then the "fans" travelled to Crookham Common in Hampshire by road. Ward won through a foul, so a re-match was organised near Stratford-on-Avon which Caunt won to declare himself "Champion of England." A few weeks later a fight was held near Holcot in Bedfordshire, to which the sporting fraternity travelled by train from Euston; one man died during the fight and the Riot Act was read as a local clergyman cut the ropes with a knife.

A fight was arranged for 2 December 1842 between Freeman and William Perry, the "Tipton Slasher." No train was laid on especially, but spectators could take scheduled ECR services to Sawbridgeworth and the station there soon became crowded. The fight organisers decided to avoid the problems of too many spectators by getting out of their own train at Harlow for the site at Hatfield Heath. This was broken up by the magistrates and many of the crowd flocked back to Bishops Stortford station, but the organisers re-arranged the fight on the canal towpath near Sawbridgeworth station.

The fight was still going after 70 rounds when it became too dark to continue, so it was re-arranged for the following week a little further north at Littlebury. The "Slasher" travelled by train to Bishops Stortford but police disrupted the fight so much that it all finished too late to get a scheduled train back to London.

Most of these early events depended on timetabled services, but in February 1844 a special excursion was arranged instead - for which the railway company must have been fully aware of the purpose. The train left London Bridge an hour late, full of mainly well-to-do people, and it reached Horley at about 11am, with the fight taking place on Horley Common in a spot hidden from the railway by trees. Perry emerged victorious when Parker was disqualified after 133 rounds.

With the importance of avoiding the Police, flexibility was crucial and some of the excursions seem to have been free to ramble the rails howsoever they wished. In 1849 the LSWR put on a train where "The captain (driver) started with sealed orders, and had a sort of roving commission as to the place at which he should cast anchor." This train went first to Bishopstoke, then to a point between Andover and Winchfield, and then stopped in a deep cutting near Woking Common; this left everyone with the difficulty of clambering up and down the steep sides of the muddy cutting. At least when the SER ran an excursion to a point near Edenbridge in September 1850 it set down the passengers on an embankment but provided steps cut out for the passengers to use; the pugilists then enjoyed the luxury of seeing two fights. This was so successful that another fight was held there on 27 October, but this was interrupted by the authorities and the train took them back to Redhill but darkness stopped the fight.

Clergymen often took the lead in complaining about the practice. In April 1850 the vicar of Frimley reported the LSWR to the Home Secretary after two fights in his district - one of which was held in a field near the National School - and on 21 May 1850 the vicar of Woking complained of "frequent" fights and special trains[9].

One of the most extraordinary fights was that between Orme and Jones on 10 May 1852, which the ECR assisted by running a special from Shoreditch. The train stopped for water at Great Chesterford, then surprised most of the passengers by heading along the old Newmarket Railway which had been officialy closed since October 1851. The plan was to pick up Orme at Six Mile Bottom but too many police were around, so, with ECR officials on board, they continued to Newmarket itself. Various sources disagree a little as to the exact itinerary, but it seems likely that Orme met the train at Newmarket and returned with it to Bourne Bridge - some suggesting that he guided it to a conveniently remote spot while sitting on the tender.

The fight at Bourne Bridge lasted only nine rounds before the shout of "Peelers!" went up, so all piled back into the train and they headed east to Warren Heath beyond Newmarket. There they managed a further 23 rounds before heading back west along the "disused" line, still with Orme on the tender. Back at Great Chesterford, Jones spoilt the fun by refusing to get out to fight anymore.

The GWR was also involved in this doubtful trade, firstly for the Broome v Terry fight at Shrivenham in 1846, then for the Mace v Goss contest in September 1863 for which an excursion fare of £2-2s was charged. This train was arranged in secrecy to prevent too many "criminal" types coming along, but a planned departure from Paddington at 2am was delayed by two hours and there was almost a riot by fight-fans who could not get onto it. A stop was made at Didcot to pick up Oxford University's finest, then the train was shunted into a siding at Wootton Bassett ready for the fight. When Police arrived the organisers hoped the GWR would take them somewhere else, but they refused to go anywhere else except back to Paddington - undeterred, everyone rushed over to Fenchurch Street and the fight was concluded at 3.30pm on Purfleet Marshes!

In April 1853 the ECR ran another excursion to milepost 108 between Ely and Thetford; the choice of location was because the lower classes had gone up earlier by scheduled train and gathered at the favourite spot of Mildenhall Road, while Police were waiting at Lakenheath. The latter was used for a fight on 18 October 1853 when the little station was completely taken over by 400 excursionists. On 14 February 1853 Mildenhall Road was the scene of a contest where Poulson's head was "beaten almost to a pulp."

In May 1856 it was clear that the ECR did its best to help the fight organisers avoid the Police. One special was arranged and then another put on for a more exclusive group of gentlemen said to include an Indian prince. The first train collected the pugilist Broome from Stratford and stopped at Manningtree to collect intelligence about the Suffolk police. The organisers surprised their opponents by going much closer to Ipswich than expected, the fight taking place close to Belstead Bank.

In September 1859 an excursion was booked with the SER, who put two engines on a train of 36 carriages of which "every one had at least its full complement of travellers, and many were over-full." This trundled down to Ashford, where Sayers was triumphant.

Trips such as this were described in loving detail in the book *Pugilistica*, by a sporting journalist H D Miles. Miles went to see Sayers v Heenan in April 1860, for which the SER laid on two "monster trains" from London Bridge. The first steamed out at 3.30am with 33 full carriages, the second at 4.20am. As dawn broke, police were seen to be guarding the countryside with "cutlasses drawn", apparently positioned at most possible sites between London, Brighton and Dover! But the trains took the Reading line at Redhill, stopping for water at Guildford, and reaching Farnborough at about 7am. A meadow next to the railway was chosen and 37 rounds fought before police arrived. This caused chaos as the referee resigned but Heenan continued the fight, battering his opponent's helpers and then running off in a "wild scramble". He had to be carried back to the train, which deposited him a couple of hours later at Bricklayers Arms - a discrete

Great Chesterford station, south of Cambridge, which saw unusual traffic in 1852 during an attempted prize fight between Orme and Jones. This extraordinary affair saw the fighters, spectators and Eastern Counties Railway officials taking a special train over the closed Newmarket branch in an attempt to evade police!

destination. The excursion trains made a profit of £500 for each of the fighters, and more for the organisers. This excursion resulted in a Parliamentary debate on the subject.

The Home Secretary became especially concerned after the LCDR ran a train from Pimlico on 31 December 1861, "for the purpose of getting off a Prize Fight on any part of the Line they might find unguarded by the Police." This fight was between Brettle and Rook for £1000 a side, and resulted in the Home Secretary's attention being drawn to "the unusual facilities afforded by the LCDR Company to the large bodies of people entering the County of Kent with the avowed intention of committing breaches of the peace."[10]

The LCDR train was shunted off the main-line at Meopham so that the ring could be set up in a nearby "Bottom", but the police soon intervened. Three hours later the train set off for Sittingbourne and stopped at Milton Meads Marsh. Attempts by police to arrest the key personnel caused a riot by the mob.

On 7 January 1862 the Home Secretary received a letter from Kent police, and a complaint was made to the LCDR. On 7 February the LCDR wrote to the Home Office agreeing not to provide any further special trains for fights, a concession clearly intended to avoid a new law being introduced.

However, this was not the end of the business as other companies became involved. On 14 December 1863 the Home Secretary was rather shocked to read a report in the *Morning Star* that Metropolitan Police had attended London Bridge station to help load passengers into a SER special train going to a prize-fight! This was the battle between King and Heenan at Wadhurst on 8 December. Commissioner Mayne was summoned to explain and said that he had sent officers to the station to protect the public, but had also warned the SER. He reported that the SER had actually applied for police assistance as the crowd was endangering other passengers:

"The noise of the mob could be heard at a long distance off all of the morning, and the violence of the ruffians composing it was such that foot passengers were violently assaulted and plundered, cabs seized and the passengers plundered before they could alight, windows of the railway station were wilfully broken....murder would have been committed had not prompt and energetic arrangements of Police been made."[11]

The trouble started at about midnight, when the mob began to assemble - up to a thousand of them. Tickets for a special train went on sale at 4.30am and this departed at about 6.20am with about 500 of the "roughs", but the crowd that assembled were unable to afford the high fares charged and wanted to follow by service train - but did not know where to go to. In their frustration they began to attack other passengers and launched an assault on the Brighton side of the station - "armed with bludgeons of all sizes and shapes."

The prosecution of troublemakers proved difficult. Some evidence was forthcoming - Mr Windham had been dragged from his cab, his clothes torn and then held aloft by the heels to make the money fall out of his pockets! PC Blow had been struck on the head, but other people who had been robbed refused to report the crimes to the police and two larceny cases had to be dismissed by magistrates as the prosecutors did not attend court.

The Home Secretary issued another warning to the SER, where

Police were positioned at most possible sites between London, Brighton and Dover in April 1860 when two special trains left London Bridge before dawn for a prize fight between Sayers and Heenan. The South Eastern Railway outflanked them by running the trains to Farnborough, where 37 rounds were fought before the law arrived. One of the specials can be seen in the background.

Alexander Beattie was both a director and a JP, although the company had said it was ceasing to run specials for fights in September 1859; in fact it had broken its promise after six months. The reason why is obvious - the December 1863 romp netted the SER a sum around £3000. Beattie wanted to see a new law banning railway companies from running prize-fight trains; he argued that until this was introduced, railways did not have the powers to refuse people a train. However, the counter-argument was made that the SER could quite easily inform magistrates if they knew something illegal was being arranged!

What really killed off this trade for the railways was that the great money to be made from the excursions became a temptation to "fleece" the public and also the persistent problem with "roughs". The former was partly addressed by a clause in Lord Redesdale's Bill of 1859, which introduced a penalty of a £5 fine or two month's hard labour for fradulently selling excursion tickets. A fight on 3 December 1862 was badly marred by thieves and "roughs" who surrounded Fenchurch Street station, robbing many of money and their tickets. In 1866 the LCDR ran an excursion to Longfield Court, for which the organisers charged two guineas first class and £1-10-6d second; Miles was disgusted that the only action provided was "much waiting for the Police" and concluded there was never any intention to fight. In April 1867 a SER excursion proved a flop when only one boxer turned up.

Suggestions that the law should be changed so that railway companies could be prosecuted for putting on these trains were continuously put aside until a clause was included in the Regulation of Railways Act, 1868; by that stage the enthusiasm for these contests was on the wane, and the ability of the police to prevent them was much improved.

Railway Disorder

During the peak years of railway growth there were many disputes between railway companies, though in general these were settled within the processes of the civil law and only occasionally spilled over into criminal disturbances.

For example, in April and May 1848 the Great Northern ran into opposition from the MSLR which refused it access to water at Retford and obstructed it at Grimsby, whilst in 1851 the GNR had to go to court again to gain an injunction establishing its right to run trains over the MSLR to New Holland.

In March 1849 the Lancaster & Carlisle and Maryport & Carlisle almost came to blows over stations in Carlisle, the former company moving in 150 navvies to protect property from its rival after a court ruling. The GNR was also involved in two famous instances of railway lines being "blocked" by a rival. In the same month there was a famous dispute at Clifton Junction, near Manchester, between the LYR and the East Lancashire. The LYR objected to through ticketing from the ELR and tried to prevent trains passing onto its line without the passengers having all re-booked. The ELR summoned the police, who watched from the ELR's signalbox as the LYR blocked the tracks in advance of the ELR train. Crowbars, light engines and a stone train were all used to reinforce the barricades and many trains were delayed. A similar dispute at Daisy Field between the East Lancashire and the Blackburn, Bolton, Clitheroe & West Yorks led to Blackburn magistrates complaining to the Railway Commissioners.

In May 1849 the GNR gained powers to run trains through from Peterborough to King's Lynn via Wisbech, partly requiring use of ECR and EAR tracks but when it attempted to run a train on 10 July it found the points had been blocked with vehicles chained to the points connecting the two stations at Wisbech. Though the EAR laid on buses between the two the GNR had made a fatal error in that the connection had not been approved by the Inspecting Officer, while the ECR maintained the connection should have been "at" the station, not "near" it.

The GNR ran into further problems at Nottingham in 1852, when starting a through service over the Ambergate Railway's line from Grantham. When the GNR engine reached Nottingham it was forced into a disused Midland Counties shed and the rails taken up behind it. A court ruled that the Midland Railway was acting lawfully in doing this as the GNR engine was "wrongfully encumbering their lines", but it has also been argued that the engine was technically on loan to the Ambergate company and therefore quite legitimate[12].

Pity the poor passenger who unwittingly got embroiled in this dispute. A lady passenger on MSJAR in 1857 tried to get out at Manchester London Road and found herself being questioned for trespass after the LNWR brought police in to close its station off to the other company. In December an attorney, connected with the LNWR's enemies, brought a case of assault in a similar situation, but his suit was dismissed as "trivial".

There was a noisy confrontation at Havant in December 1858 when the LBSCR and LSWR were battling for supremacy in Portsmouth. The LBSCR removed the points to the LSWR's Petersfield line and blocked it off with an old engine until the LSWR brought in its own men and the police. The LBSCR "switchman" had to be threatened with arrest. The LBSCR tried to prosecute the LSWR's men for assault and won nominal fines of 1s.

Railways occasionally found themselves in legal trouble for other matters. By the turn of the last century concern over animal welfare had led to new laws about the transport of animals, which were easily broken. Between 1894 and 1914 a succession of Diseases of Animals Acts were passed which regulated the movement of livestock at times of disease, leading to a number of cases against railways. The experience of the SECR shows us some typical cases, for example in 1903 it was fined £5 for delivering 42 Scottish sheep to Bickley without the authority of Kent County Council and in 1905 fined £10 after gross overloading caused the death of five sheep at Gravesend. In 1912 sheep and pigs were sent together in a van from Maidstone to Gravesend for which the company was fined £106, so after that incident it ceased mixing different types of animal. In September 1921 the SECR was fined for conveying sheep from Tenterden to Gravesend in coal trucks, with an average of 48 in each - several died.

The question of how liable railways were for fire damage caused by their engines also exercised many legal minds, but as there was no question of negligence it was a civil matter. In 1860 the case of Vaughan v Taff Vale Railway ruled that the engines which caused the damage were operating under the TVR's statutory powers so it was not liable for damages; this was eventually overturned by the Railway Fires Act of 1905 following which there were many claims for damages, usually from farmers.

The Great Northern was often in trouble in Lincoln where the High Street level crossing impeded traffic. In 1868 the Council got the Board of Trade to impose a ban on shunting across it, after which the Council employed a watchman at both this crossing and at Pelham Street to record any occasions of railway misbehaviour. Shunting across the road was logged as obstructing the highway and summonses issued en masse - 21 in one go in 1877! The Council suffered a defeat when the magistrates ruled that a short goods train from the station to the goods yard did not count as "shunting", leaving the ratepayers out of pocket.

1 *Railway Times*, 3 August 1840, says they travelled 19 miles in 19.5 minutes.

2 *Railway Times*, 10 April 1841

3 F C Mather, *Public Order in the Age of the Chartists*, Manchester, 1959, p.161

4 HO 45/729

5 This was thur Dyson, apparently a "railway engineer" or more likely a labourer: H M Walbrook, *Murders & Murder Trials*, London, 1932

6 F McKenna, *The Railway Workers*, London, 1980: p.34

7 L James, *The Law of the RailwayThe Law of the Railway*, London, 1980

8 BTC *Police Journal*, January 1959

9 HO 45/3074

10 HO 45/T363

11 HO 45/7447

12 J Wrottesley, *The Great Northern Railway*, p.78

CHAPTER ELEVEN:
NAVVIES &
OTHER RIOTS

Wages Disputes

In March 1840 navvy bricklayers employed by contractor John Stephenson went on strike on the Manchester & Leeds, so Stephenson hired new men from North Shields. When they arrived, they were offered 35s each to go home, but when this failed to persuade them threats of violence were used. Each offender was sentenced to three months by Rochdale magistrates. A notorious practice was the paying of navvies in "tommy shop" tickets, which was illegal under the Truck Acts. These tickets were in lieu of cash, and were redeemable at specified shops where - strangely - prices had a tendency to be higher than normal. In May 1842 the well-known contractor Edward Betts was nearly embroiled in a case where one of his sub-contractors, Painter, was issuing tickets for Mr Ralph's shop. Betts employed a skilled counsel, who argued there was no *obligation* for the men to take the tickets but they were really "letters of credit" to help the "improvident" men.

Early in 1843 three navvies on the Maryport & Carlisle complained to local magistrates that one of the contractors, McKay, did not pay cash wages and that they had to buy goods from a dealer who charged high prices. Magistrates looked into it and agreed with the complaint, but found that railway labourers were not covered by the Truck Acts - they suggested Lord Ashley should investigate the problem[1]. All the magistrates could do was order McKay to pay the cash wages due, but the navvies lost their jobs. Despite this, seven others made a complaint in Carlisle as they had not been paid cash after 44 days; magistrates found the tommy shop was overcharging by 25% and ordered cash wages to be paid. In a third case involving McKay, tea was found to be charged at 6s per lb rather than 4s and magistrates ordered prices to be reduced by 15%.

In 1846 a contractor on the Keymer to Lewes line was paying his men in "tickets" which could be exchanged in the Lewes shops; two clerks took advantage of this to produce hundreds of forgeries!

In 1847 there was considerable unrest around the country about high food prices, occasionally giving rise to an old-fashioned "bread riot" as people tried to push prices down. On 18 May 1847 navvies on the South Devon Railway were encouraged to invade Torquay in support of a bread riot there, but the police were organised and made a number of arrests. Local rioters received more severe sentences than the two navvies convicted, the latter getting only two weeks.

Non-payment of wages led to prosecutions over the money and sometimes riots due to the anger of the navvies.

A tangled case involved Ephraim Weaver, who brought a case against a gangsman named John Edwards on the Eastern Counties Railway. Weaver had been involved in a fight, so a "jury of the oldest railroaders" decided to fine him the price of a gallon of beer - 1s 6d - which they then drank in his absence. The money was deducted from his wages, thus causing the dispute. The case was dismissed.

A riot at Milnthorpe, Cumberland, in January 1845 was caused by the failure of a subcontractor to pay all the wages due. During the Sunday, the navvies drank heavily and, "having got into a beastly state of intoxication, they commenced fighting in a most brutal manner." Having gathered on the village green, they caused especial offence by continuing to fight during church service times. One of them, Wills, had a pair of pistols and tried to shoot a man while the deputy constable refused to arrest anyone as there was no safe place to keep prisoners - the people of Milnthorpe thereupon starting a subscription to build a lock-up!

Another problem with wages was their tendency to disappear with the wrong person. For example, James Marine, who worked for the contractor Thornton on the London & Brighton in 1840, decamped with £40 of navvy wages. In September 1841 subcontractor Douce, who was working on the ECR at Ingatestone, ran off with the wages of 98 men.

Disputes over wages led to frequent "wildcat" strikes, some of which involved violence. In August 1841 there was a strike among navvies on the Manchester & Birmingham Railway at Manchester, with some navvies attempting to intimidate others; one man was arrested for knocking another out with a stone. At Cork in 1845 striking navvies put up a notice with a coffin at the bottom to deter strike-breaking.

Navvies at work on the London, Chatham & Dover Railway's extension through the City of London in 1864. The contractor, Peto, was known to maintain good order among his workers – although other employers were not always so skilled and navvy riots were at one stage a frequent occurrence.

Working Practices

Sunday work was frowned upon in many areas of the country and, under certain circumstances, could lead to a prosecution. Churchwardens at Chelmsford successfully brought a case against a contractor named Pain in 1840, who was fined 5s for making his men work on the Sabbath - which was not approved of by the ECR Board. Railway contractors William and Henry Oldham were fined 5s each in April 1841 for "pursuing their worldly calling on the Sabbath" whilst in Essex the bringing of charges became quite common during summer 1841. However, the fines were generally insufficient to deter contractors. The *Railway Times* felt that a strict interpretation of the law was that it was illegal for railway staff to travel on Sundays, but not their passengers!

Navvies Behaving Badly

One of the main problems with navvies was that large numbers of men were brought into areas where the established practices of law and order were inadequate to cope with an upsurge of violence and drinking. In Scotland, a new law from 1845 gave Sheriffs the powers to compel a railway to form a police force during the period of construction.

Navvies had to provide their own entertainment, and fighting was one method. In April 1837 navvies arranged a prize-fight at Kilsby which attracted over 200 spectators until the authorities arrested the main characters; a rescue attempt was then mounted and the army had to be called in to restore order. Fights were also used to settle disputes, the navvies having their own concept of a "fair fight". One of these was organised at Bathampton on the GWR in July 1847, but two constables tried to stop the battle. The crowd turned on the police and attacked them, with the result that PC Bailey died. A navvy called Perry had been a "second" at the fight and was known to have been present when the death occurred, so he was singled out for trial and sentenced to life transportation.

Railways were rarely the victim of bad behaviour by navvies, but one group managed to behave appallingly at Wigston on Christmas Eve, 1840. Six of them, who worked for the well-known contractor Edward Betts, arrived at the station and asked for the expected through train to stop and pick them up. It was not scheduled to stop, so they abused the stationmaster and then tried to alter the signals so that a red light would show. They threatened to throw the crossing gates across the track and to shoot the stationmaster. Then they started walking along the line, but one was so drunk that he fell across the track as the train was approaching and had to be rescued by the stationmaster. Their fines varied up to £5.

Drink invariably fuelled many navvy problems. In September 1841 Colchester was described as "plagued" by drunken navvies. In August 1847 it was reported from Stoke Canon that "the finest part of the village [had been] destroyed" and that the GWR felt obliged to pay half the costs. On the Rugby & Stamford railway in the same month one navvy was arrested after a drunken riot, only to be "liberated" from police custody by 200 colleagues.

In 1855 the town of Haslemere had attracted a number of navvies who were working on the Portsmouth line and one of the contractors, Mr Goodeve, opened a brickyard in the town to supply his needs. On 28 July the five navvies went to the *King's Arms* to celebrate Saturday night, but this was an inn with regular problems at closing time. The combined might of the Surrey Constabulary in the town - two men - were on duty to ensure good order. Inspector Donaldson and Constable Freestone went into the *King's Arms* ten minutes after closing time where Thomas Woods proved especially reluctant to go home. Later in the Market Place Woods squared up for a fight and was pushed over by Freestone; when he got back to his feet, Freestone hit him so hard on the head with his truncheon that it broke.

As the police attempted to arrest and incarcerate one of the navvies, others joined in to rescue him in typical navvy fashion. Woods used an iron bolt to strike the Inspector on the head and David Smith kicked him while he was on the ground. Carried back to his house, Donaldson's last words were, "My dear wife, I am dying." The police managed to arrest all the navvies involved, only Smith having made an attempt to escape. Four were found guilty of manslaughter and one of assault; Woods received the heaviest sentence of twenty years transportation.

In 1871 a group of navvies working on the Devon & Somerset Railway arrived at the Castle Inn at Landkey near Barnstaple. As they were already drunk the landlord refused to serve them, but the navvies in turn refused to leave the premises. The police had to be brought in and the navvies began to walk back to their lodgings in Barnstaple, followed by the police at a safe distance. Only when they had got back to town was an attempt made to arrest them - unsurprisingly a fight broke out in which PC James was knocked to the floor and attacked with a hatchet.

Racial Riots

Tension between different racial groups was a common cause of trouble. During the period 1838-41 there were many problems across the Midlands and the North, so that detachments of Metropolitan Police were stationed at sites such as Rotherham, Wakefield and Clay Cross as anti-Irish riots occurred on the works of the North Midland and Manchester & Leeds. These were mainly caused by the practice of Irish navvies being paid less than the English, and so putting them out of work. On 10 October 1838 the Irish navvies were driven off the railway works at Masborough Common and into Rotherham, although the contractor John Stephenson tried to protect and pacify them. He took them into the yard of the Sheffield & Rotherham Railway at Westgate and gave out ale.[2] The cavalry were summoned from Sheffield but on the next day 400 English navvies attacked Stephenson's house and had to be driven off by artillerymen. Problems continued around Leeds and Bradford and in July 1839 sentences of between two and six months were handed out for riotous conduct.[3]

In 1840 drunken English men attacked Irish navvies on the York & North Midland contract at Methley; the contractor was again John Stephenson, who tried to calm the mob but was hit by a stone. The Metropolitan Police arrived armed with cutlasses and pistols, commandeering a boat on the nearby canal to take their prisoners to Wakefield gaol.

At Kinghorn in May 1845 a riot broke out between Scots and Irish navvies after 200 Scottish navvies met on the beach to plot how to get rid of the Irish; they were cautioned by the Sheriff.

At Oakham a number of men appeared in court after navvy riots on the Syston to Peterborough line on 15 July. English navvies did not want any of the work being done by the Irish, so 100 of them attacked a group of 17 Irishmen and drove them away. Two months hard labour was the standard punishment.

In February 1846 the town of Penrith was plunged into chaos by sustained fighting between English and Irish navvies. The English burnt down the huts of the Irish navvies, but then 500 Irish navvies arrived from other sites and the English fled. As rumours of trouble had spread, so 2000 English navvies from around the district flooded into the town and by 13 February there was a considerable trail of destruction with further riots in Kendal. Military assistance was needed to quell the trouble and one of the rioters, John Hobday, was given a sentence of 15 years transportation after beating Denis Salmon.

Feeling was also strong in Wales; on 22 May 1846 Welsh navvies objected to Irish joining their gang at Aber near Bangor and this spilled over into a campaign to drive out all Irish. Police made one arrest and the man was locked up in Bangor, but a rescue was organised and he climbed out using a ladder. The 68th Foot were summoned from Chester, making the journey by rail to Liverpool and then by coastal steamer.

Later the same year there was trouble at Gorebridge, near Dalkeith, after a hawker was tricked out of two watches by Irish navvies in a pub. Police arrested two men but the Irish sought to release them and gain revenge, attacking two constables they met by chance and causing the death of PC Richard Pace on 28 July. This caused an outburst of anti-Irish feeling and the Irish camp at Fushiebridge was attacked. The Irish population in Edinburgh began to plan to march out to gain further revenge and police had to prevent this movement. Four people who were ringleaders in the initial violence received sentences of seven years transportation.[4]

In Kent there was trouble at Mark Beech in August 1866 when contractors Waring Bros brought in French and Belgian navvies to undercut the rates paid to Englishmen working on the Surrey & Sussex Railway. English navvies had been paid 8s a day, but the continentals were prepared to work for less than 4s. Superintendent Dance of Tunbridge became worried at the situation, but trouble erupted before he could bring in extra men. At 10.30pm the English navvies massed near Cowden and armed themselves with staves and bludgeons; from there they marched to the navvy camp at Mark Beech tunnel where they drove out the French. At 11.30pm 50 English navvies attacked Brooke House, which was being used as a lodging for the foreign navvies, but most of them escaped. 200 English navvies blocked off the mouth of the new tunnel. The English then pursued the French to Edenbridge but the Chief Constable telegraphed for 100 soldiers from Shorncliffe Camp and the crisis was averted. Seven men received sentences of one year.

Organised Riots

Some riots occurred with the support or encouragement of higher powers. There was a fight near Pontefract on the Askern branch in September 1847, just after navvies had begun work. The landowner decided to change his mind about allowing the works, got together a gang of 250 men, "plied them with ale", and commenced a frontal attack. Sundry individuals were arrested and sent for trial.

In July 1850 there was a notable confrontation at Wolverhampton between the LNWR and the Shrewsbury & Birmingham Railway during the building of the Stour Valley Railway. The S&B decided it wished to transfer mineral traffic to a canal and began some works, which the SVR contractors - Hoof, Hill & Moore - tried to prevent. Moore was arrested for obstructing traffic but the magistrates rejected the case and refused to bind him over to keep the peace.

The following day, 13 July, Hill and Moore organised a large number of men to prevent the S&B works being carried out. Anticipating trouble, the Mayor of Wolverhampton and the Chief Constable arrived at 11am, but so did 200 navvies brought in by train to support the S&B; these had red tapes round their arms to identify which side they were on. When they tried to start work, the Hoof, Hill & Moore men threw away planks they were using and the Chief Constable scuttled off to Wolverhampton to get more police and some soldiers.

When the 48th Regiment arrived with bayonets fixed, the Mayor "addressed the multitude in energetic language, declaring his determination to maintain the public peace, and threatening the conviction of any person who interfered with the workmen."[5] He then read the Riot Act, which encouraged most of the crowd to move away.

Hill and the SVR men then called upon the Mayor to stop the S&B works and, when he ignored their demands, called on their own navvies to stop it by force. Hill was promptly arrested and fighting broke out. Hill's men blocked the S&B line near Cannock Road bridge, but this was cleared by police with cutlasses although a Shrewsbury train was delayed.

Another riot occurred at Mickleton tunnel on the Oxford, Worcester & Wolverhampton in July 1851. The engineer of the line, Brunel, was experiencing problems with contractors Williams & Marchant which was further complicated by the presence of a subcontractor, George Cole, who Marchant believed to be trying to get the contract for himself. Brunel decided to take possession of the works, but the contractors organised a defensive force and the Riot Act had to be read on 12 July. Brunel decided to arrange for the well-known firm of Peto & Betts to take over, but when they arrived on 21 July a fight broke out and Marchant threatened to shoot them. The Riot Act had to be read a second time until Marchant bowed to the inevitable.

A similar dispute occurred on the Mistley, Thorpe & Walton in Essex, a minor line that was never completed. James Cooke, the company's engineer, was unhappy with the progress of contractor William Munro and tried to replace him with Frederick Furness. Furness refused to take over the materials which Munro had already paid for so Munro refused to give up possession or he would have been ruined financially. A battle then took place between Munro's navvies, led by his agent Fryer, and a number of Harwich longshoremen brought in for the occasion under the control of Cooke. Fryer grabbed a good defensive position at the head of the cutting, but the superior numbers of the Harwich men led to him being captured and removed from the property. Resourceful and determined, he then escaped from their care and regrouped his forces but was quickly overwhelmed.

[1] Lord Ashley was already famous for his pioneering work with the Factory Acts, later inheriting the title of Earl of Shaftesbury by which he is better known today.
[2] G Body, *Great Railway Battles*, Peterborough, 1994
[3] D Brooke, *The Railway Navvy*, Newton Abbot, 1983
[4] Brooke, p.116
[5] *Railway Times*, 20 July 1850

CHAPTER TWELVE:
SUICIDE

Attempted suicide was a criminal offence in Victorian times, and some magistrates persisted in punishing it with a prison sentence. Encouraging others to commit suicide was also criminal until the 1960s, the 1961 Suicide Act replacing this archaic concept by stipulating that a 14 year sentence could be imposed if a person took part in a suicide pact and lived. However the number of suicides was relatively low in the early days of the railways - there was only one actual suicide in the six months ending December 1847. By 1850 this had increased to only 4 and to six by 1864; figures then rose sharply to 34 ten years later and 112 in 1894, 160 in 1905 and reaching 224 in 1925 so that in most years far more were killed through their own actions than in railway accidents. Suicide became a particular problem on the London Underground where "suicide pits" had to be provided to reduce the mortality rate. So the Victorian period was one of reasonable calm in this respect, before the growing problems of the Twentieth Century and the events at Stepney Junction in September 1867 must have been unusual - a woman who had only been married for a month threw herself under a train, and two nights later another woman also killed herself at the same spot.

In September 1841 a sentence of two months hard labour was handed out for attempted suicide at Chippenham, whilst on the same day an offender from Wrington on the Bristol & Exeter received one month.

With drunks, it was sometimes difficult to tell whether attempted suicide was the case or not, and it was often easier to fine someone for obstruction. On the Edinburgh & Glasgow near Kirkintilloch in April 1844 a drunken workman was found lying across the rails, and the train just managed to stop in time; he was fined 40s.

The same problem might occur with a lunatic, for feigning madness might be an alternative to going to court for attempted suicide. In July 1874 a man was seen lying across the track near Summer Lane, Barnsley, and the driver of an approaching train did his best to stop. In the event the "guard" of the locomotive pushed him off the track and the man ran away. When captured, he explained that he only wanted to stop the train and so was taken to an asylum.

The press could be very harsh about suicides. The *North British Railway*

Journal, in November 1847, described a woman suicide at Pennylee near Paisley as "a worthless, drunken character, though well-connected, who had left her husband....and had been dissipated ever since." A 16 year old youth was described as "of morose and stubborn temper" after attempting suicide at Limehouse in 1867; he jumped in front of a train but fell beneath the rails, being caught by the locomotive ashpan which turned him over and over until it stopped. Both his legs were amputated. Kate Green who committed suicide at Duffield in 1871 was described in *The Times* as "a girl of weak intellect" suffering from "religious monomania."

As suicide became more common, only cases involving more elevated members of society reached the press. Thus the suicide of James Allan at Waterloo in November 1849 was considered worthy of comment as he had been a navy surgeon; he stepped off the platform in front of an approaching train, knelt down and put his head on the rail. Despite the shouts of a policeman, his head was almost severed. The Headmaster of Plympton Grammar School was another noted victim in 1889, suffering from money problems.

Failure to achieve death in these situations often meant that a person was tried for the criminal offence of attempted suicide. This happened to Michael Callan, a printer's machine-hand, in 1868. He was first seen by Inspector Croucher of Cannon Street station, lying across the rails two feet in front of an engine which was heading up a train "due to depart in half an hour or less." When seen by Croucher he got up onto the platform but was taken into custody and found to have a phial labelled "Poison" in his possession. Three letters were in his pockets, one directed to the City Coroner. Callan's position was a sad one as he had worked for the *Times* for 15 years but had lost his job due to illness caused by "sitting in a cramped position." He was discharged on a promise not to try again and his desperately poor mother given £20 from the Poor Box.

The magistrates usually dealt mercifully with attempted suicides given that a prison term could be enforced. Lawton Ford was arrested on 6 July 1867 when he climbed over the LBSCR fence at Forest Hill and lay on the track facing an oncoming train; however, as it approached he clearly changed his mind and rolled over, although his head was knocked by the step of the brake van. He was arrested for trespass, rather than the attempted suicide which was clearly his plan due to financial problems, and bailed for good behaviour.

Arthur Hibblewhite was remanded in custody for a few weeks after attempting suicide on the NLR at Dalston in July 1868. He got off the platform and lay down in front of an approaching train; an engine-driver ran across the tracks and pulled him out of the way in the nick of time. The signalman jumped through the window of his box, a fall of 12ft, in order to arrest him.

Trains were also used by some suicides as a place to shoot yourself. A man shot himself dead in a 1st class compartment between Preston and Poulton in 1889. In the same year auctioneer's clerk Hubert Fenton was arrested for trying to shoot himself in a train at Wandsworth. In August 1891 an express arrived at Bedford with a young lady who appeared to be asleep in a 1st class compartment, but who was then noticed to be bleeding from a chest wound. The wound was caused by a bullet but no gun could be found, and the young woman was conscious enough to deny a suicide attempt. She told a sensational story about how she had been attacked by a young man just before Leicester, who had shot her and then got out at the next station. However this story fell apart when the revolver was found further south near Desborough, with two barrels discharged. The girl, who gave a false name at first, was identified by a man from Leeds and handed over to his care. In October 1903 a young couple were found shot dead in a SECR compartment at Beckenham Junction; C Spiller had shot his girlfriend, Alize Cook, then turned the gun on himself. In May 1911 a man shot himself dead with a revolver on the 4.30pm Euston to Coventry.

In February 1936 people were shocked to read of the attempted murder of Arthur Mead, a butcher, on the Great Western near Princes Risborough on the 5.42pm Aylesbury to Paddington. Two sharp cracks were heard from the compartment, but at High Wycombe it was assumed the man inside was asleep. At Beaconsfield the guard realised he was ill and when taken out, Mead told the doctor he had been shot. A search of the lineside revealed a humane killer had been thrown from the train, and the connection of this with Mead's profession soon led to the discovery of the truth - he had attempted suicide when depressed about money, and had tried to make it look like a violent robbery.

Another case that started off with discussion of murder occurred on 20 April 1959. The 10.25pm train arrived at Grantham with an offside carriage door ripped off as it swung open in the path of a parcels train. Inside the doorway a man's hat and coat were found. A search of the lineside was ordered, but at 5.40am it was not a man that was found but a crying baby at Fletton. This led to the discovery of a badly injured woman nearby, then a man's body was found at Essendine. However the case was not as dramatic as first appeared, for there was no connection between the two: the man had jumped from the 10.25pm while the woman and baby had come from the 4am down Leeds train. If the woman had jumped with the baby in her arms she was guilty of both attempted suicide and attempted murder; in the event mercy prevailed and she was placed on probation for three years for attempted suicide and given one day's prison for abandoning the baby.

Sources

P S Bagwell, *The Railwaymen*, London, 1963

B Bailey, *George Hudson*, Stroud, 1995

P Begg & K Skinner, *The Scotland Yard Files*, London, 1992

G Body, *Great Railway Battles*, Peterborough, 1994

D Brooke, *The Railway Navvy*, Newton Abbott, 1983

G Dilnot, *The Trial of Jim the Penman*, London, 1930

D M Evans, *Facts, Failures & Frauds*, London, 1859

A Griffiths, *Mysteries of Police & Crime*, London

J T Howard Turner, *The London Brighton & S Coast Railway*, London, 1977

L James, *The Law of the Railway*, London, 1980

J Janaway, *Surrey Murders*, Newbury, 1988

E MacDermot, *History of the GWR*, London, 1964

F McKenna, *The Railway Workers*, London, 1980

F C Mather, *Public Order in the Age of the Chartists*, Manchester, 1959

H D Miles, *Pugilistica*, London, c.1880

C Nash, *The Railway Robberies*, various papers in the PRO, 1846

L O'Broin, *Fenian Fever*, London, 1971

PRO papers on Irish nationalism, use of telegraph etc, principally HO144 and FO5 classifications

P P Read, *The Great Train Robbers*, London, 1978

J Richards & J MacKenzie, *The Railway Station: A Social History*, Oxford, 1986

L T C Rolt, *Red for Danger*, London, 1971

A & M Sellwood, *The Victorian Railway Murders*, Newton Abbott, 1979

J Simmons & G Biddle, *Oxford Companion to British Railway History*, Oxford, 1997

K Short, *The Dynamite War*, Dublin, 1979

H M Walbrook, *Murders & Murder Trials*, London, 1932

J R Whitbread, *The Railway Policemen*, London, 1961

Periodicals

Bedfordshire Mercury
Daily Telegraph
The Graphic
Great Eastern Railway Magazine
Herapath's Railway Magazine
The Illustrated London News
Journal of the Railway & Canal Historical Society

Lincolnshire Chronicle
Railway Gazette
Railway Magazine
Railway Record
Railway Times
The Times

INDEX